Frederick Gustavus Burnaby—soldier, traveller, writer, and pioneer balloonist—was born on 3 March 1842, the son of a sporting country parson. Educated at Bedford Grammar School (where a house is named after him), Harrow, and privately in Germany, he joined the Household Brigade as a cornet in 1859, finally commanding his regiment in 1881. In 1875, on a one-man Great Game mission, he rode to Khiva in Central Asia, and the following year set out from Constantinople for eastern Turkey. In 1885 he was speared to death while campaigning in the Sudan, where he is buried somewhere in the desert.

Peter Hopkirk, author of *The Great Game* and four other books on imperial rivalry in Central Asia, first travelled in this region in the late 1960s, although it was not until 1982, a century after Burnaby's visit, that he managed to get to Khiva, hitherto closed to foreigners.

In addition to Frederick Burnaby's *On Horseback Though Asia Minor*, the following books by Peter Hopkirk are also available from Oxford Paperbacks:

The Great Game
On Secret Service East of Constantinople
Foreign Devils on the Silk Road
Setting the East Ablaze
Trespassers on the Roof of the World
Quest for Kim: In Search of Kipling's Great Game

A RIDE TO
KHIVA

Travels and Adventures
in Central Asia

Frederick Burnaby
Capt. Royal Horse Guards

With a preface by
Peter Hopkirk

OXFORD
UNIVERSITY PRESS

OXFORD
UNIVERSITY PRESS

Great Clarendon Street, Oxford OX2 6DP

Oxford University Press is a department of the University of Oxford.
It furthers the University's objective of excellence in research, scholarship,
and education by publishing worldwide in

Oxford New York

Auckland Bangkok Buenos Aires Cape Town Chennai
Dar es Salaam Delhi Hong Kong Istanbul Karachi Kolkata
Kuala Lumpur Madrid Melbourne Mexico City Mumbai Nairobi
São Paulo Shanghai Singapore Taipei Tokyo Toronto
and an associated company in Berlin

Oxford is a registered trade mark of Oxford University Press
in the UK and in certain other countries

Published in the United States
by Oxford University Press Inc., New York

© Preface by Peter Hopkirk 1997

British Library Cataloguing in Publication Data

Data available

Library of Congress Cataloging in Publication Data

Data available

ISBN 0-19-280367-0

1 3 5 7 9 10 8 6 4 2

Printed in Great Britain by
Clays Ltd., St. Ives plc

PREFACE BY PETER HOPKIRK

Whichever way you looked at him, Captain Frederick Burnaby was distinctly larger than life. Indeed, that very phrase might have been specifically invented for him. Of giant stature and prodigious strength, this son of a Church of England canon stood six-foot-four in his stockinged feet, weighed in at fifteen stone, and boasted a forty-seven-inch chest.

Reputed to be the strongest man in the British Army, if not in the whole of Europe, Burnaby could, it was said, lift and carry a small pony under his arm—one under each arm, some claimed. Other Herculean feats of his included grasping the tip of a billiard cue between his middle and index fingers, and holding it out horizontally, with his arm fully extended. Also, despite his massive bulk, he could vault clean across the billiard table in the officers' mess of his regiment, the Blues.

But Frederick Gustavus Burnaby, known universally as Fred, was more than just a Goliath or mere fighting-machine, though no one doubted his talents on the battle-field—even if he did once attract the opprobrium of the House of Commons for introducing a double-barrelled shot-gun to modern warfare in the Sudan. Early on he demon-strated that behind his brawn and belligerence lay a first-class brain. At the age of sixteen he passed his army entrance exam-ination—the youngest of 150 candidates—to be gazetted a cornet, then the lowest commissioned rank. Educated at Bedford Grammar School and Harrow, he was fluent in French, Italian, German, Russian, and Spanish, later picking up a working knowledge of Turkish and Arabic.

On top of all this, Burnaby had an insatiable appetite for adventure and hazardous exploits—he was a pioneer military balloonist, making nineteen ascents, including a solo crossing of the English Channel at a height of 10,000 feet. This craving for adventure he combined with a vigorous and colourful prose style, which very soon brought him to the notice of certain Fleet Street editors. The result was that during the generous periods of furlough then enjoyed by British officers in peacetime, Burnaby was employed by *The Times* and other journals to report foreign campaigns.

It was in 1874, while reporting the war in the Sudan, where he had just interviewed General Gordon, that he first hit on the idea of trying to reach Khiva, then one of the most remote and exotic cities on earth. What particularly attracted him to it was a newspaper report that the whole of Central Asia had been closed to British travellers by the Russians, who were relentlessly advancing across it, gobbling up khanate after khanate, and getting ever closer to India's northern frontiers. Khiva was the latest such victim of Russian expansionism, and Burnaby was determined to see for himself what precisely the Russians were up to there. For many British strategists believed Khiva to be a perfect staging-point for an invasion of India. From Khiva, Burnaby hoped to ride on to Merv, the Turcoman stronghold, which had not yet fallen to the Tsar's armies, and after that to Kabul, the Afghan capital. From there he would enter India via the Khyber Pass. Altogether it was an immensely ambitious undertaking, especially in midwinter, which was when Burnaby intended to set out, and in the light of Anglo–Russian relations, which were at a near all-time low.

The ancient caravan city of Khiva, for which Burnaby left London's Victoria Station on November 30, 1875, had enjoyed an evil reputation among travellers since the Middle Ages. One of the two great slave markets of Central Asia— Bokhara being the other—it was regularly supplied with fresh stock by marauding bands of armed Turcoman tribesmen who dwelt in the deserts of Transcaspia. One young British officer, disguised as an Afghan, who took his life in his hands and ventured into Turcoman territory in 1840, came upon a pitiful caravan of manacled men, women, and children who had been seized north of Herat and were destined for the Khivan slave-market.

'He who once enters Khiva abandons all hope, as surely as one who enters Hell,' noted that intrepid officer in his diary, adding: 'His prison house is girdled with trackless deserts, whose sole inhabitants are the sellers of human flesh.' Many of the slavers' victims were Persians and fishermen from the nearby Caspian Sea, together with their families. But there were also large numbers of Russians, often children, who had been snatched by the 'man-stealing Turcomans' from the outskirts of Russian settlements to the north of Khiva.

The Turcoman threat had, over the years, led to a number of Russian military expeditions to Khiva, in an attempt to free the slaves and punish their captors. The first of these, led by Prince Alexander Bekovich in 1717, had ended in disaster, when the Khivans pretended to welcome the Russians, and then massacred their all-too-trusting guests. Other expeditions followed, whose fortunes—or more often misfortunes— I have described in detail in *The Great Game*. One, led by General Perovsky in the autumn of 1839, was driven back by the terrible Central Asian winter, with the loss of more than a thousand men through frostbite and nearly 9,000 camels, without a shot being fired, or the death of one Khivan soldier.

When this ill-fated expedition left Orenburg, the British in India had reacted with alarm. Were the Russians really sending 5,000 troops to Khiva merely to free a few slaves, or was this simply a cover for St Petersburg's expansionist plans in Central Asia, across which lay the strategic approaches to India? Fortunately the snowdrifts that had engulfed Perovsky and his troops had temporarily removed any such threat. But to ensure that the Tsar could not use the presence of Russian slaves in Khiva as an excuse for sending a far larger expedition, two British officers—Captain James Abbott in

1840, and Lieutenant Richmond Shakespear later that same year—were sent to try to talk the tyrannical Khan of Khiva into freeing all the slaves, thereby robbing the Russians of their pretext for marching on Khiva again.

The adventures of Abbott and Shakespear I have described fully in *The Great Game*, so I will not attempt to retell them here, except to say that Shakespear did succeed in rescuing the slaves, whom he led to freedom in one of the most bizarre rescues of all time, and for which he was awarded a knighthood by Queen Victoria and promoted to captain by his superiors. He was also formally thanked in St Petersburg by Tsar Nicholas for freeing, at grave risk to his own life, so many Russian subjects from their heathen captors. But it was no secret in court circles that privately the Tsar was infuriated by the young British subaltern's unsolicited action.

Finally, in 1873, Russian patience with the Khivans snapped. By this time they had captured Tashkent, Samarkand and Bokhara, and so had troops within easy striking distance of Khiva. When the Khan saw that the game was finally up, he fled ignominiously, leaving his entire harem and household behind. What the British in India had long feared had now happened. Although nominally autonomous, Khiva had overnight become part of the Tsar's Central Asian empire, and it was not long before it was decreed by St Petersburg that no foreigners would be allowed to travel in 'Russian Central Asia'. This was too much for Fred Burnaby, who immediately began to plan his own daring and clandestine one-man expedition to Khiva. He was most careful, however, not to let the British authorities get wind of his intentions, since they would immediately put a stop to these for fear of their worsening London's already badly-strained relations with St Petersburg.

In this book, one of two Great Game classics that Burnaby wrote, he describes in graphic detail what followed. Its Russophobic tone, which matched the mood of the British public at that time, guaranteed its success and led a year later to a sequel, also a best-seller, entitled *On Horseback through Asia Minor*. Reissued by Oxford University Press in paperback in 1996, it describes a mid-winter journey he made across Turkey to its bloodstained frontier with Russia, to see what the Russians were up to in this then remote corner of the Great Game battlefield. By a stroke of good luck, for Burnaby anyway, war broke out between these traditional foes just as his book appeared, guaranteeing it instant success.

Throughout his career Fred Burnaby was attracted to danger like a moth to a candle flame. But on January 17, 1885, fate finally caught up with him. On that day, at the age of forty-two and by now a colonel, he met his end in a manner which would have met with his full approval—speared to death, facing overwhelming odds, during ferocious hand-to-hand fighting in the Sudan. There, beneath the desert sands, lie his remains, together with those of seventy-three of his comrades. Around them, it is said, were found the corpses of some eleven hundred of the enemy.

When news of Burnaby's death reached London, the nation was plunged into a frenzy of grief, for he was a much loved figure among all classes and ranks. This universal mourning was shared by all but his liberal foes and critics, who included the poet and anti-imperialist Wilfred Blunt. 'It serves him right, for he was a mere butcher . . .' noted the latter in his diary. But then it was Blunt who claimed to have sung with joy in the train all the way down to his Sussex estate on hearing of General Gordon's somewhat similar fate, some nine days earlier, also at the hands of the Sudanese. Coming from Blunt, whom he greatly despised, Burnaby would certainly have taken it as a compliment.

PREFACE.

THE title explains the nature of this work. It is
merely a narrative of a ride to Khiva. I have added
a short account of Russia's Advance Eastward.

In the course of my journey I had the opportunity
of conversing with many Russians in Central Asia.
India was a topic which never failed to produce
numerous comments.

A work has been lately published in St. Petersburg. The author dilates at considerable length on
the Russo-Indian Question. His opinions on this
subject are similar to those which I have heard
expressed. The author's remarks are as follows :—

"Another advantage which we have gained consists
in the fact that from our present position our power of
threatening British India has become real, and ceased
to be visionary. In this respect our Central Asian
possessions serve only as an *étape* on the road to
further advance, and as a halting-place where we can
rest and gather fresh strength. If in the time of
Paul I. an overland expedition to India was considered feasible, it is certainly much more so at the

present time, when we have shortened the interval by such an immense stretch of country.

"Asia will not of course ever form the avowed object of dispute between England and Russia, but in the event of a war produced by European complications, we shall clearly be obliged in our own interests to take advantage of the proximity to India which is afforded by our present position in Central Asia.

  *   *   *   *   *

"Besides the English," the author continues, "there is another nation whose attitude is also one of expectancy for the Russians—namely, the natives of India.

"The *East India Company* is nothing less than a poisonous unnatural plant engrafted on the splendid soil of India—a parasite which saps away the life of the most fertile and wealthy country in the world.

"This plant can only be uprooted by forcible means; and such an attempt was made by the natives of the country in 1857, though it failed for want of sufficient skill.

"Sick to death, the natives are now waiting for a physician from the North. Some time will naturally elapse before they care to repeat the experiment of 1857; and, as far as can be foreseen, the English will have to deal only with disconnected outbreaks; but it cannot be said with any certainty that such small sparks of rebellion may not, if supported by an impetus from without, produce a general conflagration throughout the length and breadth of India. In this case the

British Government will be unable to reckon on the support of the native troops, numbering 124,000 out of a total of 200,000, and the small remnant will barely be sufficient to guard the most important points."

Such are the observations of Captain Terentyeff in his recent work called " Russia and England in the East."

In my own opinion Russia, from her present position, has not the power of even threatening British India.   However, she has the power of threatening points which, should she be permitted to annex them, would form a splendid basis for operations against Hindostan.   Merve, Balkh, and Kashgar would make magnificent *étapes*. The former locality is richer than any of the most fertile corn-growing countries in European Russia.   Merve is close to Herat; and should the Afghans join with Russia, a direct advance might be made upon India through the Bolan Pass. If Kashgar were permitted to fall into the Tzar's possession, we should lose our *prestige* with the Mohammedans in Central Asia; whilst the occupation of Kashgar would prove a disagreeable thorn in our side, and give rise to endless intrigues.

Balkh, from Bokhara, is only a twelve days' march, and from Balkh to Cabul, through the Bamian Pass, it is the same distance.   This road, though blocked by the snow in winter, can be traversed by artillery in the summer and autumn months; whilst Bokhara could supply Balkh with any quantity of provisions which might be required. Should Russia be permitted to annex Kashgar, Balkh, and Merve, India would be liable to attack from three points, and we should have to divide our small European force. We have learnt how much trust can be placed in a Russian statesman's promises. Russia ought to be clearly given to understand that any advance in the direction of Kashgar, Balkh, or Merve, will be looked upon by England as a *casus belli*. If this is done, we shall no longer hear from the authorities at St. Petersburg that they are unable to restrain their generals in Turkistan. At the present moment Great Britain, without any European ally, can drive Russia out of Central Asia. If we allow her to keep on advancing, the same arms which we might now employ will one day be turned against ourselves.

THE AUTHOR.

Somerby Hall, Leicestershire,
September, 1876.

CONTENTS.

———•———

CHAPTER XII.

CHAPTER XIII.

CHAPTER XIV.

CHAPTER XV.

CHAPTER XVI.

CHAPTER XVII.

CHAPTER XVIII.

CHAPTER XIX.

CHAPTER XX.

CHAPTER XXI.

CHAPTER XXVII.

CHAPTER XXVIII.

CHAPTER XXIX.

CHAPTER XXX.

CHAPTER XXXI.

CHAPTER XXXII.

CHAPTER XXXIII.

CHAPTER XXXIV.

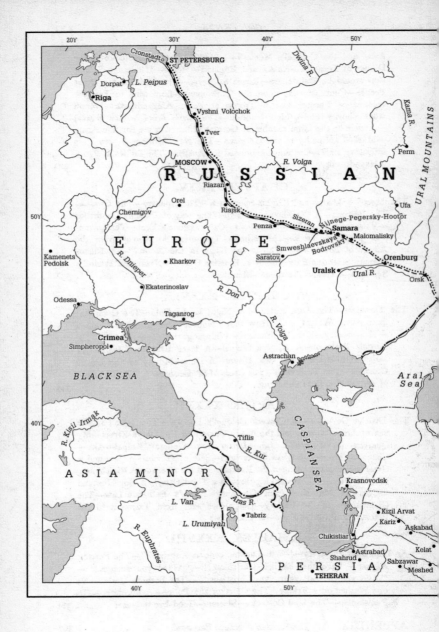

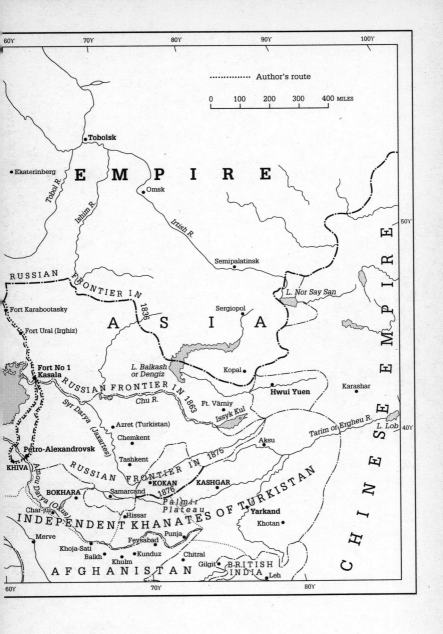

.... Author's route

0   100   200   300   400 MILES

•Tobolsk

•Ekaterinberg   E M P I R E

•Omsk

Tobol R.

Ishim R.

Irtish R.

50Y

RUSSIAN

Fort Karabootasky

Fort Ural (Irghiz)

F R O N T I E R I N 1836

A   S   I   A

•Semipalatinsk

L. Nor Say San

Sergiopol•

Fort No 1
Kasala

RUSSIAN FRONTIER IN 1863

Syr Darya (Jaxartes)

L. Balkash
or Dengiz

Chu R.

Kopal•

Hwui Yuen

Karashar•

Petro-Alexandrovsk

KHIVA

Azret (Turkistan)•

Chemkent•

Tashkent•

Ft. Várniy

Issyk Kul

RUSSIAN   F R O N T I E R   I N   1875

Aksu•

Tarim or Ergheu R.

L. Lob

40Y

C H I N E S E   E M P I R E

Amou Darya (Oxus)

BOKHARA

Char-jui•

KOKAN

Samarcand•

1876

KASHGAR

Pámir
Plateau

K H A N A T E S   O F   T U R K I S T A N

Yarkand•

Hissar•

I N D E P E N D E N T   K H A N A T E S

Khotan•

Merve•

Khoja-Sati

Balkh•

Khulm•

Kunduz•

Feysabad•

Punja•

Chitral•

Gilgit•

B R I T I S H
I N D I A

Leh•

A F G H A N I S T A N

A RIDE TO KHIVA.

———✦———

INTRODUCTION.

A LOW room, with but little furniture, and that of the
simplest kind ; a few telegraphic instruments scattered
about here and there in out-of-the-way corners, and
mixed up promiscuously with rifles and wooden boxes,
some filled with cartridges, others containing provisions
for a journey ; two or three bottles, labelled "Quinine,"
on a rickety wooden table ; several men of various
nationalities all talking at the same time, and a Babel
of different languages ;—such was the scene around the
writer of this work, who was leaning against the
window-sill, and glancing from time to time at an old
number of an English newspaper.

The host was a German gentleman, now several
thousand miles from the Fatherland, which he had been
induced to leave by an offer of the post of superinten-
dent and general manager on a long and important line
of recently-constructed telegraph. A graceful girl, with
large dark eyes and pearl-white teeth, but whose olive
complexion and Oriental dress showed that she was in
no way akin to the fairer beauties of Europe, was
engaged in handing round small cups of coffee to the
most excited talkers of the party, an Italian, Arab, and

Englishman, the former gesticulating wildly in an endeavour to interpret between his two companions, who were evidently not at all in accord about the subject of conversation. A bright sun, its rays flashing down on a broad stream, nearly the colour of lapis-lazuli, which flowed hard by the dwelling, had raised the temperature of the room to an almost unbearable heat. It was the month of February. In England people were shivering beside their fires or walking in slush or snow; but I was at Khartoum, having just returned from a visit to Colonel Gordon, Sir Samuel Baker's successor, on the White Nile.

It may seem strange thus to commence the narrative of a journey to Central Asia in Central Africa, and yet, had it not been for a remark made by one of the men in the low square room to which I have just referred, in all probability I should never have gone to Khiva. The conversation had lulled, the Arab and Englishman having, by means of the Italian, settled the knotty point as to whether the son of Albion, an officer late in the Khedive's service, was to receive the salary due to him in its entirety or not; the Mohammedan being of opinion that the Christian ought to be paid the amount subject to a deduction, the native Egyptian officials having always to submit to this system of taxation. However, my English friend did not see it in this light: he had agreed to serve for a certain sum—that sum he must receive—and if the Arab did not pay, why, he would complain to the Khedive. This last remark having been at length translated to the official, the latter succumbed. My compatriot, the question being settled to his satisfaction, came and looked out of the window by my side.

It was indeed a picturesque scene. The Blue Nile,

here nearly half a mile from shore to shore, lay smooth
and unrippled like a sea of glass almost at our feet.
On its vast surface were barges and native boats
innumerable, whilst many *nuggers*—the huge sailing
barques of the Arabs, and much used by them in
former years when engaged in the slave-trade—were
anchored here and there. Gangs of workmen, black
as ebony, and stripped to the waist, their well-
developed muscles standing out like knotted cords,
were busily engaged unloading a freight of ivory
bound for Cairo. An enormous *saquieh*, or water-
wheel, for irrigation purposes, was slowly revolving,
put in motion by the united exertions of a bullock
and a donkey. The wild yells of a negro lad, whose
duty it was to goad the animals should they ever flag,
mingled strangely with the creaking sounds of the
ponderous woodwork.

"I wonder where we shall all be this time next
year," suddenly remarked my companion. "God
knows," was my answer; "but I do not think I shall
try the White Nile again; if I come to Africa another
time I shall select a new line of country." At that
moment my eye fell upon a paragraph in the paper.
It was to the effect that the Government at St. Petersburg had given an order that no foreigner was to be
allowed to travel in Russian Asia, and that an Englishman who had recently attempted a journey in that
direction had been turned back by the authorities. I
have, unfortunately for my own interests, from my
earliest childhood had what my old nurse used to call
a most "contradictorious" spirit, and it suddenly
occurred to me, Why not go to Central Asia? "Well,
I shall try it," was my remark. "What, Timbuctoo?"
said my friend. "No, Central Asia;" and I showed

him the paragraph. "You will never get there; they will stop you." "They can if they like, but I don't think they will." And this trifling incident was the first thing which put the idea into my head of again attempting to reach Khiva.

I had intended to go there some few years ago, when the Russians were about to invade the country. I had even started on my journey, meaning to try and find a way into Khiva, *viâ* Persia and Merve, and, if possible, be with the Khivans at the time of the Russian attack. But this project was never realised. A typhoid fever, caught as I was rapidly travelling through Italy, laid me for four months on a bed of sickness. My leave thus was spent in a very different manner from that originally intended, and I had, as it is commonly termed, a much closer shave for my life than I believe would ever have been the case even if I had been taken prisoner by the most fanatical Turkomans in Central Asia. But the campaign was over. There would be no fighting to see. Our statesmen had learned how to appreciate a Russian's promises at their true value. Samarcand had been annexed to the Tzar's dominions, the Black Sea Treaty had been repudiated, and Russian troops were quartered in Khivan territory.*

According to some politicians Khiva was a long way from India, and it really did not signify to England whether Russia annexed it or not. Again, it was urged by others, if Russia does eventually reach our Indian frontier so much the better for England. We shall have a civilized nation as a neighbour instead of the barbarous Afghans. A third argument brought

* See Appendix A, The Russian Advance Eastward.

forward to defend the action of the Liberal Government was, that India did not signify so much to us after all, that she was a very expensive possession, and one which we should very likely have taken from us, but one certainly not worth fighting for. This was the opinion of some men who were high in office, and who thus lightly valued one of the brightest jewels in the British crown. The majority of our rulers did not trouble their heads much about the matter. India will last my time was the remark; Russia is still a long way off; and our grandchildren must look after themselves. Sufficient for the day is the evil thereof; and after me the Deluge. Thus the question was allowed to drop, and the minds of our legislators were speedily engrossed in studying the important question as to which would be the better course to pursue—to allow Englishmen to go into public-houses after eleven o'clock at night, or to send them thirsty and supperless to bed.

The following autumn the Carlist War was going on, so I went to Spain. After a time my thoughts were no longer occupied with the state of affairs in Central Asia. It was only when my friend, in reply to my observation, had observed, "You will never get there; they will stop you," that it occurred to me to ask what possible reason the Russian Government could have for pursuing a line of policy which, easily understood when adopted by a barbarous nation like China, was a singular one for even a semi-civilized power. It was the more remarkable, as, from the days of Peter the Great, the regenerator of Russia, his successors have invariably encouraged the inhabitants of Western Europe to visit and freely circulate throughout the Imperial dominions. If it were not for the German

element, which is so largely diffused throughout the
governing classes, Russia would never have arrived at
even her present state of advancement.   Of all the
Tzars of Muscovy during the last 200 years the
present Emperor is perhaps the sovereign most keenly
alive to the advantage of raising the standard of
civilization throughout his dominions, by admitting
foreigners, particularly Germans, to every office in the
empire.   The repressive order to which I have alluded,
thus absolutely cutting off Asiatic Russia from almost
all contact with the more civilized inhabitants of
Europe, was in striking contrast to the line of conduct
which had previously characterized his reign.

There was, then, something behind the scenes—
something that it was desired to hide from the eyes of
Europe.

What could it be?

Were the generals in Central Asia treating the
inhabitants of the conquered districts so cruelly, that
the fear of this reaching the Emperor's ears—not
through Russian sources, as this would be impossible,
but through the medium of a foreign press—was the
origin of the order?   Or could it be that though no
absolute cruelty had been shown to the people in the
recently-acquired territory, they were being badly
governed, and that the bribery and corruption which
goes on in Western Russia had taken deeper root
when transplanted to the far-off East?   Or was it that
the authorities in Turkistan, the enormous territory
acquired by Russia within the last few years, were
afraid of letting Europe know that instead of having
raised the tone of morality amidst the inhabitants of
Central Asia, the latter had in many instances brought
the Russians down to an Oriental level, and that the

vices and depraved habits of the East were actually being acquired by some of the conquerors?

Judging from the accounts of the few travellers who have succeeded in making a way into this comparatively speaking unknown country, any of the hypotheses above alluded to might have been the origin of the order. But I could not help thinking that there was something more behind the scenes than the mere wish to blind the eyes of Europe to these matters, or to appear as the apostles of Christianity—one of the pleas put forward by the Russian press to defend the system of annexation so steadily persevered in by the Government. There was something beyond all this; and in that something I felt convinced that the interests of Great Britain had a share. Peter the Great's will, or rather wishes, have not been forgotten by his successors. The proof of this is best shown by looking at a map of Russia as it was in his days and as it now exists; whilst in a recent staff map of Turkistan, 1875, the compiler has not even dotted in the boundary line from N. lat. 39°2′, E. long. 69°38′, to N. lat. 44°40′, E. long. 79°49¾′, thus showing that the boundary line, in his opinion, has not yet been reached. When will that limit be attained? When is the Russian advance to be barred, and where? By the Himalayas, or by the Indian Ocean? This is a question, not for our grandchildren, nor our children, but for ourselves.

CHAPTER I.

HAVING once resolved to go to Central Asia, the next question was how to execute my intention. On returning to England from Africa I eagerly read every book that could be found, and which seemed likely to give any information about the country which I proposed to visit. Vambéry's " Travels," Abbott's " From Herat to Khiva," and MacGahan's " Campaigning on the Oxus," were each in turn studied. Judging by the difficulties that the gallant correspondent of the *New York Herald* had to overcome before he carried his project of reaching Khiva into execution, I felt convinced that the task I had laid out for myself was anything but an easy one.

The time of year in which I should have to attempt the journey was another obstacle to the undertaking. My leave of absence from my regiment would only commence in December. I had already, in previous journeys through Russia, discovered what the term " cold " really means in that country. After reading of the weather experienced by Captain Abbott when travelling in the month of March, in a latitude a good deal to the south of that which seemed to me the most practicable, I felt certain that very careful preparations must be made for a ride through the steppes in mid-winter, or that I should inevitably be frozen. The cold of the Kirghiz desert is a thing unknown I believe in any other part of the world, or even in the Arctic regions. An enormous expanse of flat country, extending for hundreds of miles, and devoid of everything save snow and salt lakes, and here and there *saksaool*, a species of bramble-tree, would have to be traversed on horseback ere Khiva could be reached. The winds in those parts of Asia are unknown to the inhabitants of Europe. When they grumble at the so-called east wind, they can little imagine what that wind is like in those countries which lie exposed to the full fury of its first onslaught. For there you meet with no warm ocean to mollify its rigour, no trees, no rising land, no hills or mountains to check it in its course. It blows on uninterruptedly over a vast snow and salt-covered track. It absorbs the saline matter, and cuts the faces of those exposed to its gusts. The sensation is more like the application of the edge of a razor than anything else to which it can be compared.

There was, besides this, something else to be taken into consideration. I was well aware that no assistance could be expected from the Russian authorities. They might not content themselves by indirectly throwing obstacles in my path, but might even stop me by sheer force if they found all other ways fail. The account of the prohibitory order which I had seen published in the English journal was, I had every reason to believe, correct. Should I not find, after crossing the Ural river, and entering Asia, that my long sleigh journey had been to no purpose, and have to retrace my steps through European Russia? These were my first impressions on arriving in

England; but on talking the matter over with some Russians of my acquaintance, they assured me that I was entirely mistaken; that, on the contrary, the authorities at St. Petersburg would readily permit English officers to travel in Central Asia. It was observed that the order to which I had alluded referred only to merchants or people who tried to smuggle contraband goods into the recently-annexed khanates.

A few months later I had the honour of making the acquaintance of his Excellency Count Schouvaloff, the Russian Ambassador in London, and formerly the head of the secret police at St. Petersburg. He was excessively kind, and promised to do what he could to further my plans, but in answer to a straightforward question as to whether I should be permitted to travel in Russian Asia or not, his reply was, " My dear sir, that is a subject about which I cannot give you any answer. The authorities at St. Petersburg will be able to afford you every possible information." It was a diplomatic answer—one which bound the Count to nothing—and I went away charmed with the tact and affability of the Russian Ambassador. Apparently there was nothing to be learned officially from Russian sources; but unofficially, and one by one, many little bits of information crept out. I now first learned that General Milutin, the Minister of War at St. Petersburg, was personally much opposed to the idea of an English officer travelling in Central Asia, particularly in that part which lies between the boundaries of British India and Russia. According to him, a Russian traveller, a Mr. Pachino, had not been well treated by the authorities in India.* This gentleman had

---

* This I believe to be incorrect, as also the other statement—that Mr. Pachino was not permitted to enter Afghanistan.

not been permitted to enter Afghanistan; and, in consequence, General Milutin did not see why he should allow an Englishman to do what was denied a Russian subject.

Another peculiarity which I remarked in several Russians whose acquaintance I at that time had the honour of making, it may here be not out of place to mention. This was their desire to impress upon my mind the great advantage it would be for England to have a civilized neighbour like Russia on her Indian frontier; and when I did not take the trouble to dissent from their views—for it is a waste of breath to argue with Russians about this question—how eager they were for me to impress their line of thought upon the circle of people with whom I was the more immediately connected. Of course, the arguments brought forward were based upon purely philanthropic motives, upon Christianity and civilization. They said that the two great powers ought to go together hand in glove; that there ought to be railways all through Asia, formed by Anglo-Russian companies; that Russia and England had every sympathy in common which should unite them; that they both hated Germany and loved France; that England and Russia could conquer the world, and so on.

It was a line of reasoning delightfully Russian, and though I was not so rude as to differ from my would-be persuaders, and lent an attentive ear to all their eloquence, I could not help thinking that the mutual sympathy between England and Germany is much greater than that between England and Russia; that the Greek faith as practised by the lower orders in Russia is pure paganism in comparison with the Protestant religion which exists in Prussia and Great

Britain; that Germany and Great Britain are natural
allies against Russia, or any other power aggressively
disposed towards them ; that Germans and Englishmen, who are well acquainted with Russia, understand
by the term "Russian civilization" something diametrically opposite to what is attributed to it by those people
who form their ideas of Muscovite progress from the
few Russians whom they meet abroad ; and that the
Honduras railway would be a paying concern to its
English shareholders in comparison with an Anglo-
Russian line, to be constructed in Central Asia with
English capital and Russian directors.

The time was wearing on, November was drawing
to a close, my leave of absence would begin on the first
of the following month. On that day I must commence
my travels. Preparations were rapidly made. Under
the advice of Captain Allen Young, of Arctic fame, I
ordered a huge waterproof, and, consequently, air-proof,
bag of prepared sail-cloth. The bag was seven feet
and a half long, and ten feet round. A large aperture
was left on one side, and the traveller could thus take
up his quarters inside, and sleep well protected from
the cold winds. The bag would also be useful in
many other ways, and I found it of great convenience
for every purpose save the one for which it was
originally intended. The manufacturer, not calculating
on the enormous dimensions an individual assumes
when enveloped in furs, had not made the aperture
large enough. The consequence was that the difficulties, when I attempted to take a header into the
recess of my sleeping apartment, were almost insur-
mountable. Only on one occasion, and when somewhat lighter clad than usual, I succeeded in effecting
an entrance. Four pairs of the thickest Scotch fishing

stockings were also ordered; and jerseys and flannel shirts of a texture to which people in this country are but little accustomed. Then came a suit of clothes, made by Messrs. Kino, of Regent Street, and in which they assured me it would be impossible to feel cold. The clothes, I must admit, were exceptionally well made, and well suited to be worn under a sheepskin attire, but I cannot wish my worst enemy a greater punishment than forcing him to sleep out on the steppes in winter time with mere cloth attire, no matter how thick. Fur or skins of some kind must be worn, or without this precaution the traveller, should he once close his eyes, will undergo a great risk of never opening them again. Two pairs of boots lined with fur were also taken; and for physic—with which it is as well to be supplied when travelling in out-of-the-way places—some quinine, and Cockle's pills, the latter a most invaluable medicine, and one which I have used on the natives of Central Africa with the greatest possible success. In fact, the marvellous effects produced upon the mind and body of an Arab Sheik, who was impervious to all native medicines, when I administered to him five Cockle's pills, will never fade from my memory; and a friend of mine, who passed through the same district many months afterwards, informed me that my fame as a "medicine man" had not died out, but that the marvellous cure was even then a theme of conversation in the bazaar.

So far as I could learn from the books which related to Central Asia, there would be but little game, and nothing particular in the shape of sport. I determined not to take a rifle. The cartridges would have considerably added to the weight of my luggage, the prime object being to travel as light as possible.

However, as it was as well to have some sort of a gun in the event of falling in with wild fowl, which I had been told abounded in some places, I took a favourite old No. 12 small-bore, and amongst other cartridges a few loaded with ball, in case I should encounter any bears or wolves. A regulation revolver, with about twenty cartridges, made up my defensive arsenal in the event of an attack from the Turkomans.

The next thing to be thought of was a cooking apparatus. If I had taken the advice of many kind friends, I should have travelled with a *batterie de cuisine* sufficient for the wants of M. Soyer himself. But canteens could not be thought of for a moment, on account of the extra weight, so I limited myself to two soldiers' mess tins, and admirable little utensils they are too, whether for cooking over a spirit-lamp or on a fire, and far superior to any of the more costly and cumbersome articles especially invented to get out of order and perplex the traveller. A trooper's hold-all, with its accompanying knife, fork, and spoon, completed my kit, and with a thermometer, barometer, and pocket sextant by way of instruments, I was ready to start. Even this amount of luggage was much more than was desirable, and when placing the baggage for my journey—consisting of the sleeping sack, a pair of saddle-bags, railway bag, and gun—into the scales, I found that it weighed exactly eighty-five pounds. An officer in the Foot Guards—my friend K.—wished very much to accompany me in my journey. He would have been a most cheery and agreeable companion, as he was accustomed to travel, and capable of roughing it to any amount, but he was ignorant of Russian. By this time I was thoroughly aware of the difficulties that would most likely be thrown in my way, and of the little chance I had of getting to Khiva alone, so I was compelled to decline his proposal.*

The day before my departure from London I received a very courteous letter from Count Schouvaloff. He said that as I was provided with letters to General Milutin, the Russian Minister of War, and to General Kauffmann, the Commander-in-Chief of the Forces in the Government of Turkistan, it only remained for him to give me a letter of introduction to his brother at St. Petersburg, and to wish me God speed on my journey. He also added that he had sent off a despatch to the Minister of Foreign Affairs at St. Petersburg, asking him to do everything he could to aid me in my proposed journey. And so at the last moment I began to flatter myself things looked a little brighter, but some observations from Mr. MacGahan, whose acquaintance I was so fortunate as to make at the house of a mutual friend, a few evenings previous to my departure, made me still rather doubtful of success. "You will get on very well as far as Fort Number One," had been the remark, "and then you will have to pull yourself together and make your rush, and again in the same way when you leave Russian territory for India; but it is to be done, though the odds are rather against you." He had also given me some valuable hints about acquiring a knowledge of the Tartar language, and travelling as light as possible.†

---

* K. was determined not to be idle during his leave, and, as he could not go with me to Russia, went by way of a change to Abyssinia, where, I believe, he had some interesting adventures.

† To Mr. MacGahan, and subsequently to Mr. Schuyler, First Secretary at the Russian Embassy at St. Petersburg, I am greatly indebted for much valuable information with reference to my journey.

CHAPTER II.

THE 30th November, 1875, broke cold and damp. It
was one of those disagreeable days that depress and
lower the barometer of the human spirit to a semi-
despondent level; but I had finished all my regimental
duty, and having provided myself at Thornhill's with
a strong waist-belt to contain the amount of gold I
thought necessary for my journey, and which by the
way was a most uncomfortable bedfellow, I drove to
the Victoria Station, to start by the night mail.

I had determined not to take a servant—they are
generally in the way, unless they know something of
the country travelled in. Under other conditions
master and man have to change places. I must say,
however, that I was sorry to leave behind my faithful
fellow; he had been with me in several parts of the
world, and was able to make himself understood by
signs and the few broken words of the language he
might pick up, in a manner to me quite incomprehen-

sible, but Russian *moujiki* (peasants) and Tartar camel-drivers would have been too much even for him. Besides, he was a married man, and I did not wish to be saddled with his wife and family in the event of a disaster.

Our iron horse galloped merrily over the distance between London and Dover. The passage to Ostend was a favourable one, and the following afternoon at 4 P.M. I found myself again in the familiar old station of Cologne.

Two or three hours' delay, waiting for the night express to Berlin, and once more *en route.* The capital of Germany was reached the following morning, but I had no time to stop, much as I should have liked to visit the many well-loved old nooks and corners familiar to me in my student days. As it was, I could barely catch the train for St. Petersburg, when I found the carriages very much overcrowded, and with difficulty secured a place.

Two Russian gentlemen were in the same carriage. In the course of conversation I found that one had been employed in the diplomatic service in Italy. He said that he had suddenly received a telegram from Prince Gortschakoff, at that time at Berlin, requiring his presence there immediately. The clothes worn in Italy, even in winter, are not necessarily of the warmest texture, and my fellow-traveller, who, by the way, looked in very delicate health, found his journey northward anything but a pleasant one. But his troubles on arriving at the capital were only beginning, for the Prince said to him, " I am going to St. Petersburg, and will give you your orders there ; leave by the next train." It was very cold weather, and the unfortunate secretary, unprovided with the necessary wraps, was miserable at the way the fates had served him. He was an Anglo-phobist, and much chuckled as he told his companion that a violent article against England had appeared in the *Nord* —a paper which, according to him, is inspired by the Ministry at St. Petersburg—with reference to Mr. Disraeli having purchased the Viceroy of Egypt's Suez Canal shares.

"The English are a great nation, but very mad," observed another Russian. "They are sufficiently sane when their interests are concerned," said the secretary, "for they have bought these Suez shares, which they will make pay, financially as well as politically speaking. Two years ago they nearly inveigled the Shah into a treaty with Baron Reuter, and that would have given them the control of the whole of Persia; but, thank goodness, our people checkmated them there, and I do not think England will try that game on again just at present; as to Strausberg, he is a joke to that fellow Reuter. A nice business the latter would have made out of it, and the English too for the matter of that."

The day wore away, and the night came on cold and bleak, as we rattled northward on our course. The secretary sat shivering in the corner, and the rest of us, enveloped in furs, sought the arms of Morpheus. It was an unusual thing to experience such cold in a North German railway-carriage, as generally they are well warmed by means of stoves, and the more frequent fault to find with them is overheating and stuffiness; but for some reason or other the stupid attendant had let the fire out, and the result was anything but an agreeable night. Presently we reached the boundary limit between Germany and Russia. A few minutes later I found myself, with the rest of the passengers, in a large high hall, set aside for the examination of luggage and inspection of passports.

It was not a pleasant thing to be kept waiting in a cold room for at least three-quarters of an hour, whilst some spectacled officials suspiciously conned each passport. The Russian secretary himself was not at all impressed with the wisdom of his Government in still adhering to this system, which is so especially invented to annoy travellers. "What nonsense it is," he remarked; "the greater scoundrel a man is the greater certainty of his passport being in the most perfect order. Whenever I go to France, and am asked for my passport, I avoid the difficulty by saying, ' Je suis Anglais; no passport;' and the officials, taking me for an Englishman, do not bother me, or make me show it."

I was myself a little uneasy about my own pass. It was one which had done service about five years previously, and I had forgotten to send it to the Russian Consulate previous to my departure from London. However, after looking at the document for some time, and scrutinising its owner very carefully, the official returned it to me.

The customs' examination was easily got through. The only part of my luggage which puzzled the *douane* officer was the sleeping-bag. He smelt it suspiciously, the waterproof cloth having a strong odour. "What is it for?" "To sleep in." He put his nose down again, and apparently uncertain in his own mind as to what course to pursue, called for another official, who desired me to unroll it. "And you sleep in that big bag?" was the question. "Yes." "What extraordinary people the English are!" observed the man who had inspected my passport, and *sotto voce,*

" he must be mad ;" when the other bystanders drew
back a little, thinking that possibly I was dangerous
as well.

Forward again, in a most commodious and well-
arranged carriage—well warmed, fairly lit, and containing every convenience the traveller could require
during the journey. The Russian trains are constructed on the American principle. You can walk
from one end of them to the other if you like, whilst
two attendants in each carriage supply every want of
the traveller. I must say that in this respect railway
travelling in Russia is far better arranged than in
England, and the refreshment-rooms are unequalled by
any in this country. Everything you ask for is ready
at a moment's notice, the dishes are hot and good,
whilst the attendance and the bill—a very important
adjunct to a traveller's pleasure—leave nothing to be
desired, the charges being exceedingly moderate. But
with all these advantages there is one great drawback,
and that is the slowness of the pace, which, when
travelling through a vast country like Russia, is a
matter of considerable importance. Extreme cold
would seem to have the same effect upon the human
mind as extreme heat. The indifference to time which
characterizes the Russian is only equalled by the low
estimation in which it is held by the Spaniard ; whilst
the Russian word *zavtra* ("to-morrow") is used as
frequently by the Muscovite as its Spanish equivalent,
mañana, by the inhabitant of the Peninsula. But there
is something else which may account for the slowness
of pace of the trains of Russia, and that is the careless
way in which the lines have been constructed. The
Government inspectors, by all atcounts, are easily
suborned. The golden metal has charms for them

greater than the lives of their countrymen. If the engine-drivers were to attempt even a moderate rate of speed, the sleepers and rails would inevitably give way. This was the explanation given me by a fellow-traveller, when referring to the subject.

St. Petersburg was at last reached, the journey having been accomplished in three days and a half from Charing Cross. I had but little delay in obtaining my luggage. In this respect things are well managed in the Russian stations, and I shortly afterwards found myself comfortably lodged in Demout's Hotel. The day was still young. Determining to take advantage of the early hour, I took a sleigh and proceeded to call upon General Mílutin, the Minister of War.

The foreigner, unaccustomed to St. Petersburg, is at first a little astonished at the way he is beset, on leaving the portico of his hotel, by the numerous sleigh-drivers who are congregated outside. "Where to? Where to?" they cry: when, hearing the stranger stammer out the name of the street, and the name of the person to whom the house belongs—for in Russia, as a rule, houses are known by the name of their proprietors, and are not numbered as elsewhere—a brisk competition ensues. "I will take you for a rouble, sir. Look what a beautiful sleigh I have, and what a fine trotting horse." "He knows nothing about it!" shouts another; "I will take the gentleman for sixty kopecks!" and his face assumes an expression as if by his offer he had conferred on you a favour unequalled in the annals of sleigh-drivers. The other fellows then wait a few seconds, to see if the stranger will succumb to the offer; but if not, and you walk forward two or three steps, the drivers change their tone, from sixty to forty, and from that to twenty kopecks (about sixpence in English money), this being about the value of an average "course" in St. Petersburg, for there is no established tariff. The result is that foreigners are more robbed by the sleigh-drivers in that city than even by our London cabmen.

General Milutin was not at home, so I was informed by a tall servant, the hall porter, when, leaving the letter of introduction and my card, I returned to the hotel. There was no Russian piece going on in any of the theatres that evening, although there were French and German plays, besides an Italian opera. In St. Petersburg there is one capital Russian theatre, the Alexandrensky, and also a national opera house, the Marensky; but the Alexandrensky is often used for German plays, and thus it sometimes occurs, as on the day when I arrived, that there is no performance going on, in the national idiom, in any theatre in the capital. But, after all, this can be easily explained by the intense dislike many apparently well-educated Russians have to their own language. I have often heard them say, " It does very well for the *moujiki* (peasants), but the language for society is French." This remark has been made by Russians from the provinces of the interior, whose knowledge of French was so imperfect, and their accent so atrocious, that it jarred on the ear when listening to them. There is no doubt that there is an intense contempt amongst the higher circles throughout the empire for everything purely Russian; it must be foreign to be eagerly sought after. This weakness on the part of the well-to-do classes has a very discouraging effect on the industries of the nation. It would rather surprise people in this country if an Englishman were to address his wife in a foreign language, and if the correspondence between members of the same family were never carried on in English; or should the daughter of the house be unable to write a letter, save in French, without making the most outrageous faults in grammar as well as spelling. But this surprises no one in Russia. There is not that love of everything national amidst the higher classes; and to study the real Russ you must not visit St. Petersburg. For there the native is so veneered over with foreign polish, that it is not easy to discover what exists below the surface. A French fencing-master is infinitely preferred to a Russian Socrates. The present Emperor, it is said, has done everything in his power to check this weakness on the part of his subjects. He is a far-seeing man, and the empire owes more to him and to his beneficent rule than to any of his predecessors; but a deep-rooted custom cannot be ousted in one generation. It will take many years to teach the inhabitants of the capital that this running after everything foreign, to the detriment of national enterprise, will never add to the prosperity of Russia. Another influence which has a deterrent effect on the development of the commercial and agricultural interest throughout the country is the high importance given to military rank, as a Russian country gentleman once bitterly remarked to me, " In my country a man is nobody unless he eats the bread of the State. He must wear a uniform, he must have a *tchin* (military rank) or its equivalent, should he serve in the civil service. He must be a consumer instead of a producer; and then, and then alone, is he a man to be respected and looked up to." The result is, that all the energies of the nation are expended in what will never bring grist to the mill; but, if this system be persisted in, it will eventually cause a national bankruptcy.

As I was reading a Russian newspaper that after-noon, I came upon a short paragraph which so thoroughly displays the weakness for strong liquors which prevails throughout the empire, that I am tempted to reproduce it.

It appeared that in a certain large village a spirit merchant wished to open a drinking establishment; to do this he had to obtain the consent of the inhabitants. It was determined to put up to auction the right of establishing a house of that sort. This fetched the sum of 3,500 roubles, which, divided amongst the population, made exactly 7½ roubles a head.

The money was paid, and, according to the corre-spondent, the proprietor must have got back the amount he had given in the first three days, as unusual drunkenness prevailed during all that time. When the money was spent things once more took their usual course.

Drunkenness is not looked upon with nearly the same feelings of abhorrence in Russia as in England—amongst the military class especially. An officer who can drink all his comrades under the table is looked upon as a hero. The climate undoubtedly has a great deal to do with these ovations to Bacchus; and when the thermometer is below zero, the body requires much more caloric, both externally as well as internally, than in more temperate zones.

The Russian officers, by way of thoroughly keeping out the cold, have invented a singular drink. They call it jonka. After dinner, and when champagne, claret, and liquors have been drunk to an extent of which people in this country have no conception, a huge silver bowl is produced; brandy, rum, spirits, and wines of all kinds are poured in promiscuously, apples and pears, with all the fruits on the dessert-table, are cut up and tossed into the liquid. It is then set on fire, and when in this state the flaming mixture is poured out into large goblets, which are handed round the table. It is a high trial if the drinking bout has been persisted in for several hours. It is calculated to try the stomachs as well as the heads of the guests. But we are in Russia, *et à la guerre comme à la guerre.* Until this excess of drinking goes out of fashion with the upper circles, we cannot be surprised if the lower ones remain equally addicted to it.

That evening I dined at the *table d'hôte.* This is comparatively speaking a new institution in Russia, where to dine *à la carte* is preferred. For any one not accustomed to them, Russian dinners are rather remarkable. Previously to sitting down at table the guests are taken to a side buffet; here in profusion are sardines, caviare pressed and fresh—a delicacy unknown in this country, where the so-called fresh caviare is invariably a little salted—anchovies, and every conceivable relish. Cigarettes are smoked, a glass or so of liquor drank, and the party adjourns to the dinner-table. With the soup little *patés* made of meat and rice are eaten in lieu of bread. The soups, particularly those made of fish, are excellent, and well suited to a Russian climate, where an enormous quantity of nitrogen must be consumed to keep up the animal heat.

I found myself seated next to a Russian officer, a general in the Engineers, and had a long conversation with him about India. " You English," he said, " are always thinking that we want India; but you are apt to forget one equally important point, which is, that some day the natives of that country may wish to govern themselves. I study the course of events in India very closely ; and what do I see ? why, that you are doing everything you possibly can to teach the inhabitants their own strength. You establish schools ; you educate the people ; they read your language— many of them even your newspapers ; and the leading men know what is going on in Europe just as well as you yourselves. But the day will come when some agitators will set these thinking masses in motion ; and then what force have you to oppose to them ? If ever there was a nation determined to commit suicide it is England. She holds India, as she herself allows, by the force of arms, and yet she is doing everything in her power to induce the conquered country to throw off the yoke."

"But do you not think," I observed, "that when our frontiers touch, as your statesmen wish, there will be more agitators than even now in India ?"

He did not reply to this question, but lit a cigarette and turned the conversation. There was a great deal of reason undoubtedly in what he had urged. However, there is one argument in favour of further education in India, which is, that the better educated the natives of India become, the greater probability of their seeing that their own interests are far more likely to be cared for under a British than a Russian rule. But this still leaves open the question of whether they might not prefer to govern themselves, which undoubtedly will some day be the case.

I remember once meeting a highly-educated Hindoo on board a Peninsular and Oriental steamer, and having a long conversation with him. He had

travelled in England, where he had been extremely
well received. On my asking how the English were
liked in India, he simply replied, "You are a great
nation. The English people are devoted to their
national institutions. How should you like a foreign
ruler to establish himself in your country ? "

The following day I called at the British Embassy,
but there was no one at home save the Military
Attaché, and he was so engaged in having a lesson
that he had no time to see me. Later on, I met
some old friends, and conversed with them about my
proposed journey. They all took a pessimist view
of the case. "Get to Khiva!" said one man. "You
might as well try to get to the moon. The Russians
will not openly stop you, but they will put the screw
upon our own Foreign Office and force the latter to do
so. The Russians are as suspicious as Orientals, and
they will imagine that you are sent by your Government to stir up the Khivans. They will never believe
that an officer, for the mere sake of travel, and at his
own expense, would go to Khiva." "Why," observed
another, "only a short time ago an officer who was
about to start for Turkistan, wanted to take an English servant with him. The man, I believe, had been a
private in the Second Life Guards. Somehow or other
this got to the ears of a Russian General. He sent
for the servant, and said, 'Did you ever correspond for
the *Times ?*' The man, who looked upon the question
as one put to prove his capabilities, answered, 'Never
did, sir ; but have no doubt I could, if you wish it.' 'I
tell you what it is,' said the General, 'if I catch you
writing a line to England about what you see when you
are with us, I will have you hanged.' The man became
alarmed. He could clean a horse, and his ideas did

not soar above that calling; but to be told that he was to be hanged if he wrote a letter! Why he might want to write home to his friends! He went to some authorities at St. Petersburg and asked them their advice. The result was, he started with his master, but only got as far as Kazan, for, on arriving at that point, an order was sent to have him turned back."

The Russian soldiers, it seems, are not very particular what they do in Central Asia, and General Kauffmann greatly dislikes publicity. Judging from accounts subsequently given me by eye-witnesses of what has taken place, I cannot help thinking that the General is wise in his generation.

In the afternoon I called upon Mr. Schuyler, the United States' Secretary of Legation at St. Petersburg. He had been to Tashkent and Bokhara, having travelled as far as Fort Number One with Mr. MacGahan, the energetic correspondent of the *New York Herald.* Mr. Schuyler had been able to gather a great deal of most valuable information in the course of his travels. He is, I believe, the only diplomatist the Russians have ever permitted to visit their Eastern possessions, and is a very keen observer, besides being a thorough master of the Russian language. He had been able to dive considerably below the surface in his endeavours to master the state of affairs in Turkistan. His report was forwarded to Washington, and subsequently published in a blue-book; the authorities in Turkistan not being very pleased at the way he exposed their administration.* Mr. Schuyler gave me some useful hints

* Mr. Schuyler exposes the weak points in the Russian Administration in Turkistan; but in other respects he is favourable to the Russians and to their policy in Central Asia. He thinks that it is for the interests of the United States for the Russians to be firmly established in Central Asia, so as to act as a counterpoise to British influence in the East.

as to what I should require for my journey.. He was engaged in writing a book on his travels. From the first day of his arrival at St. Petersburg he had studied hard to master the Russian language, probably feeling that a diplomatist in a land where he cannot read the newspapers .or converse with all classes of society, if necessary, is rather like a fish out of water, and receiving a salary which he has not fairly earned.

The German Chancellor showed what he thought of this matter. The very first thing he did, many years ago, when at the Russian Embassy in St. Petersburg, was to study the Russian language, which he eventually mastered. Bismarck's example is not a bad one to follow ; but until the language be made a compulsory one at the examination of candidates for our Foreign Office, I fear that the business of the British Embassy at St. Petersburg will continue to be transacted through an interpreter.

Later on I called upon Count Schouvaloff's brother —to whom the Count had so kindly given me a letter of introduction—but he was abroad, so I was informed by the servant, and consequently the letter was of no use.

I began to be a little anxious about the letter which I had left at the house of General Milutin, the Minister of War, particularly as I had omitted to fee his hall porter—a great omission on my part, as I was informed by an Englishman, an old resident at St. Petersburg ; and he added, "nothing whatever can be done in Russia without a judicious disposal of presents. From hall porters to the mistresses of those officials, who give out the railway contracts all have their price. You will find gold, or rather its equivalent in rouble paper, an open sesame throughout the Russian Empire."

I must say, that for my part, I did not share this opinion about the porter's venality. However, as I had written to ask the General if I could have the honour of an interview, and no reply had been sent, I determined to write another letter, which was couched in the following terms :—

"To General Milutin, the Minister of War.

"Sir,—I trust that you will pardon the liberty I am taking in writing to you without having the honour of your personal acquaintance.

"I wish to have the permission to go to India, *viâ* Khiva, Merve, Cabul. But as I had read in some English papers, previous to my departure from London, that the Russian Government had issued an order forbidding Englishmen to travel in Russian Asia, I thought that I ought to address myself to Count Schouvaloff, the Russian Ambassador in London. He said to me, 'I cannot personally answer your question; but when you arrive at St. Petersburg, the authorities there will give you every information.' Before I quitted London I received a letter from Count Schouvaloff, informing me that he had written officially to the Minister of Foreign Affairs at St. Petersburg with reference to my journey, whilst the Count enclosed me a letter of introduction to his brother, and concluded by wishing me a happy journey. Now, sir, I should much like to know if I can have this permission. If it cannot be granted me, will you do me the honour of writing two lines and tell me frankly, Yes or No. If the answer is No, I shall leave St. Petersburg immediately, because my leave of absence will soon be over, and I do not wish to remain here longer than it is necessary to receive your answer.

"I have the honour to be, etc."

Having dispatched this letter, I began to be a little easier in my mind. I did not think that the General, who, by all accounts, is a most gentlemanlike man, would purposely delay replying to my note; nor was I wrong in my surmises. In the meantime I was trying to get all the information I could about the route to Khiva.

CHAPTER III.

MR. SCHUYLER thought that the best way to go to
Khiva would be by Astrakhan and the Caspian to
Krasnovodsk, and from there across the steppes on
horseback to Khiva. This, undoubtedly, would have
been the shortest and easiest journey; but a paragraph
which I read in a paper that afternoon showed me that
this route was out of the question. The paragraph
was to the effect that the accumulation of ice had
already prevented navigation in the Caspian, and that
the Volga was frozen.

I tried to obtain some information from a few
Russian officers whose acquaintance I accidentally
made, but all to no effect. They did not know themselves. They believed that there was a post to Khiva,
and that the Tartars had carried letters there on horseback, but whether from Orenburg or from Tashkent no
one knew.

I now determined, should the reply to my letters to
General Milutin be in the affirmative, to go to Orenburg and seek for further information in that town. In

the event of General Milutin's answer being in the negative, I had made up my mind to go straight to Persia, and then, skirting the Russian boundary-line, pass *viâ* Merve and Bokhara to India.

It would have been an interesting journey, though very difficult to know the exact boundary-line in some parts, for, as I have noticed before, in the last Russian Staff Map of Turkistan, dated 1875, the boundary-line extending over a large track of country is not marked by a dotted line, as in other parts of the map; thus showing that there is a doubt in the mind of the officer by whom it was compiled as to how far Russia extends in that direction.

All sorts of reports were circulating with reference to General Kauffmann, the Governor-General of Turkistan, some to the effect that he had sent in his resignation. Again, it was said that he had only received a jewel-mounted sword in return for his services, and that one of his subordinates had been similarly rewarded. One thing, however, seemed very certain, which was, that the General had left Tashkent, and was on his road to St. Petersburg. But whether on account of the recent disturbances in Kokan, or for General Milutin to consult him with reference to a further advance upon Kashgar, were mooted points, and to which no one could give an answer. In fact, there is no country, perhaps, in the universe where reports are so rife as in Russia. The press is gagged, owing to the strict system of censorship which prevails. Gossip runs rampant. Each man embellishes the story he has heard from his neighbours; when it eventually acquires greater dimensions than that of the three black crows, so happily told by one of our English authors.

The letter to General Milutin produced the effect

I anticipated. The result was a reply, directed, singularly enough, to the British Embassy, although in my own letter I had distinctly written my address as Demout's Hotel. The communication was to the effect that the Commandants in Russian Asia had received orders to aid me in my journey through the territory under their command : but that the Imperial Government could not give its acquiescence to the extension of my journey beyond Russian territory, as the authorities could not answer for the security or the lives of travellers beyond the extent of the Emperor's dominions.

Now this was so self-evident a statement that I was much surprised at General Milutin for making it. Of course the Russian Government could not be responsible for my safety beyond the Emperor's dominions, any more than could Her Majesty's Government be responsible for the life of a traveller passing through Natal to Central Africa.

Merve and Herat no more belong to the Emperor of Russia than Central Africa to the Queen of Great Britain ; then how could the Imperial Government at St. Petersburg imagine itself liable for anything happening to me outside Russian territory ?

There were only two inferences to be drawn from the letter : either that the General, who is by all accounts a most kind-hearted man, valued my life at a greater price than I did myself—which was exceedingly amiable on his part—or that, for certain military and political reasons, he did not wish me to go to Central Asia.

I must say that I was very much surprised at the way he endeavoured to deter me ; and Russian officers must be very different to English ones, if the mere fact of there being a little risk is sufficient to stop their travelling.

I should have much liked to ask General Milutin one question, and to have heard his answer—not given solemnly as the Russian Chancellor makes his promises, but face to face, and as a soldier—Would he, when a captain, have turned his face homeward to St. Petersburg simply because he was told by a foreign government that it could not be responsible for his safety? I do not think so; and I have a far higher opinion of the Russian officers than to imagine that they would be deterred by such an argument if used to them under circumstances similar to those in which I found myself.

However, there was the letter in black and white. The only thing left for me to do was to write and thank the General for permitting me to travel in Russian Asia, adding in a final postscript that I should probably return either by Tashkent or Teheran. My intention was to go from Khiva to Merve, and so on to Meshed, when I should have been in Persian territory. I could have then gone *viâ* Herat and the Bolan Pass to Shikarpoor, and returned either through Cachemire, Kashgar, and Tashkent, or by Cabul, Bokhara, and Kasala to European Russia.

The final preparations for the journey were soon made, all my superfluous clothes sent back to England, a pair of high cloth boots, commonly known as valenki, bought to keep out the cold, and the following evening at 8 P.M. I found myself at the railway station *en route* for Orenburg. A marvellous ignorance seemed to exist amidst the clerks at the booking office when I asked them how far the line extended in the direction of that town. Did it go to Samara? No. Could I

take my ticket to Orenburg? No. Well, how far
could I book? None of them could tell me; so,
taking a ticket as far as Penza, which I knew was
on the line, I proceeded to register my luggage.

The box containing my cartridges struck the
attention of an official who was standing beside the
scales, and "Pray what may this be?" he observed,
looking suspiciously at the case. "It is very heavy."

He was quite right; cartridges are heavy, and the
four hundred which made up my ammunition—and
which travelled to Khiva and back again—were often
a source of great annoyance to myself as well as my
camels.

"They are little things which contain some lead,"
I answered. "Oh! instruments which contain lead,"
he said. "Yes," I replied; "very useful instruments;
pray be careful with them;" upon which he gave me
the receipt.

The carriages between St. Petersburg and Moscow
are, if possible, more commodious than those which
run from the capital to the German frontier. They are
also well supplied with sleeping compartments, so the
journey can be performed as comfortably as if travelling in a Cunard's steamboat.

Upon taking my seat, two ladies, dressed in the
deepest black, entered the carriage, and solicited sub-
scriptions from the different passengers for the wounded
insurgents in Herzegovina.

"I suppose some of this money will go to the main-
tenance of the hale as well as the sick," observed a
fellow-traveller. "Poor fellows, they want arms very
badly."

"I would give anything to drive out those
Mussulmans," remarked his companion, producing a

well-filled purse, and making a large donation to the fund.

His example was followed by all the other Russians in the carriage. Not wishing to appear conspicuous by not subscribing, I added a trifle, my *vis-a-vis* saying, "Thank you, brother. It will help to keep the sore open; the sooner the Turk falls to pieces the better. What is the good of our having a fleet on the Black Sea unless we can command the Dardanelles? The longer this affair continues in Herzegovina the more likely we are to reach Constantinople."

"What will the English say to this?" I inquired. "Oh, England! she goes for nothing now," he replied. "She is so bent upon money-making that it will take a great deal of kicking to make her fight. Why, she did not do anything when Gortschakoff repudiated the Black Sea treaty."

"He (Gortschakoff) chose the right time for this," added a fellow-traveller; "it was just after Sedan."

"After Sedan or before Sedan," continued the first speaker, "it would have been all the same; England is like an overfed bull, she has lost the use of her horns."

"What of her fleet?" I inquired. "Well, what can she do with it?" was the answer. "She can block up the Baltic — but the frost does that for six months in the year, and she can prevent the corn from our Southern Provinces reaching her own markets; bread will be dearer in London, that is all. England will not land troops in the Crimea again."

"God grant that she may," said another; "our railway to Sevastopol is now open."

I here remarked that England was not likely to declare war without having an ally. "But what if Germany or Austria were to join her?"

"As for those pigs of Germans, we must fight them some day or other," replied the previous speaker, and when the Tzarevitch is Emperor, please God we will beat them well, and drive every German brute out of Russia; they fatten on our land at the expense of our brothers."

"But supposing they get the best of it?"

"Well, what can they do? they cannot stop in Russia, even if they should be able to assail us. We can play the old game—keep on retiring. Russia is big, and there is plenty of country at our back."

"They might take the Baltic Provinces," I remarked.

"Take them! I hope Gortschakoff will give them to Bismarck before long, and arrange that Germany does not interfere with us when we march upon Constantinople," said another of the travellers.

"Arrange with Bismarck! you might as well arrange with the devil!" said the first speaker; "he will take everything he can, and give us nothing. He is the greatest enemy we have—except perhaps the people at Vienna! However, they do not count for much, as with the Czechs and Hungarians, they have plenty on their hands; but we must give those Austrians a beating before long."

"Which would be most popular, a war with Austria or one with Germany?" I inquired.

"With Austria," was the unanimous reply, "because we know that we can march to Vienna without any difficulty. We are not prepared for Germany; our army is not yet sufficiently organised to compete with Moltke's forces. We must bide our time. Besides this, the Emperor likes his uncle too much. When the Tzarevitch is on the throne then we shall have a war.   Bismarck, too, does not want to fight at present.   He would like to see Russia fight England, Austria, and Turkey; the old fox would sit still himself, and do nothing ; but if we got the best of Austria, he would take Vienna and Holland as his share of the spoil, and as a reward for his exertions; whilst, if we were beaten, he would take the Baltic Provinces. But perhaps you are a German," said one of the travellers.   "No, I am an Englishman," was my answer, "and I am very much obliged to you for this interesting conversation."

Moscow was reached early the following morning. Finding that there would be no train to Penza till the afternoon, I took a sleigh, and drove to call on Her Majesty's Consul, a Mr. Leslie, whose acquaintance I had made during a previous visit to Moscow. His post is a purely honorary one, but perhaps in no other Consulate in Europe is so much hospitality shown to Englishmen.   Mr. Leslie, from his long residence in Russia, is well acquainted with the character of the people with whom he has to deal, and is a very valuable member of our Foreign Office.

Moscow, with its wide streets, the long distances from one part of the city to the other, its world-renowned Kremlin, the palaces of its nobles, embracing vast suites of apartments, parquet floors, and almost Oriental magnificence, has so often been described by travellers, that I will not trouble my reader with a description.   If I were to do so it would be the account of what I had seen during previous visits, and not the experiences of my present journey.   As it was, I had barely time to pay a rapid visit to my friends at the Consulate, drink a glass of tea in the Moscow Traktir, and hear a well-remembered tune from the old organ in that time-honoured restaurant, when I was once more dashing through the streets to the station, my half-drunken Jehu shouting out at the top of his voice, "*Beregis, beregis!*" (take care). He generally contrived to utter the warning sound just after he had driven into the sleigh of some fellow-Jehu. The latter, in return for the collision, used that peculiar class of language which is not exclusively confined to Russian drivers.

CHAPTER IV.

Railway Officials—Unpunctuality of Trains—Frauds on the Railway Companies—
Old Spirit of Serfdom—Socialistic and Nihilist Tendencies—The Emperor
Alexander and the Religious Influence in Russia—The Ecclesiastical Hier-
archy more powerful than the Tzar—Waiting-rooms at Riajsk—Superstition
and Dirt—Sizeran.

On the track again, but this time alone in my com-
partment, till I was joined by an official whose business
it was to inspect the line between Moscow and Riazan.
His chief object was to find out if any unnecessary
delays took place at the different stations on this
railway, a number of complaints having been lately
made about the unpunctuality of the trains. It was
supposed to be the station-masters' fault, and that
these officials, being slack in the performance of their
duty, were the main cause of the delay. "I could
easily find them out," remarked the inspector, "if it
were not for the confounded telegraph, but that beats
me. The rogues are all in collusion the one with the
other, and as soon as ever they see me on the platform
they telegraph the intelligence to their brethren down
the line."

It appeared that there used formerly to be a great
deal of fraud committed on the railway companies in
Russia by the guards of the trains. They would ask a
passenger when about to take his ticket at the booking
office—"What class are you going by?" If by the first
or second, the guard would say, "Take a third-
class ticket; give me a few roubles, and I will let you go

first class, as I am guard of the train by which you will travel." But, according to the inspector, this system of roguery has now been put down. The result is a better return on the railway capital, although up to the present time the lines have been anything but remunerative as an investment. From the inspector I found out that I ought to have taken my ticket to Sizeran. This was the temporary terminus of the line in the direction of Orenburg. It was too late now to pay the difference; I must wait till we arrived at Penza, when I should just have time to get a new ticket and re-label my luggage.

It was a bitterly cold night, in spite of all our furs. At Riazan, where it was necessary to wait an hour, and to change trains, a Russian nobleman, who had entered the carriage at an intermediate station, was furious with an old man, the stoker. The latter had omitted to keep up the fire. The nobleman lost his temper, and swore fearfully at the old fellow : the culprit trembling and crying out as if he were under the lash of a whip.

It will take a long time to thoroughly eliminate the spirit of serfdom in Russia. It is several years since the peasants were emancipated, but the men who have been brought up as slaves find it difficult to get rid of a feeling of awe when they are in the presence of their superiors. Perhaps it is as well that things follow on in this groove. It would be a bitter day for Russia should the socialistic and nihilist tendencies which are being developed in her larger towns become extended amidst her rural population. At the present moment the love for the Emperor predominates over every feeling but one amidst the peasantry. This devotion to their Father, as he is termed, is well deserved, for

the Emperor Alexander underwent an enormous personal risk when at one stroke of the pen he did away
with slavery in his dominions. It was a step which
required great moral courage on the part of its origi-
nator. Few Emperors would have risked mortally
offending the upper classes of the country to do an act
of justice to the lower.

Probably the only influence which could be brought
to bear upon a peasant's mind, to such an extent that I
believe it would counterbalance his affection for the
Tzar, is the religious one. In perhaps no country in
the world has this element so powerful a sway as in
Russia. In religion, coupled with superstition, lay a
power which could even thwart the wishes of the
Emperor Nicholas himself. The ecclesiastical hier-
archy is certainly more powerful than the Tzar.
Hitherto the two dominant influences have gone hand
in glove together. It is as well that it should be so,
for any rupture between them would inevitably lead to
a revolution.

In the waiting-room at Riajsk waiters were hurrying
about with glasses of scalding tea, which were eagerly
called for by the traveller. In fact, the amount of this
beverage that a Russian can drink is somewhat astonish-
ing to a stranger. The traditional washerwoman of
our country, whose capabilities in this respect are
supposed to be unrivalled, would have no chance whatever if pitted against a subject of the Tzar. A large
samovar (a brass urn) stood on the refreshment table.
The water was kept to boiling point, not by a spirit
lamp, as in England, but by a funnel which fitted into
the centre of the urn, and was filled with red-hot
charcoal. Economy was evidently the order of the
day with some of the travellers. Instead of putting

the sugar in their glasses, they would take a lump in their mouths, and thus sweeten the scalding draught.

I took advantage of our delay at Riajsk, and walked through the other waiting-rooms. These were crammed with third-class passengers. It was a strange sight to see the mixture of different nationalities, which, huddled together like sheep, lay in different attitudes on the floor. Here a Tartar merchant, his head covered with a small yellow fez, whilst a long parti-coloured gown and pair of high boots completes his attire, was fast asleep in a corner. A woman, her face covered with a thick white veil, lay folded in his arms, whilst a child, enveloped in a bundle of rags, was playing with the fur cap of its parent. Next to them a man, whose peculiarly-shaped nose showed a distinct relationship to the tribe of Israel, was breathing hard through his nasal organ. From time to time he clutched convulsively at a small leather bag, which, half hidden beneath a greasy-looking black coat, was even in his dreams a source of anxiety. Peasants in every posture, their well-knit frames clad in untanned leather, which was tightly girt about their loins with narrow leather belts studded with buttons of brass and silver, re-echoed the Hebrew's melody. An old Bokharan in flowing robes sat listlessly with his legs twisted up under him, beside the stove. He appeared to be under the influence of opium, and was possibly dreaming of celestial houris and bliss to come. A smart-looking lad, perhaps his son, judging from the likeness between them, had withdrawn a little from the rest of the throng, apparently not very well pleased by his vicinity to the Russian peasants.

The Mohammedans of Central Asia have certainly one great advantage over the moujik, and that is in their love for water. If the Russian peasant could be persuaded to be more particular in his ablutions, it would be conducive, if not to his own comfort at least to that of his fellow-travellers. Superstition and dirt are twin brothers in Russia. I have frequently observed that the more particular a peasant is in his adoration of the various idols (*obrazye*) which are prominently displayed on the threshold of every cottage, the more utterly he is forgetful of the advantages of soap and water.

At Penza I had barely time to secure another ticket on to Sizeran, where my railway travelling would terminate. Presently I found myself in a large saloon carriage. Here almost every seat was taken, and the porters had piled upon them some railway bags and parcels belonging to passengers travelling in another carriage. These articles had been put in whilst the owners were in the waiting-rooms, the object being to diminish the length of the train. This was attained, but at the cost of considerable discomfort to the travellers, who were eagerly searching for their lost property by the dim light of a smoky tallow dip.

In the course of conversation with one of the party, a tall and very stout middle-aged man, I discovered that my shortest route to Orenburg would be through Samara. He said that he was going to the last-mentioned town, and proposed that we should hire a *troika*—a three-horse sleigh—and travel together. I readily embraced the offer, when after a few hours' more travelling we stepped out on the platform of the station at Sizeran. Here my companion was evidently well known, for the railway officials and porters respectfully saluted him, and hastened to bring our luggage to the waiting-room. I must say that I was surprised to find so good a refreshment-room so far from the capital. With but very short halts, for the purpose of changing trains, we had been travelling for more than sixty hours, and all this time in the direction of Asia, on nearing which you expect at each stride to leave civilization farther and farther in your wake. But the buffet at Sizeran left nothing to be desired. In a very short time as good a breakfast was supplied as could be obtained in any French restaurant.

We now had to think over the preparations for our sleigh journey. After a little bargaining my companion made arrangements with a farmer in the neighbourhood to supply us with a sleigh and relays of horses as far as Samara. The distance is about eighty-five miles, and there is no regular government postal station between the two towns.

CHAPTER V.

"You had better put on plenty of clothes," was the friendly caution I received from my companion as I entered the dressing-room. "The thermometer marks 20 degrees below zero (Reaumur), and there is a wind." People in this country who have never experienced a Russian winter have little idea of the difference even a slight breeze makes when the mercury stands low in the thermometer, for the wind then cuts through you, furs and all, and penetrates to the very bones. Determining to be on my guard against the frost, I dressed myself, as I thought, as warmly as possible, and so as to be utterly impervious to the elements.

First came three pairs of the thickest stockings, drawn up high above the knee. Over them a pair of fur-lined low shoes, which in their turn were inserted into leather goloshes, my limbs being finally deposited in a pair of enormous cloth boots, the latter reaching up to the thigh. Previously I had put on some extra thick drawers and a pair of trousers, the astonishment of the foreman of Messrs. Kino's establishment, "Lord love you, sir!" being his remark, when I tried them on, "no cold can get through them trousers anyhow." I must confess that I rather chuckled as my legs assumed herculean proportions, and I thought that I should have a good laugh at the wind, no matter how cutting it might be: but Æolus had the laugh on his side before the journey was over. A heavy flannel under-shirt, and shirt covered by a thick wadded waist-coat and coat, encased my body, which was further enveloped in a huge shuba, or fur pelisse, reaching to the heels. My head was protected with a fur cap and bashlik, a sort of cloth headpiece of a conical shape made to cover the cap, and having two long ends which tie round the throat.

Being thus accoutred in all my armour, I sallied forth to join my companion, who, an enormous man naturally, now seemed a very Colossus of Rhodes in his own winter attire. How people would have laughed if they could have seen us in Piccadilly in our costumes! "I think you will do," said my friend, scanning me well over; but you will find your feet get very cold for all that. It takes a day or so to get used to this sleigh travelling, and though I am only going a little beyond Samara I shall be uncommonly glad when my journey is over."

He was buckling on his revolver; and as we were informed that there were a great many wolves in the neighbourhood, I tried to do the same. This was an impossibility, the man who made the belt had never foreseen the gigantic proportions my waist would assume when clad in this Russian garb. I was obliged to give it up in despair, and contented myself by strapping the weapon outside my saddle bags.

For provisions for possibly a thirty-six hours' journey, and as nothing could be bought to eat on the road, I provided myself with some cutlets and chicken, which fitted capitally into the mess tins. My companion agreed to furnish the tea and bread, the former an article without which no true Russian will ever travel. He had not much baggage with him, and my own had been reduced to as little as possible; but we soon discovered that it was impossible to stow away the luggage in the first sleigh that had been brought for our inspection. When my railway bag, saddle bags, cartridge box, gun, and sleeping sack had been put inside, and were well covered with straw, I essayed to sit upon them, but found that there was too little distance from the improvised seat to the roof. My back was nearly bent double in consequence.

" Bring out another sleigh," said my friend. " How the wind cuts; does it not?" he continued, as the breeze whistling against our bodies made itself felt in spite of all the precautions we had taken. The vehicle now brought was broader and more commodious than the previous one, which, somewhat in the shape of a coffin, seemed especially designed so as to torture the occupants, particularly if, like my companion and self, they should happen to be endowed by Nature with that curse during a sleigh journey—however desirable appendages they may be when in a crowd—long legs. Three horses abreast, their coats white with pendent icicles and hoar-frost, were harnessed to the sleigh. The centre animal was in the shafts, and had his head fastened to a huge wooden head collar, bright with various colours. From the summit of the head collar was suspended a bell. The two outside horses were harnessed by cord traces to splinter-bars attached to the sides of the sleigh. The object of all this is at make the animal in the middle trot at a brisk pace. His two companions gallop, their necks arched round in a direction opposite to the horse in the centre. This poor beast's head is tightly reined up to the head collar.

A well-turned-out troika with three really good horses, which get over the ground at the rate of twelve miles an hour, is a pretty sight to witness, particularly if the team has been properly trained, and the outside animals never attempt to break into a trot, whilst the one in the shafts steps forward with high action. But the constrained position in which the horses are kept must be highly uncomfortable to them. It is not calculated to enable a driver to get as much pace out of his animals as they could give him if harnessed in another manner.

Off we went at a brisk pace, the bell dangling from our horse's head collar, and jingling merrily at every stride of the team.

The sun rose high in the heavens. It was a bright and glorious morning, in spite of the intense cold, and the amount of oxygen we inhaled was enough to elevate the spirits of the most dyspeptic of mankind. Presently, after descending a slight declivity, our Jehu turned sharply to the right; then came a scramble, and a succession of jolts and jerks, as we slid down a steep bank, and we found ourselves on what appeared to be a broad high road. Here the sight of many masts and shipping which, bound in by the iron fetters of a relentless winter, would remain embedded in the ice till the ensuing spring, showed me that we were on the Volga. It was an animated spectacle, this frozen highway, thronged with peasants who strode beside their sledges, which were bringing cotton and other goods from Orenburg to the railway. Now a smart troika would dash by us, its driver shouting as he passed, when our Jehu, stimulating his steeds by loud cries and frequent applications of the whip, would vainly strive to overtake his brother coachman. Old and young alike seemed like octogenarians. Their short thick beards and moustaches were white as hoar-frost from the congealed breath. According to all accounts the river had not been long frozen, and till very recently steamers laden with corn from Southern Russia had plied between Sizeran and Samara. The price of corn is here forty kopecks the poud of forty pounds, whilst the same quantity at Samara could be purchased for eighteen kopecks. An iron bridge was being constructed a little further down the Volga. Here the railroad was to pass, and it was said that in two years' time there would be railway communication, not only between Samara and the capital, but even at far as Orenburg.

Presently the scenery became very picturesque as we raced over the glistening surface, which flashed like a burnished cuirass beneath the rays of the rising sun. Now we approach a spot where seemingly the waters from some violent blast or other had been in a state of foam and commotion, when a stern frost transformed them into a solid mass. Pillars and blocks of the shining and hardened element were seen modelled into a thousand quaint and grotesque patterns. Here a fountain perfectly formed with Ionic and Doric columns was reflecting a thousand prismatic hues from the diamond-like stalactites which had attached themselves to its crest. There a huge obelisk, which, if of stone, might have come from ancient Thebes, lay half buried beneath a pile of fleecy snow. Further on we came to what might have been a Roman Temple or vast hall in the palace of a Cæsar; where many half-hidden pillars and monuments erected their tapering summits above the piles of the *débris*. The wind had done in that northern latitude what has been performed by some violent Pre-adamite agency in the Berber desert. Take away the ebon blackness of the stony masses which have been there cast forth from the bowels of the earth, and replace them on a smaller scale by the crystal forms I have faintly attempted to describe. The resemblance would be striking.

Now we came to some fishing-huts, which were constructed on the frozen river. The traffic in the finny tribe which takes place in this part of Russia is very great, the Volga producing the sterlet (a fish unknown in other rivers of Europe) in large quantities. I have often eaten them, but must say I could never appreciate this so-called delicacy. The bones are of a very glutinous nature, and can be easily masticated. The taste of a sterlet is something between that of a barbel and a perch, the muddy flavour of the former predominating. However, they are an expensive luxury, as to be in perfection for the table they should be taken out of the water alive, and put at once into the cooking-pot. A good-sized fish will often cost from thirty to forty roubles, and sometimes even a great deal more. The distance to St. Petersburg from the Volga is considerable.

In most of the restaurants in the capital the proprietors keep sterlet alive in small ponds. The intending purchaser goes there to select a fish for his dinner, the owner of the restaurant dragging it out of the water with a landing-net for his customer's inspection.

" The Cossacks of the Ural have a singular way of

catching sturgeon," observed my companion, "and it is a method, I believe, unknown in any other part of Europe. At certain times in the winter the men assemble in large numbers by the side of the river, and, dismounting from their horses, cut a deep trench across the stream from one of its banks to the other. They lower their nets into the water, and arrange them so as to block up the entire channel, when, getting on their horses, they will ride for seven or eight miles along the banks. They then form a line of horsemen reaching from shore to shore, and gallop down in the direction of the nets. The fish, hearing the clatter of a thousand hoofs, swim away from the sound, and dart like lightning in the opposite direction. Here their course is at once arrested, and they become entangled in the trammels. The quantity of sturgeon is at times so large," he continued, "that the sheer weight of the fish is sufficient to force a passage through the nets, a blank day being the result to the fishermen."

In England the sturgeon is looked upon as being rather coarse eating, and as unfit for the table, but in Russia it is highly appreciated. When served up in cold slices, with jelly and horseradish sauce, it is by no means to be despised, and I have eaten many a worse dish on this side the Channel. The part of the sturgeon most liked by the Russians is the roe (the far-famed caviare). A Russian will take this out whilst the fish is almost alive, and devour it with the greatest gusto, for the fresher the caviare is the more it is liked. There are three kinds of caviare in Russia—the quite fresh, when no salt whatever has been added; then the slightly salted, which is the caviare generally exported to this country and to other parts of Europe; and finally, the pressed caviare, which is the second quality pressed into cakes. This is used for sandwiches and other relishes. A little pressed or fresh caviare and a glass or so of Russian vodki, taken a minute before sitting down at the dinner-table, gives a wonderful stimulus to the appetite, and is a strong incentive to thirst.

CHAPTER VI.

THE road now changed its course, and our driver
directed his steeds towards the bank. Suddenly
we discovered that immediately in front of us the ice
had broken beneath a horse and sleigh, and that the
animal was struggling in the water. The river here
was fortunately only about four feet deep, so there
would not be much difficulty in extracting the quadruped, but what to ourselves seemed far more
important was to solve the knotty problem of how to
get to land. For between our sleigh and the shore
was a wide gulf, and there seemed to be no possibility
of driving through it without a wetting. "Pleasant,"
muttered my companion, "pleasant, very; let us get
out and have a good look round, to see if we cannot
find a place where we can get across in safety."

"I will pull you through," observed our Jehu, with
a broad grin on his lobster-coloured countenance, and
apparently much amused with the state of things.

"No, O son of an animal," retorted my companion;
"stay here till we return."

After considerable search we found a spot where
the water channel was certainly not much more than
twelve feet across. Some peasants who were fishing
in the river came up and volunteered their assistance.

One of them produced a pole about eight feet long, with which, he said, we could jump the chasm. My companion looked at me with a melancholy smile, in which resolution and caution struggled for the mastery. "It is very awful," he said, "very awful, but there is no other alternative, and I much fear that we must."

With these words he seized the pole, and carefully inserted one end of it in the muddy bottom. "If the ice gives way when I land on the other side!" he suddenly observed, releasing his hold of the leaping-bar. "Why, if it does, you will get a ducking," was my remark, "but be quick, the longer you look at it the less you will like it, and it is very cold standing here; now then, jump over."

"I have been just thinking," went on my companion, "whether it would not be better to be pulled through in the sleigh, for then I shall only get the lower part of my body wet. But if the confounded ice breaks, which must also be taken into consideration, for I am not at all light" (this was certainly the case, as with his furs and other clothes he must have weighed at least twenty stone), "nor am I so active as I was, why, I shall get in, and very likely be frozen to death in consequence."

At this moment his apprehensions were very nearly realised. The ice gave way under one of his feet, and let it in to about a foot of water. Retracing his steps rapidly, my companion remarked, "I shall be dragged through, and not for all the joys of Paradise will I entrust myself to that confounded pole."

It was an awful moment, and I cannot say that I relished the situation. There are minutes in a man's life when the heart has a strong inclination to jump into his mouth. It is a very disagreeable sensation, and one which I have sometimes experienced when riding at a Leicestershire so-called bullfinch, not being quite aware of what was on the other side; but then there was a gallery of other men looking on, a wonderful incentive. This time there were no spectators save a few grinning moujiki and my companion, who, as he had not faced the obstacle himself, thought that it would be better and more dignified if I were to follow his example.

Dignity appeared to me to be out of the question, particularly when placed between the two alternatives of being dragged through the water or risking a jump into the channel. It was a disagreeable choice, but I selected the latter, at the same time being a little annoyed at the chaffing remarks of the grinning peasants. They greatly enjoyed our discomfiture, and were passing *sotto voce* observations on the size of my companion and myself, eminently true, but highly disrespectful. " How fat they are !" said one. " No, it's their furs," observed another. " How awkward he is," continued a third; " why, I could jump it myself!" " I tell you what it is, my friend," I at length observed, " if you continue this conversation I think it very likely you will jump either over or in, for I want to find out the exact distance, and am thinking of throwing you over first, in order to satisfy my mind as to how wide it is, and how deep."

This remark, uttered in rather a sharp tone, had the desired effect. Seizing the pole convulsively, I prepared for the leap, which, nothing to a man not clad in furs, was by no means a contemptible one in my sleigh attire. One, two, three! a bound, a sensation of flying through the air, a slip, a scramble, and I found myself on the other side, having got over with no more damage than one wet leg, the boot itself being instantly covered with a shining case of ice.

"Come along quick!" cried my friend, who by this time had been dragged through; "let us get on as quickly as possible." And without giving me time to see if my cartridges or other baggage on the bottom of the sleigh had suffered from the ducking, we rattled off once more in the direction of Samara.

Estates have become much dearer in the neighbourhood of Sizeran since the railway has been opened up to that town. A *desyatin* of land (2·7 acres) now costs twenty roubles, whilst in Samara it can be purchased for half that price. Land gives a good return for the capital invested upon it in Russia. A proprietor thinks that he has reason to grumble if he does not receive from six to eight per cent. on the purchase-money, clear and free from any deductions.

An English gentleman, a well-known M.P., foreseeing the rise which would take place in the value of property near Samara, had bought a large and beautiful estate in that neighbourhood. According to my companion he would double the capital invested should he in the course of two or three years wish to part with his purchase.

We were now gradually nearing our first halting-place. It was a farmhouse known by the name of Nijny Pegersky Hootor, twenty-five versts distant from Sizeran. Some men were engaged in winnowing corn in a yard hard by the dwelling. The system they employed to separate the husks from the grain

probably dates from before the flood, for, throwing
the corn high up into the air with a shovel, they let
the wind blow away the husks, and the grain descended on to a carpet set to catch it in the fall.
It was then considered to be sufficiently winnowed,
and fit to be sent to the mill. The farmhouse was
fairly clean, and for a wonder there were no live
animals inside the dwelling. It is no uncommon
thing in farmhouses in Russia to find a calf domesti-
cated in the sitting-room of the family, and this
more particularly during the winter months. But here
the good housewife permitted no such intruders, and
the boards were clean and white, thus showing that a
certain amount of scrubbing was the custom.

The habitation, which was of a square shape, and
entirely made of wood, contained two good-sized, but
low rooms. A large stove made of dried clay was so
arranged as to warm both the apartments. A heavy
wooden door on the outside of the building gave
access to a small portico, at the other end of which
there was the customary obraz, or image, which is to
be found in almost every house in Russia. These
obrazye are made of different patterns, but generally
take the form of a picture of saints or of the Trinity.
They are executed in silver-gilt on brass relief, and
adorned with tawdry fringe or other gewgaws. The
repeated bows and crosses made by the peasantry
before these idols is very surprising to an Englishman, who may have been told that there is little difference between the Greek religion and his own, but if
this is the case, the sooner the second commandment
is omitted from our service the better. It may be said
that the Russian peasantry only look upon these
images as symbols, and that in reality they are praying

to the living God. Let any one who indulges in this delusion travel in Russia, and talk to the inhabitants with reference to the obrazye, or go to Kiev at the time of a pilgrimage to the mummified saints in that sanctuary. I think he will then say that no country in the world is so imbued with superstitious credences as Russia.

Above the stove, which was about five feet high, a platform of boards had been erected at a distance of about three feet from the ceiling. This was the sleeping resort of the family, and occasionally used for drying clothes during the day. The Russian moujik likes this platform more than any other part of the habitation. His great delight is to lie there and perspire profusely, after which he finds himself the better able to resist the cold of the elements outside. The farmhouse in which I now found myself had cost in building two hundred roubles, about twenty-six pounds of our money. Her home was a source of pride to the good housewife, who could read and write, an accomplishment not often possessed by the women of this class in the provinces of Russia.

By this time our former team had been replaced by three fresh horses. The driver who was to accompany us had nearly finished making his own preparations for the sleigh journey. Several long bands of cloth, first carefully warmed at the stove, were successively wound round his feet, and then having put on a pair of thick boots, and stuffed some hay into a pair of much larger dimensions, he drew the latter on as well, when, with a thick sheepskin coat, cap, and vashlik, he declared that he was ready to start.

The cold was very intense when we quitted the threshold. The thermometer had fallen several

degrees during the last half-hour. The wind had increased, and it howled and whistled against the eaves
of the farmhouse, bearing millions of minute snowy
flakes before it in its course. Presently the sound of
a little stamping on the bottom of the sleigh announced
to me that the cold had penetrated to my companion's
feet, and that he was endeavouring to keep up the
circulation.

CHAPTER VII.

VERY soon that so-called "pins-and-needles" sensation, recalling some snowballing episodes of my boyish days, began once more to make itself felt. I found myself commencing a sort of double shuffle against the boards of the vehicle. The snow was falling in thick flakes. With great difficulty our driver could keep the track. His jaded horses sometimes sank up to the traces in the rapidly-forming drifts. They floundered heavily along the now thoroughly hidden road. The cracks of his whip sounded like pistol-shots against their jaded flanks. Volumes of invectives issued from his lips.

"Oh! sons of animals!"—[whack].

"Oh! spoiled one!"—[whack]. This to a brute which looked as if he had never eaten a good feed of corn in his life. "Oh! woolly ones!" [whack! whack! whack!].

"Oh! Lord God!" This as we were all upset into a snow-drift, the sleigh being three-parts overturned, and our Jehu precipitated in the opposite direction.

"How far are we from the next halting-place?" suddenly inquired my companion, with an ejaculation which showed that even his good temper had given way, owing to the cold and our situation.

" Only four versts, one of noble birth," replied the struggling Jehu, who was busily engaged endeavouring to right the half-overturned sleigh. A Russian verst about nightfall, and under such conditions as I have endeavoured to point out to the reader, is an unknown quantity. A Scotch mile and a bit, an Irish league, a Spanish legua, or the German stunde, are at all times calculated to call forth the wrath of the traveller, but in no way equal to the first-named division of distance. For the verst is barely two-thirds of an English mile, and when, after driving for another hour, we were told that there were still two versts more before we could arrive at our halting-place, it began fully to dawn upon my friend that either our driver's knowledge of distance, or otherwise his veracity, was at fault.

At last we reached a long straggling village, formed of houses constructed much in the same way as that previously described. Our horses stopped before a detached cottage. The proprietor came out to meet us at the threshold. " Samovar, samovar!" (urn), said my companion. " Quick, quick, samovar!" Hurrying by him, and hastily throwing off our furs, we endeavoured to regain our lost circulation beside the walls of a well-heated stove.

In a few minutes, and when the blood had begun once more to flow in its proper channels, I began to look round and observe the other occupants of the room. These were for the most part Jews, as could easily be seen by that peculiarity of feature which unfailingly denotes any members of the tribe of Israel. Some half-open boxes of wares in the corner showed their trade. The men were hawkers of fancy jewellery and other finery calculated to please the wives of

the farmers or better-to-do peasants in the neighbourhood.

The smell was anything but agreeable. The
stench of sheepskins, unwashed humanity, and some
oily cooking going on in a very dirty frying-pan, at last
caused my companion to inquire if there was no other
room vacant. We were shown into a small adjoining apartment. Here the smell, though very pungent,
was not quite so disagreeable as in the one inhabited
by the family. "This is a little better," muttered my
companion, unpacking his portmanteau, and taking out
a tea-pot, with two small metal cases containing tea and
sugar. "Quick, Tëtka, Aunt!" he cried (this to the old
woman of the house), "quick with the samovar!" when
an aged female, who might have been any age from
eighty to a hundred, for she was almost bent double by
decrepitude, carried in a large copper urn, the steam
hissing merrily under the influence of the red-hot
charcoal embers.

By this time I had unstrapped the mess-tins, and
was extracting their contents. "Let me be the carver,"
said my friend, at the same time trying to cut one of
the cutlets with a knife; but he might as well have tried
to pierce an iron-clad with a pea-shooter, for the meat
was turned into a solid lump of ice. It was as hard as
a brickbat, and when we tried the bread it was equally
impenetrable; in fact, it was only after our provisions
had been placed within the stove for about ten minutes
that they became in any way eatable. In the meantime
my companion had concocted a most delicious brew,
and with a large glass of pale or rather amber-coloured
tea, with a thin slice of lemon floating on the top, I
was beginning to realise how pleasant it is to have
been made thoroughly uncomfortable. It is only after

having experienced a certain amount of misery that you can thoroughly appreciate what real enjoyment is. "What is pleasure?" asked a pupil of his master. "Absence of pain," was the philosopher's answer, and let any one who doubts that a feeling of intense enjoyment can be obtained from drinking a mere glass of tea, try a sleighing journey through Russia with the thermometer at 20° below zero (Reaumur), and a wind.

In about an hour's time we were ready to start. Not so our driver; and to the expostulations of my companion, he replied, "No, little father, there is a snowstorm, we might be lost, and I might be frozen. Oh, Lord God! there are wolves; they might eat me; the ice in the river might give way, and we might all be drowned. For the sake of God let us stop here!"

"You shall have a good tea present," * I observed, "if you will drive us."

"Oh, one of noble birth," was his answer, "we will stop here to-night, and Batooshka, little father, also," pointing to my companion; "but to-morrow we will have beautiful horses, and go like birds to the next station."

It was useless attempting to persuade him. Resigning ourselves to our fate, my companion and self lay down on the planks to obtain what sleep could be found, notwithstanding the noise that was going on in the next room. The Jew pedlars were occupied in trying to sell some of their wares, and drive a bargain with the antique mistress of the house. Notwithstanding her age, she was keenly alive to her own interests. The shrill female accents mingling with the nasal ejaculations of the Hebrews were not at all conducive to slumber.

---

* A Russian term for a money gift to an inferior.

Presently another pedlar, enveloped in sheepskin and covered with snow, strode into our room. He began to cross himself and perform his devotions before an obraz which was attached to one of the walls. As soon as this act of worship was finished, he commenced bargaining with the owner of the house, trying to persuade the man to let him have a horse to drive to the next station at a lower rate than the one ordinarily paid. But the proprietor was proof against all this kind of eloquence, and the pedlar, finding that his entreaties were useless, returned once more to our room, and kicking off his boots by the side of my companion's head, announced his intention of passing the night in our company. This the Russian gentleman objected to in very strong terms. In addition to the smell of the pedlar's body and his garments, there was good reason to believe that a vast amount of what it is not necessary here to mention inhabited his beard and clothes. " No, brother," said my companion, firmly, at the same time taking up the pedlar's sheepskin between his finger and thumb, when holding it at arm's length before him he deposited the filthy garment in the other room. " Go there, brother, for the sake of God, and pass the night with your fellows."

It was in vain attempting to sleep. The new arrival had brought a still further element of discord amidst the assembled pedlars. They were a strange party in that room, the proprietor, his mother, his wife, and her sister, two or three children, and five pedlars, all huddled together promiscuously, and adding by their number to the foul air which poisoned the interior of the dwelling. What surprised me most was to see how healthy the children looked. I should have imagined that they would have been poor, weak, delicate little things, but no; and the eldest, a chubby lad about ten years old, apparently the picture of health, looked as if bad smells and want of ventilation decidedly agreed with him.

The Russian peasants are not ignorant of the good old maxim that the early bird gets the worm. The few hours' daylight they enjoy during the winter months makes it doubly necessary for them to observe this precept. We were all up a good hour before sunrise, my companion making the tea, whilst our driver was harnessing the horses, but this time not three abreast, for the road was bad and narrow. We had determined to have two small sleighs with a pair of horses to each, and put our luggage in one vehicle whilst we travelled in the other.

Off we went, a motley crew. First the unwashed pedlar who had wished to be my companion's bedfellow the night before; then our luggage sleigh, and finally my friend and self, who brought up the rear, with a careful eye upon our effects, as the people in that part of the country were said to have some difficulty in distinguishing between *meum* and *tuum*.

The sunrise was bright and glorious, and in no part of the world hitherto visited have I ever seen aurora in such magnificence. First, a pale blue streak, gradually extending over the whole of the Eastern horizon, arose like a wall barring the unknown beyond. Suddenly it changed colour. The summit became like lapis-lazuli, the base a sheet of purple. Waves of grey and crystal radiated from the darker hues. They relieved the eye, appalled by the vastness of the barrier. The purple foundations were in turn upheaved by seas of fire. The eye was dazzled by the glowing brilliancy. The wall of colours floating in space broke up into castles, battlements, and towers. They were wafted by the breeze far away from our view. The seas of flame meanwhile had lit up the whole horizon. They burst through their borders. They formed one vast ocean. The eye quailed beneath the glare. The snowy carpet at our feet reflected like a camera the wonderful panorama overhead. Flakes of light in rapid succession bound earth to sky. At last the globe of sparkling light appeared arising from the depths of the ocean of fire. It dimmed the surroundings of the picture.

Presently a sudden check and exclamation of our Jehu told us that the harness had given way, and a conversation, freely interlarded with epithets exchanged between the driver and the pedlar, showed that there was decidedly a difference of opinion between them. It appeared that the man of commerce was the only one of the party who knew the road. Having discovered this fact, he determined to make use of his knowledge by refusing to show the way unless the proprietor of the horses, who drove the vehicle containing our luggage, would abate a little from the price he had demanded for the hire of the horse in his, the pedlar's, sleigh. "A bargain is a bargain!" cried our driver, wishing to curry favour with his master, now a few yards behind him. "A bargain is a bargain! Oh, thou son of an animal, drive on!" "It is very cold," muttered my companion. "For the sake of God," he shouted, "go on!" But neither the allusion to the pedlar's parentage, nor the invocation of the Deity, had the slightest effect upon the fellow's mercenary soul.

"I am warm, and well wrapped up," he said; "it is all the same to me if we wait here one hour or ten;"

and with the most provoking indifference he commenced smoking—not even the manner in which the
other drivers aspersed the reputation of his mother
appearing to have the smallest effect. At last the
proprietor, seeing it was useless holding out any
longer, agreed to abate somewhat from the hire of the
horse. Once more the journey continued over a breakneck country, though at anything but a breakneck
pace, until we reached the station—a farmhouse—
eighteen versts from our sleeping quarters, and, as we
were informed, forty-five from Samara.

CHAPTER VIII.

THE Guardian of the Forests stepped into the dwelling
whilst we were waiting for fresh horses. He said that
there were many wolves in the neighbourhood, and
that they did a great deal of damage to the flocks; at
the same time informing us that he had shot several
wolves that winter, and one only two days before. The
keeper was a well-built, sturdy fellow, and seeing my
gun, proposed that we should stop a day or so, remarking that he could show us some capital sport. But my
companion was obliged to hasten to his property; and
as for myself, the 14th of April—the termination of
my leave of absence—rose up like a bugbear in my
mind's eye.

Every day was precious. I had no time, much
as I should have liked to accept the invitation. About
six hours more brought us to the river Samara—here
a broad stream which runs into the Volga. We dashed
over a road made on its glistening surface, when the
driver, pulling up his horses and getting down to tie
up the bell on the head collar, informed us that we
were about to enter the town. No bells were allowed
within the suburbs, for fear of frightening any horses

A rapid drive through some fine broad streets, the well-built houses announcing that the inhabitants were comfortably off in this world's goods, and five minutes later I found myself beneath the roof of the Hotel Anaeff, a much better hostelry than I should have thought to encounter so far away from a railway.

There was no time to be lost, for the day was well advanced. We at once commenced making preparations for our journey onward; my fellow-traveller leaving me at this point, as his estate was not on the road to Orenburg. I was sorry to shake hands with him and to say good-bye. He was a very cheery companion, and a drive over the steppes alone and without a soul to speak to for several hundred miles was not an inviting prospect. *Mais à la guerre comme à la guerre*, and the same saying equally applies to a winter journey through Russia. I resigned myself to the situation, speedily forgetting all cares in the bustle of laying in a stock of provisions for the road, and in the search for a sleigh which I had here to buy to convey me and my fortunes to Orenburg, or, perhaps, to Khiva.

Presently a coffin-shaped vehicle was driven up for my inspection. I now discovered that one of the runners was cracked, and not in a fit state for the journey. The owner of the sleigh used all his eloquence to persuade me that there was an advantage in having a damaged runner, and seemed much surprised when I informed him that I did not share this opinion ; however, seeing me obdurate, he promised to have the vehicle repaired, and ready to start by the break of day.

The law of libel is stringently applied in Russia, judging by a paragraph which I saw in a newspaper that evening. It appeared that the editor of the magazine *Dalo* had been summoned by a Mr. Weinberg for calling him a beggar. The editor, according to the evidence, had previously asked the plaintiff to translate a work. On its completion, Mr. W. wrote to his employer requesting the payment of fifty roubles, which would make up the difference of the amount due. No answer being returned, he called in person, and said he would not leave without the money. Upon this, the editor sent him down a rouble note, wrapped up in a piece of paper, on which was written, " I give you this for your begging," or words to that effect. The advocate for the defence apologised for his client, who, he said, was an old man ; but the Court, not seeing the point of the argument, sentenced the editor to two weeks' imprisonment—undoubtedly a well-merited punishment ; though in England I much doubt if the offender would have even been mulcted in damages for the expression. The Russian law for libel, or rather insult (oskorblenie), is very voluminous. Many words which in this country would not come within the statute for libel are followed by a heavy punishment in the Tzar's dominions.

The people at Samara were looking forward to the rapid completion of the railway from Sizeran to that town. The proprietors of land were the most interested in this matter, as then they would be able to obtain a better market for their corn. Provisions were very cheap, the best beef only costing seven kopecks per pound, and bread two and a half kopecks, while twenty bottles of vodki could be purchased for four roubles ; thus enabling the inhabitants of that highly-favoured community to get drunk, if they wished, at even a lower rate than that announced on a placard hung some years ago outside a public-house in Ratcliff Highway, and couched in the following terms : " Take notice.— Get drunk and be made happy, all for a penny."

Mutton was even cheaper than beef, and to be bought for six kopecks a pound, whilst a first-rate cow could be readily purchased for thirty roubles, and a hundred fresh eggs for one rouble and a half. When I jotted down the list of prices, which was furnished me by the polite secretary at Anaeff's Hotel, I began to think that what I had read in my boyhood about the latitude and longitude of the promised land must be a myth. Samara was evidently that much desired region, and would be an abode of bliss to all those melancholy and matrimony-in-search-of young bachelors who occasionally forward a mournful dirge to our daily press, and inquire if a man can marry on a hundred a year. Why of course he can ! Only let him go to Samara, and he can keep a seraglio into the bargain, provided he feeds the ladies on beef and mutton.

The only country I have ever visited where provisions cost less than in Samara was in the Soudan in Africa. There a fat sheep could be purchased for four shillings—a hundred eggs for the same price— whilst on the White Nile the value even of human beings was so depreciated as to be almost incredible. Many people in this country will utterly disbelieve that a mother could sell her own child for a small quantity of corn.

That child himself had not a high opinion of his paternal roof, for later on, when his master, an Englishman, who was passing by the lad's village, told him to go back to his mother, the boy began to cry, and then said, in broken Arabic, " No, sir, mother has no clothes ; you have given me clothes. Mother gave me nothing to eat, here there is plenty. Father gives me stick, and here nothing to do but eat, drink, and cook. Please let me stop!" Poor little Agau, he afterwards returned with me to Cairo, and I have no doubt by this time has quite forgotten his father, mother, and the domestic fetish, in the virtues and vices of Pharaoh's capital.

But although Samara, and, in fact, all the south-eastern part of Russia, offers many inducements to the settler on account of the low value of land and the cheapness of provisions, there is, in spite of these advantages, one great drawback to the country. This is the rate of mortality, the more particularly amongst the infantine population. Out of 1,000 children born, 345 die in the first five years, 40 in the next five, 19 in the subsequent term, and the same number ere two decades have been completed. Thus, out of 1,000 children, 423 will not reach their twentieth birthday. From another table of statistics I took the following figures :—Out of 10,000 children born, 3,830 die the first year, 975 in the second, and 524 in the third. Whether this excessive mortality is caused by the extreme rigour of the winter months, or by the love of spirit drinking on the part of the parents, which causes them to neglect their offspring, is a difficult question to answer. Probably both these influences have a good deal to do with the matter. I have frequently heard educated Russians defend this theory, and curse the foundling hospitals, which, originally started to diminish the evil, have, in their opinion, only succeeded in augmenting immorality, whilst they have greatly added to the mortality throughout the empire.

There is a regular postal road, which goes from Samara to Orenburg. The authorities have recently established a new system along this route, which has superseded the old order of things with reference to *podorojnayas*, or passports. Formerly the traveller, previously to starting, had to visit the police, tell them where he was going, and the number of horses he required for his sleigh. They would then give him a printed document, containing his description, and an order to the postmasters of the different stations to forward him on towards his destination. But now all this antiquated system has been abolished, and a *volnaya potchta*, or free post, is established between Samara and Orsk, a town about 140 miles beyond Orenburg.

All the traveller has to do is to ask at the different post-stations for the necessary horses. They will be immediately furnished him, or as soon as possible after the order has been given. The traveller pays in advance four kopecks per horse for each verst travelled.

I was called at daybreak the following morning. The few preparations required to be made were soon finished, and I found myself in my newly-purchased sleigh, which had been thoroughly repaired, driving along in the direction of Smweshlaevskaya, the first station arrived at when travelling towards Orenburg, and about twenty versts from Samara. The country was a dead flat, and of a most uninteresting description. A few trees scattered here and there made by their scarcity the bleak and naked appearance of the adjacent surroundings the more conspicuous. Naught save snow here, there, and everywhere. No signs of life save a few melancholy crows and jackdaws, which from time to time made a short flight to stretch their pinions, and then returned to perch by the side of some kitchen chimney, and extract from the rapidly rising smoke as much warmth as possible. The route much resembled the road between Sizeran and Samara; for, indeed, in winter-time everything in Russia is either alike or hidden from view, buried beneath its blanch white pall of snow.

The station-houses along the line of road I was then travelling were fairly clean. The furniture generally consisted of a horsehair sofa and some wooden chairs, whilst a few coloured prints of the Emperor and other members of the Royal Family of Russia were hung about the walls, and made up the attempt at decoration. A book in which to inscribe complaints was also kept, and any traveller who felt himself aggrieved could write down his grievance, which would be subsequently investigated by an inspector, whose duty it was to perform this task once a month. I sometimes used to while away the time whilst waiting for fresh horses by turning over the pages of the grumblers' book—occasionally, indeed, having to add my own grievance to the list—the badness of the horses being a frequent source of annoyance to the passengers.

I reached Bodrovsky, the next station, a little after sunset, only halting sufficient time to drink a few glasses of tea, in order the better to resist the rapidly-increasing cold, the thermometer having fallen to 25° below zero (Reaumur), and started again for Malomalisky, about $26\frac{1}{2}$ versts distant. I hoped to reach this point about 9 P.M., and there refresh the inner man before proceeding on my journey. It is hungry work, sleigh-driving in the winter, and the frame requires a good deal of support in the shape of food in order to keep up the vitality. However, it is no good forming any plans in which time is concerned in Russia. The natives have a Mohammedan-like indifference to the clock, and travellers must succumb, however unwillingly, to the waywardness of the elements.

Presently I became aware by some pistol-like cracks—the sounds of the whip reverberating from the backs of my horses—that there was a difference of opinion between them and the driver. A blinding snow had come on; the darkness was so great that I could not distinguish the driver. Our jaded animals were floundering about in all directions, vainly endeavouring to hit off the original track, from which it was evident that they had strayed. The man now got down from his box, and, leaving me in charge of the horses, made a wide cast round on foot, hoping to discover the road.

CHAPTER IX.

Delayed by a Snowstorm—Tchin—Russian Curiosity—A Conservative Inspector
—General Kryjinovsky—He tells me that I speak Russian—The Interest the
Paternal Government takes in my Movements—Russia and China—A Newly-
married Sleigh Driver—A Camel in Love.

THE snow all this time was falling in a manner unknown to people in this country. It was piling itself
up against the sleigh in such volumes that I foresaw, if
we did not speedily reach the station, we should inevitably be buried alive. After about half an hour's
search the driver returned, and said to me, "Oh, Lord
God!—you are a misfortuné. Let us turn back." I
replied, "If you have lost the way, how can you turn
back? Besides, if you know the road, we are now half-
way, so it is just as easy to go forward as to return."

He had found the track, but by this time the sleigh
was so buried in the snow that the horses could not
stir it. There was only one thing to do, which was
for me to get out and help him to lift the vehicle, when
we eventually succeeded in regaining the path.

The fellow was a good deal surprised at this action
on my part, for Russian gentlemen as a rule would
almost prefer to be frozen to death than do any manual
labour. Presently he said, "One of noble birth, what
shall we do now?" "Go on." But at last, finding that
it was no use, and that the snow in front of us had
drifted over the track to a much greater extent than
over that part of the road which we had left behind, I

was reluctantly obliged to give the order to return. This he obeyed with the greatest alacrity, the horses as well as the driver showing, by their redoubled exertions, that they were well aware of the change of direction.

There is nothing so disheartening to a traveller who wishes to get forward rapidly as the frequent snowstorms which occur in winter in this part of Russia. Days upon days of valuable time are thus lost, whilst any attempt to force a way through at all hazards will only lead to the extreme probability of your being frozen to death, without enabling you in any way to accelerate your arrival. The inspector at the station laughed heartily when we returned, and said that it was very fortunate I had not to pass the night out in the open. He had previously advised us not to attempt the journey that evening, but wait for daylight. However, I did not believe him, and consequently had to buy my experience.

He was very anxious to know what my *tchin* (rank) was; whether I was *voennye* (military) or *statsky* (a civilian); and the spelling of my name caused him a good deal of perplexity.

Of all the countries in which it has been my fate to travel, the land where curiosity is most rampant is decidedly Russia. Whether this comes from a dearth of public news and subjects for conversation, or from something innate and specially characterising the Sclavonic race, it is difficult to say. The curiosity of the fair sex, which in other countries is supposed to be the *ne plus ultra* of inquisitiveness, is in the land of the Tzar far outstripped by the same peculiarity in the male inhabitants. Of course I am alluding the more particularly to the lower orders, and not to the upper classes, though even with the latter it is a feature that cannot help striking the foreigner.

The inspector was a thorough old conservative, and greatly mourned the new order of things, and that he could no longer demand the traveller's *podorojnaya*, or pass. " Why," he said, " I do not know who I am addressing ; I may be talking to a shopkeeper, and call him your Excellency, or address a Grand Duke as simply one of noble birth." " Yes," chimed in some travellers who were benighted like myself, " and rogues can travel now, for they are not obliged to go to the police." I was rather amused at this. There was decidedly a wish on the part of the other wayfarers to know who I was ; so, pulling my English passport out of my pocket, I said to the inspector, " There, you can look at my *podorojnaya.*" He turned it upside down ; and then said, " Ah, yes ! you are a Greek, but what a beautiful crown that is on it ! You must be some great personage, going to Tashkent." " Perhaps so," I replied, assuming an air of importance. " There is a royal highness coming through soon," said the inspector ; " I heard it from a pedlar who went by yesterday ; and one of his officers is travelling on in front to make preparations. Perhaps his Excellency," turning to me, " is that gentleman." " No," was my answer, when one of the company, who appeared a little annoyed at my evident unwillingness to undergo this process of pumping, remarked that there had been several robberies in the neighbourhood. " Yes, there have," said another, and the assemblage all looked at me as much as to say, " You are the man ; now, do not deny it ; we shall not believe you."

So the evening wore on, till one by one we laid ourselves down to rest, when a sound, very suggestive

of a pigsty, awoke the echoes of the night.   On
looking out at daybreak, I found that the wind had
subsided, and the thermometer had risen to within a
few degrees of freezing point.   There was no time to
be lost, particularly as I could not tell how long this
exceptional order of things would last ; so, ordering
fresh horses, I recommenced the journey.   A great
deal of snow had fallen during the night, and it was
fortunate that we had returned to the station, as in
some places, only a little distance beyond the spot
from which my driver had retraced his steps, were
drifts eight and ten feet deep.   "Praise be to God
that we did not fall in !" said my Jehu, pointing
them out to me as he drove by ; "I might have
been frozen."

A single line of telegraph ran along the side of the
road, being part of the wire which connects the capital
with Tashkent.   The high poles from which the line was
suspended served as a capital landmark to point out
the route which we must follow.   Presently the scenery
changed, and some plantations here and there relieved
the eye, tired by continually gazing over the endless
waste.   Low trucks on wooden runners, drawn by two
or four horses, and laden with iron rails for the construction of the railway, encountered us on the path.
In many places we had great difficulty in passing,
owing to the narrowness of the road.   My Jehu's
vocabulary of expletives was more than once thoroughly
exhausted upon the heads of the sleighmen.   They
had, as it appeared, purposely tried to upset our
sleigh by charging it with their heavily-laden vehicles.

A few stations further on the road I met General
Kryjinovsky, the Governor of the Orenburg district,
who was on his way to St. Petersburg, accompanied by

his wife and daughter. He had highly distinguished himself in his early career in Turkistan, and to this he owes the important post entrusted to his charge. He is a little spare man, with a keen glance and determined eye, and if I might be allowed to judge from our brief interview, he was not the sort of individual who would care to give me much information about my journey, of which he did not seem to approve.

"You must remember," he said, "on no account are you to go to India or to Persia. You must retrace your steps to European Russia along the same road by which you go. You speak Russian, I hear?" he suddenly remarked, looking fixedly at me. Our conversation up to that time had been carried on in French.

"Yes," I replied; "but how clever you are to have made this discovery, considering that we have not spoken one word in your language, and you have never seen me before." This took the general a little aback, and he slightly changed colour.

He had evidently received a communication from some authorities at St. Petersburg, to the effect that I was acquainted with Russian, generally an unknown tongue to foreigners, and to a certain extent had let the cat out of the bag. He now observed, "Oh, I only supposed you did so." In the meantime his wife and daughter were taking off their furs in the same apartment. The accommodation for ladies is of the most meagre kind in these roadside stations, there are no retiring-rooms whatever, and the fair sex have in this respect to put up with much more discomfort than the men.

As I drove away after our interview I pondered the general's words well over in my mind—"You must not go to India; you must not go to Persia; and you must retrace your steps exactly by the same route you go." It was really very extraordinary to see how much interest this paternal government in St. Petersburg took in my movements. Here I was travelling in a country where the rulers defend the despoliation of the inhabitants in Central Asia, and the annexation of their territory, on the ground that it is done for the purpose of Christianity and civilization. And yet the government of this civilized nation made as much fuss about my travelling in Central Asia as any mandarin at Pekin, whose permission I might have had to ask for a journey through the Celestial Empire.

It will take the Russians a long time to shake off from themselves the habits and way of thought inherited from a barbarous ancestry. *Grattez le Russe et vous trouverez le Tartare, ça c'est une insulte aux Tartares.* This is a hackneyed expression; however, it is a true one. It requires but little rubbing to disclose the Tartar blood so freely circulated through the Muscovite veins.

Some distance further on the road I observed a strong disinclination evinced by the man whose business it was to drive me to the next halting-place. He was a fresh-looking, sturdy fellow, and I could not understand the evident dislike he had for his fare, the more particularly as I had made a point of well tipping the respective drivers in order to get on as fast as possible. "What is it?" I inquired of the station-master. "Is he ill?" "No," was the reply; "he was married yesterday, that is all." It seemed somewhat cruel to tear away the poor fellow from the conjugal bliss that awaited him in the next room, but there was no help for it. No other driver could be procured, and the duty must be performed. If I had not before remarked that there was something amiss with the fellow, I should very soon have found it out by the extraordinary motions his horses imparted to the sleigh.

He lashed the animals. They kicked and jumped, performing antics which slightly resembled the convulsive twitchings of an individual suffering from St. Vitus. I was thrown in the air and caught again by the rebound; upset, righted, and upset again, without having had time to realise the first disaster; cartridge-cases, gun, saddle-bags, and self, all flying in the air at the same instant, the enamoured driver forgetting everything in the absorbing influence of his passion, save the desire to return to the side of his adored Dulcinea.

I once rode a camel in love; this was in the Great Korosko desert. He was known by the name of the Magnoon, or the Mad Camel; but whether on account of his susceptible heart or not I cannot say. I shall never forget on one occasion, when the amorous quadruped had accidentally become separated from the Juliet of his affection, a sweet creature, that carried the sheik of our party. She was very old, but this was no deterrent in the eyes of her ardent admirer, who was miserable when not at her side. I had ridden on a little ahead of the party when the voice of Juliet, who was being saddled in the desert, and who vented her woes in weird squeals and sounds appropriate to her race, was wafted by the breeze to the attentive ears of her admirer. He was a very long and a very tall camel, and in an instant he commenced to rear. My position became both ludicrous and precarious. Ludicrous to every one but myself, who was interested in the matter more than any one except Romeo. I found that I was, as it were, slipping down the steep roof of a house, with nothing to hold on by but a little peg about four inches long, which projected from the front part of the saddle.

It was an awful moment, but he did not keep me long in suspense. Performing an extraordinary movement, he suddenly swung himself round on his hind legs, and ran as fast as ever he could in the direction of the fair enticer. A camel's gait is a peculiar one; they go something like a pig with the fore, and like a cow with the hind legs. The motion is decidedly rough. At this moment my steed was seized with a strange and convulsive twitching which threatened to capsize the saddle. My position became each second more ridiculous and appalling. I was a shuttlecock, Romeo's back was the battledore. At every moment I was hurled into the air. The fear of missing the saddle and falling on the ground was continually in my mind. The little projecting knob, which seemed an instrument of torture like the impaling sticks used to punish the unfaithful in China, was also a source of consternation. I do not think I have ever felt a more thorough sensation of relief than when, on arriving at our encampment, Romeo halted by the side of his Juliet.

The episode with Romeo had been an alarming one. It was nothing to being driven by this amorous young Russian as a charioteer. At last, after having been deposited with all my luggage for the third time in the snow, I resolved to appeal to his feelings by a sharp application of my boot. "Why do you do that?" he said, pulling up short. "You hurt, you break my ribs."

"I only do to you what you do to me," was my reply; "you hurt, you break my ribs, and property besides."

"Oh, one of noble birth," ejaculated the fellow, "it is not my fault. It is thou, oh, moody one!"— to his offside horse, accompanied by a crack from his lash. "It is thou, oh, spoilt and cherished one!"— to his other meagre and half-starved quadruped. (Whack!) "Oh, petted and caressed sons of animals" (whack, whack, whack!), "I will teach you to upset the gentleman!"

CHAPTER X.

IT was hard work, this perpetual travelling. Wherever the roads were passable I kept steadily journeying onward, and gradually diminished the distance that lay between myself and Orenburg.

For the last hundred versts there were scarcely any travellers, save at one station, where I met a few officers who were on their way to Samara. They did not much fancy the piece of road which lay before them, and told me that the winter we were having was the most exceptionally cold season they had ever experienced in those latitudes. Occasionally the road for a few miles would take quite a different aspect. A succession of ridge and furrow was formed by the wind, which had billowed up the snow before it in a strange and fantastic manner. The motion my sleigh would then assume was not at all of an agreeable character. Any person who suffers from crossing the Channel would have found that a journey in a sleigh can, under certain circumstances, be quite as disagreeable. On the evenings when there was no storm, when the roads were smooth and the horses good, it was very agreeable travelling. The stars and other constellations lit up

the heavens with extraordinary brightness, and made
the night as clear as day. The "tinkle, tinkle, tinkle"
of the sleigh-bells, changing time as the horses changed
their pace, now ringing fast and furiously, then dying
away as our animals struggled up some eminence,
helped to wile away the hours. When about sixty
versts from Orenburg, I was told that a short cut off
the road would diminish the distance considerably. I
determined to avail myself of this information, and take
the risk of not being able to find horses at the farmhouses on the road, where the farmers, if they have any
animals in their stables, are only too glad to let them
out to the travellers.

Presently we arrived at a cottage the fac-simile of
an Irish hovel. Here were some unclean four-footed
ones, sharing the habitation with the two-legged
inmates. Pigs, calves, men, women, and children
were huddled together round a huge stove, which
barely warmed the ill-built and wretched hovel. But
the horses supplied me were good, and finally we
crossed the Samara river. Once more some signs
of civilization. A few brick houses were to be seen.
My driver leaped from his seat and tied up the bell on
the horse's head collar. We were approaching a town.
Shortly afterwards we dashed up the principal street at
a good swinging gallop, my sleighman shouting cheerily
and cracking his whip at every bound. Orenburg was
reached. A few minutes later I found myself in a
well-warmed room, enjoying a wash, the luxury of
which can only be appreciated by those who have
driven 400 versts through Russia in the winter, and
who have thus practically become acquainted with the
slight respect the Russians show to the good old
maxim, "Cleanliness is next to Godliness." The latter

quality, as displayed in a Russian devotee, is more allied with dirt than anything else I can mention.

It was evident that I was rapidly leaving civilization behind me. No bed-linen could be procured. On my asking for a towel, the nearest approach to this commodity which could be obtained was a table-napkin. Russians, when journeying in these regions, carry about their own bed-linen, pillow-cases, &c., and either dispense with sheets altogether, or are contented with a rug. The architect who had designed this hotel was evidently a stranger to comfort as this is understood in other countries. To go from the dining-rooms to the bed-rooms it was necessary to pass through an open courtyard. This, as the thermometer was at that time occasionally 30° below zero (Reaumur), did not conduce to the traveller's comfort. The people staying in the inn were chiefly officers. A well-worn billiard-table in a room down-stairs was being played on incessantly night and day. The attendant at a bar where caviare, salt fish, anchovies, sour kraut, and all kinds of relishes, with spirits and liquors, could be procured, had not a spare moment to himself.

In fact, there is no country in the world, not even the United States, where so much of what is commonly termed nipping goes on as in Russia. Probably the extreme cold to a certain extent permits the inhabitants to take such liberties with their stomachs. But the increasing numbers of Russian visitors who are each summer to be seen at Carlsbad, and their general complaint—liver—is a clear sign that dram-drinking, if persisted in, eventually sows the seed of disease.

When I awoke the following morning it was with a splitting headache and a feeling of oppression, which, except when once half-suffocated by the gas out of a balloon, I cannot remember to have ever before experienced. I had a great deal of difficulty in raising myself from my bed. On opening the door of the room and breathing the cold but pure air, my legs gave way under me. Staggering forward, I fell down. It then flashed across my mind that the stove had been shut up too soon the previous evening, the consequence being that the poisonous gas from the charcoal had escaped into the sleeping apartment. Fortunately, however, the room which had been given me was a large one. The stoves in Russia, though admirably arranged so as to keep up a due degree of warmth in the house, require considerable care. Any neglect in this respect will lead to disagreeable consequences. Indeed, seldom does a winter pass without some traveller or other falling a victim.

Later in the day I drove to the house of an American gentleman, a Mr. G——, for whom I had a letter of introduction. He received me with the usual hospitality of his nation, and promised to do everything he could to further my views. But as for information about the road to Khiva, he could give me none. All the news and gossip about Tashkent, Samarcand, and about the recent disturbances at Kokan, he had, so to speak, at his fingers' ends. Khiva, however, was a sealed book to him. He recommended me to call upon a Mr. Bektchourin, a Tartar gentleman, the Professor of Eastern Languages at the Russian Military Academy, who, he said, knew more about the subject than any other man in Orenburg.

On returning to my hotel, the waiter informed me that the chief of the police had sent an order that I was to attend at the police-office immediately. It seemed a little strange his forwarding me this communication through a servant at the inn, and not through some more official channel. However, at once obeying the command, I proceeded to the residence of the police officer, and shortly afterwards was shown into the chief's room. He held, it appeared, the rank of a colonel in the army, and said that he wished to know why I had come to Orenburg. I replied that "I was going to Russian Asia;" when he remarked, "I cannot allow you to do this, unless you have permission from the authorities in St. Petersburg. There is a special order prohibiting foreigners from travelling in Turkistan." I showed him the letter I had received from General Milutin, which was written in French. He perused it with difficulty, and to all appearance was not well acquainted with that language. He then said, "By what route do you propose to go?" I replied by Kasala, and perhaps from there to Tashkent, and so on to Khiva . . . anyhow, first of all to Kasala. . . . "Yes," he said, "that is your best plan; for there you will be able to obtain information which no one here can give you." From the police-office I drove off to call upon Mr. Bektchourin, the Tartar gentleman.

On my ringing the bell Mr. Bektchourin opened the door himself. He was a tall, noble-looking old man, in a long Eastern dressing-gown. It was fastened around his waist with a sash, whilst a fez cap on his head betokened an allegiance to the faith of Islam. He was a little surprised to see a stranger, but courteously invited me to enter his abode. When I had explained the object of my visit—which was, first to know if he could give me any information about the route to Khiva, and secondly if he would recommend me a Tartar servant who could speak Russian—he said, " My good sir, I will do everything I can ; but first of all you must drink some tea." A servant entered with some glasses of this beverage. Bektchourin handed me a cigarette, lit one himself, and slowly sipped the thought-inspiring liquid.

Presently he remarked, "First of all, my good sir, as to going to Khiva ; it is winter, the Syr Darya-Jaxartes and Amou Darya (Oxus) rivers are frozen up. The difficulties and hardships will be immense. You will have to ride on horseback over 500 versts of snow-covered steppes. If it had been summer you would have had no difficulty whatever. Once arrived at Kasala, better known as Fort Number One, you could have gone in a steamer, and have been landed within a few miles of Petro-Alexandrovsk, our fort in Khivan territory. There would have been no fatigue or danger. In winter, however, it is very different. I sincerely advise you to give up the idea altogether, or to come back in the summer and then perform the journey." I here remarked that it was not likely that I should have taken the trouble to travel even so far as Orenburg in the winter without having made up my mind previously to leaving London as to what my intentions were. " Quite right, my good sir," continued the kind old gentleman, "quite right. If you mean to go I will help you ; but at the same time it was only right of me to say what my opinion is about the matter ; and, indeed," he added, "I really cannot give you any information as to the routes. At this time of the year all will depend upon how much snow has fallen in the steppes. This you can only find out at Kasala. As to recommending you a servant, I do not know of one at present, but will make every inquiry. Not that I much care about the task," he continued, "for there was an American gentleman here not long ago with the Secretary of the United States Legation at St. Petersburg, Messrs. MacGahan and Schuyler were their names. I was asked to recommend them a servant, and to get them one in twenty-four hours.

"How I toiled and slaved! My good wife, too, asked all the people of her acquaintance, and we hunted everywhere to find an honest Tartar servant; not but that there are plenty of honest Tartars," he added, "quite as many as Christians; but Mr. Schuyler required a man who could speak Russian, and who, to a certain extent, was accustomed to European ways. Well, we searched everywhere, and at the last moment a fellow offered himself for the situation. I could hear of nothing against his character, and the fact was I had no time to make inquiries. But the next thing I heard was that the servant had turned out to be a scoundrel, and that Mr. MacGahan, who wrote a very interesting book about his journey, had adverted to me in it, and said that I had recommended the man. Now, if I get you a servant, perhaps you will write a book and say the same as Mr. MacGahan has done, that is, if you are not pleased with your servant; but I tell you candidly that I cannot in any way be responsible for his character, although I will do my best to find you an honest fellow."

No one could have been kinder than Mr. Bektchourin; he assured me that he would make every inquiry with reference to the object I had in view; whilst I relieved his mind by promising to speak to Mr. MacGahan, so that when another edition of "Campaigning in the Oxus" came out, Mr. Bektchourin's explanation of the circumstances might be appended in a note. Probably on account of the military element in the hotel, the newspapers were represented by the *Invalide*. On turning over the leaves of an old number of this journal, I came across a paragraph which showed the friendly interest the Russian officer who wrote it evidently took in India.

It was to the effect that at a late exhibition of maps in Paris, the more recent British maps of the Attrek and Afghanistan were not to be found, but that an interesting map of the Punjaub, with all the various march-routes, and which the compiler had particularly not intended to be published, was to be seen in the exhibition.

The following day I called upon General Bazoulek, the Governor *pro tem* now that Kryjinovsky was away. He was a good-looking man of about five-and-forty, and a little pompous in his demeanour. In Kryjinovsky's absence he was all-powerful at Orenburg, and he duly endeavoured to impress upon me the importance of his position. He could give me no information whatever as to how to go to Khiva, his remark being the same stereotyped one repeated ever so many times before—" You must go to Kasala, and there you will be able to obtain every information." On inquiry if there was a post to Khiva, his answer was, " I believe so, but I do not know by what route it goes." In fact, the ignorance displayed by all the officials with whom I came in contact might have surprised any one aware of the great importance attached to the study of geography by the Russian military authorities. I could not explain it to myself otherwise than by assuming that the real solution of the problem consisted in the politeness of the officers, who preferred being thought ignorant to rude.

CHAPTER XI.

THE principal topic of conversation at Orenburg was
a recent *emeute* amidst the Ural Cossacks. It
appeared that the inhabitants of the town of Uralsk,
as also many of the people in that neighbourhood, had
become excessively discontented with the military law
of universal conscription. Previously to the promulgation of the new edict, the better-to-do classes had
not sent their sons to serve, and the ranks were filled
with recruits from the poorer orders. But now all was
changed; money would no longer purchase a substitute, and grievous discontent possessed the minds of
the Ural Cossacks. Most of them were Raskolniki
dissenters from the Greek Church, and belonged to the
old faith (Staroi vara). When they were ordered to
send their sons to serve they rebelled, and openly
called the Emperor Antichrist. This was too much
for the pious-minded authorities at St. Petersburg;
2,500 of the malcontents had been banished from
Uralsk to Central Asia, whilst it was said at Orenburg that 2,000 more would speedily follow.

· The delinquents had been marched from Orenburg to Kasala, and from that place it was intended to transport them to Khivan territory. A
detachment of 500 had been already sent to
Nookoos, a small fort recently constructed by the

Russians on the right bank of the Amou Darya. It appeared that the commander at Kasala had experienced much difficulty with the men when he ordered them to march under escort to Nookoos. They absolutely refused to stir. At last he ordered them to be attached to camels by cords, and then commanded the Orenburg Cossacks to flog the prisoners with their whips. This had been done with great barbarity. I was assured that three of the victims had died under the lash. The commandant of Kasala had written to St. Petersburg to know what was to be done with the remainder of the exiles.

G—— now informed me of a battue which had taken place by order of Kryjinovsky a few weeks previous to my arrival, with the object of destroying some wolves, which had been doing a vast amount of damage in the neighbourhood. Several miles of country had been enclosed by beaters, who gradually reduced the circle. However, the wolves proved too much for the sportsmen, and the latter were not able to bag a single animal.

I must say I had become rather sceptical as to the existence of these carnivorous beasts—that is to say in any large numbers ; I had now travelled over five hundred versts of country and had not seen or heard a single one. That there were wolves I did not deny, but was inclined to believe that both their numbers and depredations were much exaggerated.

Kauffmann, the Governor-General of Turkistan, was said to have sent for two more regiments from European Russia. They were to be despatched to Turkistan immediately, he himself being now on his road to St. Petersburg. People in Orenburg said that he was not in very good favour at court, for having pushed the Russian arms further in Central Asia than had been either the wish or intention of the Emperor. It was declared that the Tzar himself was very much opposed to this system of annexation in the East, and had only been induced to permit it on the representations of his generals that they were surrounded by lawless tribes, who carried off and imprisoned Russian subjects.

It is easy to make a good case if the counsel for the plaintiff is the only one heard. The Kokandians and Khivans have not had the opportunity of putting forward their side of the question, so, as is naturally to be supposed, the Russian generals have invariably carried the day. Indeed, we cannot wonder at the Tzar's officers in Turkistan being so eager to continue in their line of conquest. Taken for the most part from poor but well-born families, having no inheritance but the sword, no prospect save promotion, they thirst for war as the only means at hand for rapidly rising in the service. A life in Central Asia in time of peace is looked down upon with contempt. With everything to be gained by war and nothing by peace, we need not be surprised should every little pretext be sought for to provoke reprisals on the part of the native population. Europe then hears of the cruelties committed by the brutal fanatics in Central Asia, of Russian magnanimity, and of Mohammedan intolerance.

Exeter Hall is quieted by the idea of a crusade against the Mussulmans. The lust for conquest is cloaked in a garb called Christianity. The sword and the Bible go forth together. Thousands of the natives are mown down by that evangelical weapon, the breechloader; and one day we read in our morning newspapers that a territory larger than France and

England together has been added to the Tzar's dominions.

But it does not signify, observe some of our legislators. The sooner Russia and India touch each other the better. How much better for India to have a Russian neighbour on her frontier, instead of the barbarous Afghans! Russia herself is apparently well aware of the advantage of having civilized neighbours on her western frontier; as it is, on that frontier she is obliged to keep concentrated two-thirds of her available forces. People in this country who advocate the two empires touching are not perhaps aware that our Indian army would then have to be increased to three times its present strength, and in spite of that precaution there would be less security for ourselves.

It now wanted only two days to Christmas. I had already been four days in Orenburg, and, as far as I could see, was as far off as ever from obtaining a servant. Getting into my sleigh, I hurried off to the house of my friend Bektchourin. I found him, as usual, clad in his dressing-gown, but this time he was not alone. Several Easterns were sharing his hospitality, and imbibing large glasses of strong green tea, which, I was told, is the kind most appreciated in Central Asia.

It was fortunate that I had called at that hour. It gave me the opportunity of making the acquaintance of the Khan of Kokan, formerly a sovereign, but now an exile far from his own country, and detained in European Russia by the order of the Tzar. He was a swarthy, strong-built fellow. His captivity did not seem to have pressed much on his soul. He had readily adopted European customs, and had actually gone so far as to give a ball. This, I was informed,

had been a great success, many of the fair damsels in
Orenburg having attended it. A wicked report ran
to the effect that a great competition was going on
amongst certain of the ladies with the view of convert-
ing the handsome Khan to the Greek faith, and so on to
matrimony according to the Russian rites. But, taking
into consideration a Mohammedan's innate horror of
idols or image-worship, and that the Khan is already
blessed with four wives, this would seem rather a hopeless task. However, everything might be gained in
the event of success, and it was said that a union with
the convert would not be displeasing to some of the
less favoured fair ones of Orenburg. Fabulous reports
of his wealth were spread about the town. Great
delight was evinced in every quarter on its being
announced that he had elected to live in Orenburg,
and was about to purchase a house in the neighbourhood. He had been prompted to take this step by
his friendship with Mr. Bektchourin, and with General
Kryjinovsky, the Governor of the province. According
to my Tartar acquaintance, the Khan's wealth had
been much exaggerated. He was not by any means
the Crœsus he had been represented. On leaving
Kokan he had taken with him a large quantity
of treasure in gold and silver specie, but had been
robbed on the road. At the time of which I write
he had only 120,000 roubles—about £15,000 of our
money—not much in the eyes of an English match-
maker, but a glittering bait to the husband-seeking
dames of Orenburg.

Bektchourin now said that he had discovered a
Bokharan who would accompany me as a servant; and
that the man could speak Russian, Tartar, and Persian,
and would be very useful as an interpreter.

However, later on Bektchourin came to the hotel, and with a long face informed me that he did not think the fellow would suit. Mrs. Bektchourin had been making inquiries, and had discovered that the Bokharan's papa and mamma smoked opium, whilst it was currently rumoured that their son partook of his parents' taste. An opium-smoker as a servant would have been an intolerable nuisance. In consequence of this Mr. Bektchourin had brought with him a young Russian, who had been a clerk in a counting-office, and could speak Tartar. He was ready to accompany me. However, I discovered that his idea was to travel as an equal, and that he had no intention to act as a servant. In fact, he had so great an idea of his own importance that I felt that the Bokharan, opium and all, would have been more eligible as an attendant.

What was to be done? I began to think that I might as well search for the philosopher's-stone as for a servant in Orenburg. But Bektchourin was by no means disheartened. " I will find one," he said, " never fear;" and a few hours later another candidate for the post turned up in the shape of a man who had been to Tashkent with Mr. David Ker. He informed me that Mr. Bektchourin had sent him to the inn, and that Mrs. Bektchourin had lent him five roubles to take his passport out of pawn, a Jew having previously advanced some money on this document. As the Tartar appeared a likely sort of fellow, I agreed to accept his services, twenty-five roubles a month being the wages, and all found.

" Perhaps, one of noble birth," said the man, " you would not object to give me two months' wages on account? I have an aged mother, and should like to leave a little money to support her during my absence."

Filial affection is undeniably a good trait in a man's character. I was delighted; I had secured a prodigy. I blessed Bektchourin, who had sent me such a paragon of virtue, and I gave the servant the money, he promising to return to the hotel early the following morning. The difficulties of the journey seemed half over already, and I went to bed convinced that at last I was in a fair way to make a start.

Hope told a flattering tale. I awoke the next morning at about five o'clock, and commenced my preparations. However, no man arrived. A few hours later I rang the bell for the head waiter of the inn.

"Did you see the servant I engaged yesterday?"

"Yes, one of noble birth, I saw him."

"Why has he not come here this morning? he was to have been here at six!"

"Perhaps, one of noble birth, you gave him some money?"

"Yes," was my reply, "for his bedridden mother."

An irrepressible grin caused the lantern jaws of the head waiter to open from ear to ear. A cavernous mouth was disclosed. A few yellow teeth bristling at irregular intervals in the huge recess appeared to take their share in his amusement. Unrolling a long tongue he caressed the stumpy fangs, and licked his lips with an air of the greatest possible enjoyment.

"His bedridden mother! Hee! hee! hee! Oh! the son of an animal!" and the tears poured down the fellow's face as he became convulsed with laughter. "You will not see him again," he continued, "until he has spent the money; he has gone to *kootit*" (drink and make merry, the acme of a Russian's happiness). "Oh! the cunning pigeon!" and the head waiter left the room evidently much delighted at the way I had been taken in by his countryman. At first I could hardly bring myself to believe in the waiter's version of the matter. The delinquent had such an honest-looking countenance, and my vanity was somewhat insulted at the idea of my having been so duped. No ; it was more likely that he would turn up later. Comforting my mind as well as I could with this reflection, I went out with my friend G—— to purchase some provisions for the journey.

CHAPTER XII.

G——, though he was an American citizen, a man of the world in its fullest sense, and had travelled from the States to Orenburg, was not an efficient adviser with reference to the supply of provisions required by a traveller. Indeed, if I had taken my friend's advice I should have bought the contents of nearly every shop in Orenburg. The grocers looked delighted as G—— put aside tin after tin of preserved meats. At last I was obliged to remonstrate—"So! many thanks, but how can I carry them?"

"Carry them!" continued my imperturbable friend; "a sleigh is the most elastic piece of goods I know; it will stretch to any amount. Schuyler and MacGahan took a great deal more. I am only just beginning; we will go to another store presently. These sweet lozenges—they are excellent; try some;" and to the grocer, "Put 4lb. of this chocolate aside, and some pickles too — delicious; a few bottles — very good. Now, then, about candles and spirits for cooking, and a cooking apparatus, and a lamp. You had better have some carpenter's tools, in case the sleigh breaks, and lots of stout cord and nails. A carpet would be also a good thing to take to sit down upon; and some wine and spirits to present to the Russian officers. They like wine, and although you don't drink yourself, they do; just a dozen or so," he added with a supplicating glance. "Well, as you like— but it would be better. Then you must have presents for the natives. A few looking-glasses and ornaments. You will find them very useful."

It was really necessary to make a stand of some sort against my good-intentioned companion, who, not accustomed to travel himself, evidently thought that the entire contents of an upholsterer's or grocer's shop were indispensable requisites for a journey on the steppes.

"I tell you what it is," I observed, "I shall not take a quarter of the things which you have put aside for me, and certainly not purchase any more. It was as much as I could do to stow myself away in my sleigh when travelling without a servant from Samara here, and the vehicle would never hold half these things, which are for the most part quite unnecessary."

"Not at all," said my acquaintance, giving vent to his feelings by squirting some tobacco juice on the floor. "Not at all. Schuyler and MacGahan had two sleighs. Capital; the thing is settled." Then to the shopman. "A few pounds of cocoa. I shall soon have finished," he added.

It was useless arguing with him, and the only thing to be done was to allow the shopman to put aside the different articles, and to say that I would call another day, select what I wanted, and then pay the bill.

I now proceeded to the bank, as the amount of

Russian gold in half-imperials, which I brought from St. Petersburg, was more than would be required for my journey. The money was very heavy and cumbersome as carried in my waist-belt, and so I determined to convert a certain proportion of the precious metal into bank notes. There is a curious circumstance in connection with the paper currency in Russia which is not generally known by foreigners. On the face of every note is printed the following announcement :— ' The bank will pay the owner on demand the amount of roubles stamped on the paper in either gold or silver."* A most just and excellent arrangement if it were only carried out; but, on the contrary, it is extremely difficult to obtain gold in Russia, and during my stay at St. Petersburg I had to wait nearly an hour at Venekin's Bank whilst the clerk was sent out to buy half-imperials. Finally, I had to pay six roubles eighteen kopecks for each coin, the value stamped on it being five roubles, fifteen kopecks. On my going to the Government Bank at Orenburg and inquiring if I could change some half-imperials into paper, the cashier declined to give more than five roubles, seventy-five kopecks for each piece. I would not accept these terms, and went to the Commercial Bank, the cashier here offering six roubles. On my producing some English sovereigns he greatly admired them, and said that they were very beautiful, but refused to give me any roubles in exchange, unless I would first pay the cost of a telegram to the head of the firm in St. Petersburg, so as to inquire what price he would give. I then discovered that no one else in Orenburg would change the sovereigns on any terms whatever, and so had to accept these conditions.

* Literally in *zvonkom metala*, in ringing metal.

The following day I was informed that the Commercial Bank would change my English gold, though at a much lower rate than that which I had received at St. Petersburg. After the difficulties experienced with the sovereigns it can easily be imagined that the cashier did not look with much respect upon Coutts' circular notes, or upon a letter of credit from Cox & Co., the well-known bankers and army agents in Craig's Court. The bills might just as well have been waste paper in so far as the official was concerned, and when I told him that the paper of these two English bankers was looked upon in London as being as good as gold, the clerk shook his head, and evidently did not believe me.

In spite of the amount of silver which is supposed to be found in Russia, there is a great deficiency of this metal in the banks ; the cashiers object to pay any one more than five roubles, or fourteen shillings, in silver pieces, and confine their business almost exclusively to paper notes. When a Russian is about to leave Orenburg for a long drive by post, and a supply of silver is absolutely necessary, he has to send different people as commissioners to the bank ; each man will then receive five roubles' worth of silver, and in this manner the traveller can eventually get sufficient small change for his journey. Indeed, without a certain supply of silver coin it is almost impossible to travel in Russia, the station inspectors hardly ever having any change. The amount of paper in circulation throughout the Tzar's dominions is somewhat startling to a foreigner, and if the financial prosperity of a nation can be gauged by the amount of gold it possesses Russia must be on the verge of bankruptcy.

In the evening I dined with a party of Russian

officers, amongst others the chief of the telegraphs at Orenburg. The conversation turned on the chance of any immediate rupture with Germany; and one of the guests assured me that it would be impossible for a German army to make use of its own railway-carriages on the Russian lines, as the gauge has been made purposely of a different width to that employed in Germany and Austria. However, another of the party here remarked that, according to a recent account, the Prussians had got over this difficulty, an Engineer officer having invented a system for building carriages and engines by which the wheels can be made to fit any kind of line, and that if this statement were true a German advance would not necessarily be impeded on account of the difference of gauge. The telegraph official was very inquisitive, and asked a great many questions about my journey, finally stating to G——, " You may depend upon it we shall never see him again. He has been sent out by his Government, and when he has done what they want, he will return, but not by this road."

It was Christmas Day. I had been exactly twenty-five days on my journey—enough time to go from London to New York and back—and was still no further on my road than Orenburg. All of a sudden Mr. Bektchourin was announced, his first question being, " Have you seen the servant ? " " Yes," was my reply, " not only seen him, but engaged him, and given in advance fifty roubles, on account of his bed-ridden mother. He was to have been here yesterday morning at six, but he has not turned up."

" Oh, the dove ! " said Mr. Bektchourin ; " oh, the cunning little scoundrel. You do not know how he has deceived my wife. He came to her in my absence, and said that he had seen me, and then persuaded her to lend him five roubles to take his passport out of pawn. She gave him the money, and he has bolted with it. Oh, the cunning one!"—and Mr. Bektchourin shook his fist with rage—"but we will catch him. His little back shall smart. My dear sir, I will go to the police;" and the good man hurried off as fast as he could in that direction.

Later on I called on the same authorities, and was fortunate enough to find Colonel Dreir, the Chief of the Force at Orenburg. He informed me that Mr. Bektchourin had been already there, and that the case was in the hands of Sergeant Solovef, the most intelligent of the thief-catchers in the district. As he uttered these words, the colonel touched a bell, and desired the servant to summon the sergeant.

A moment afterwards the latter stood before us. He was a stout-built fellow, with a firm, resolute mouth, and a hawk-like nose and eye. He saluted in the military fashion, and remained at attention, standing stiff and erect before his chief.

"You have heard of this English gentleman who has been robbed by a Tartar servant?"

"I have heard."

"The rogue must be caught."

"I will catch him."

"The money must be got back."

"The money shall be got back—if he has not spent it," muttered the sergeant.

"Immediately."

"Immediately."

"Go at once," said the colonel.

"I obey," was the answer; and the sergeant, swinging round on his heel, saluted, and left the room.

The difficulties of obtaining a servant at Orenburg seemed to be so great that I made up my mind not to delay a day longer on that account, but to go alone on my travels—at all events, so far as Kasala. Once there, I could try again, and see whether in that part of the world an honest Tartar was such a *rara avis* as in Orenburg. In the meantime, Colonel Dreir gave me an order for a *podorojnaya* as far as Fort Number One (Kasala), and told me to go to the Kaznacheistvo, or Treasury, where the necessary document could be obtained. On receiving the pass, I found that it was worded as follows :—

BY THE ORDER OF

HIS MAJESTY THE EMPEROR ALEXANDER,

THE SON OF NICOLAS,

AUTOCRAT OF THE WHOLE OF RUSSIA,

etc., etc.

FROM the town of Orsk to the town of Kasala, to the Captain of the English service, Frederick, the son of Gustavus Burnaby, to give three horses, with a driver, for the legal fare, without delay. Given in the town of Orenburg, 15th Dec., 1875.

I had barely returned to my hotel, when Bektchourin was again announced ; and whilst we were drinking some tea, the clashing of a sword-scabbard on the staircase, and a considerable noise and clamour going on outside, warned us that something unusual was occurring. The head waiter now entered the room. His face wore a look of intense importance, coupled with admiration for something he had seen. He was evidently bursting to impart to me a startling piece of news ; and if he had been an English groom, I should have thought that my best horse had broken his leg.

"Well, what is it ?" I inquired. "Is the house on fire, or your wife dead ?" "No, one of noble birth ;

they have caught him." "What, the thief?" cried
Bektchourin. "Yes; the sergeant has him outside. The
rogue is weeping; the servants are all looking on—the
lodgers, too: they all know that he is caught. It is
grand; praise be to God! May the sergeant bring
him in?" "By all means," I said. A moment later the
door opened, and the delinquent was precipitated into
the room.

The sergeant followed. His mien was imposing.
He took two short steps, then a long one, advanced to
the side of the prisoner, placed his left hand on the
culprit's shoulder, and saluted majestically with the
right. It was a comical gathering—the servants in
the room, their hair bristling with awe; the lodgers
outside, eager to know what was the matter; the head
waiter wiping his perspiring forehead with a table-
napkin—which he had brought me as a substitute for
a towel—his huge mouth extended from ear to ear,
and alternately opening and shutting with astonishment; the prisoner pleading for mercy; the sergeant
erect and consequential; whilst Bektchourin, who was
more excited than I could have believed it possible for
an Oriental to become, was shaking his fist in the culprit's
face. "So they have caught you, brother. Ah! my
little pigeon, you have come back. So you wanted to
throw discredit on our race. Oh, you dear one! But
now, stick, stick, stick! you shall have it! Ah, my
love! you may cry," as the prisoner groaned at the
allusion to the whipping in store for him. "But the
money, sergeant, the money; what has he done
with it? and where did you catch him?"

The policeman was not gifted with the same
command of language as his interrogator, and to gain
time to collect his thoughts he once more saluted, then

jerked out, " He spent twenty-five roubles in drink —there are twenty-five here. Women, women— there were two with him!" and having disburdened himself of this statement, the sergeant produced the money he had taken from the culprit, and laid it on the table.

"For the sake of Heaven, pardon me," cried the prisoner, going down on his knees, and trying to kiss Bektchourin's feet; "but I drank, she drank, we all drank. I will return the money."

"Very well," said Bektchourin. "First of all the money, and then we will take into consideration the whipping; so remove him, sergeant, and see if he is able to make good the deficiency."

CHAPTER XIII.

THE excitement created in the household by the prisoner's arrival having calmed down, I set out with my friend G—— to see if I could purchase a sheepskin suit such as is worn by the Russian peasantry. In the meantime, Bektchourin very good-naturedly went off in search of a servant. "I must get you one," he said. "You shall not go alone. It shall not be said that there is not one honest Tartar servant in Orenburg." G—— drove me to a street mainly inhabited by dealers in sheepskin. On entering one of the shops, we were nearly compelled to beat a retreat, owing to the smell. A few years ago the Thames on a hot summer's afternoon, and at low water, had a bouquet peculiarly its own, and one which startled the olfactory nerves; but the odour in this little Russian shop was infinitely more disgusting. The sheepskins were in every stage of preparation. The heat thrown out by a large drying-stove was very great, and only the absolute necessity of ordering some warm clothes forced me to remain for an instant in the establishment. The things I had brought from St. Petersburg were of no use for the journey on horseback. The shuba or pelisse, which reached to my feet, would not have been suitable attire when I was in the saddle, and sheepskin garments, in spite of their disagreeable smell, are much the warmest clothes that can be worn. I was measured for a riding-coat, the wool to be worn inside, for some trousers of the same material, and for a pair of high stockings, or rather buckets, also made of sheepskin. These last would be drawn on over four pairs of fishing stockings, and in their turn be encased in some high cloth boots —experience had already taught me that any leather about the feet is a mistake—and when my new clothes were put on over those which had been made for me in London, I thought myself proof against any amount of frost.

In the evening Bektchourin returned to the hotel, accompanied by a Tartar, the most diminutive of his race, and certainly not five feet high. I was informed that he was of noble birth, his father having been an officer in the Russian army ; but the family was poor, and Nazar—this was his name—liked travelling and adventure. The man expressed himself as ready to do anything and go anywhere. He said that he never drank. I found out that he could speak Russian very well, and also the Kirghiz dialect. Bektchourin said that he could answer for the fellow's honesty, and as he wanted fifty roubles on account to leave with his wife, I agreed to advance this amount, though with a slight feeling of hesitation after the way I had been taken in by the man with the aged mother. The money was paid. Bektchourin embracing me said good-bye, and it was agreed that the servant should come to the inn the following morning, when we would start on our travels.

Long before daybreak I was up making preparations, and by the time the Tartar arrived, I had packed up most of the provisions. And then came the tug of war, for there were the servant, sleigh, horses, and luggage; but how on earth to put the luggage into the vehicle, and afterwards to find room for my legs, this was a problem which it appeared impossible to solve.

Nazar first arranged the parcels in one manner and then in another, but all to no purpose. At last, the inventive genius of the head waiter came to the rescue, when by firmly tying some of the provision boxes to the edges of the sleigh, there was sufficient space left for me to sit down. Fortunately my servant was a dwarf; his personal luggage being adapted to his stature. Balancing himself on the top of the gun-case and saddle-bags, he looked round for orders. "Off!" I cried; and away we galloped down the principal street of Orenburg, escorted by the good wishes and farewells of the inmates of the hotel.

A biting east wind, but a bright clear atmosphere, and in a few moments I was driving along the river Oural. Every now and then we encountered a caravan of camels drawing sleighs laden with cotton from Tashkent. Any one only accustomed to the camels of the Libyan sands would hardly recognise any affinity between the undersized and shaggy animals with lion-like manes which are met with in the steppes, and the huge sleek "ships of the desert" to be found in the African Sahara. Nature has supplied the Kirghiz camels with every requisite for resisting a bitterly cold clime, and the hardy beasts could be seen striding through the snow where it was four feet deep, and where horses would have been of no avail. Here a Cossack galloped by us, brandishing his long spear as he quickly vanished in the distance; and then we met some Kirghiz wanderers, their ruddy faces—red as lobsters—offering a striking contrast to the sallow-visaged Russians I had left behind.

I must say I congratulated myself on the purchase of the sheepskin clothes. In the keen air which surrounded us it was impossible to perceive the slightest smell, and for the first time during my sleigh journey I was feeling tolerably warm. We arrived at the station-house in capital time. In less than ten minutes fresh post-horses were harnessed and I was again *en route.* Nothing could have been more uninteresting than the country through which we were travelling; naught but a bleak white plain, save for the low ridge of Ural mountains which, lying far away on our left, slightly broke the monotony of the scene.

Three stations had been left behind us; I had determined to put another stage—Krasnogorsk—between myself and Orenburg. Nazar was a little famished; he had started without any breakfast, and a delighted expression passed over his countenance when I announced to him my intention of halting a short time at Krasnogorsk.

"Excellent milk there," he remarked, at the same time smacking his lips; "eggs, too. Please God we will stop."

I was myself beginning to experience a sensation of emptiness in my inner man; the glass of tea and rusk I had swallowed before leaving Orenburg were not very staying condiments, and I desired the driver to hurry on as fast as possible. However, the old proverb, "The more haste the less speed," proved, alas, to be a true one.

The afternoon was drawing to a close, and the golden orb could be seen dimly descending in the far-off west, when I became aware, by the numerous exclamations of my Tartar driver, principally consisting, as I afterwards ascertained, of strong expressions, that he was not at all contented with his horses. At starting I had remarked upon their appearance. They were as thin as laths, or, as Jorrocks would have said, "as herring-gutted as greyhounds," the ribs of the animal in the shafts looking as if they might at any moment pierce the skin. The driver had harnessed his beasts in what the Russians call goose fashion, that is to say, one in the shafts and the other two as leaders. His short whip, with lash some twelve feet long, and which previously he had allowed to trail behind the sleigh, was now continually in the air, whilst the thong, thick as my wrist at the handle end, resounded from the flanks of the over-taxed animals—sounds like pistol shots breaking the deep stillness of the snowy waste.

In answer to the question as to what was the matter, the one word "Bouran" was his answer; and, by the way, the gradually-rising gale was beginning to drift the snow across our path, it became evident that we were about to encounter a heavy storm.

Presently the atmosphere became denser with flaky particles, the cold becoming more and more intense. The last rays of the setting sun had disappeared from view, and in spite of all my wraps I began to feel the first insidious onslaught of the elements.

Darker and darker grew the shades around, till at last I could barely distinguish the driver's back; and my little Tartar servant, perched like a monkey at his side, informed me, in a melancholy tone, that we had lost our way. It was the case. We were off the track, whilst our wearied animals, up to their flanks and breast deep in the snow, were vainly endeavouring to plough a passage forward. A final effort, caused by the pitiless lash of our driver's whip, and the goaded steeds burst through the barrier. Up and down went the sleigh, bounding wildly over the treacherous furrow, till at last one of the horses stumbled and fell, breaking his rope harness, and bringing us to a dead halt.

Our team had collapsed, that was evident, and the driver seemed to have equally succumbed, for he left off swearing, and his whip, which up to that moment had never ceased cracking, lay stretched out behind the vehicle. He got off the seat, and having with difficulty succeeded in raising the fallen animal, jumped on his back and made a wide cast round in the hope of discovering the track.

"I am starving," said my little Tartar in a melancholy tone; "I had no breakfast, my belt is very loose," and suiting the action to the words he commenced tightening the strap around his waist, in order the better to resist the wolf inside. I had some bread and chocolate in my pocket, and dividing it with him, we stopped for a while the pangs of hunger.

In about an hour's time the driver returned, and in a mournful tone informed me that he had lost his way, that we must sleep out, and that in all probability we should be frozen. Not a pleasant piece of intelligence with the thermometer below zero, and a hurricane searing the face as if it were with a red-hot iron if we exposed the smallest piece of skin to its onslaught, whilst the flakes, drifting higher and higher around the sleigh, threatened, if the storm continued much longer, to bury us alive.

There was no wood in the neighbourhood—nothing with which we could make a fire—and the sleeping-sack, which I at once thought of, proved useless, owing to the small size of the aperture. We had no shovel to make a snow house, and there was naught to do save to sit it out the lifelong night.

My hands and feet first began to smart, and the nails to ache as if they were being scorched over a fire —a nasty burning, gnawing sensation which ate into the joints and then died away in a dull feeling of indescribable numbness which seized all the limbs. The pain was considerable, although it did not amount to that agony experienced from severe frostbites, and which I had to undergo later on in the journey. A heavy weight seemed to bear me down, and I dosed off for a second, till aroused once more to the reality of existence by the groaning of my little servant. He was murmuring something to himself in a low tone, but not one word of complaint ever escaped his lips.

I desired him to get inside, and giving the Tartar coachman all the furs that could be spared, we pulled ourselves together, as it is commonly termed, strung our nerves for the occasion, and determined not to go to sleep.

There was now no more pain, and my thoughts began to wander to far-off places, whilst well-known faces came and looked at me, then flitted away in the waste, and were replaced by well-spread banquet-halls, laden with viands which vanished as in my dream I strove to partake. It was over, and I was lost to consciousness, when I was suddenly aroused by a sharp tap on my elbow and a violent shaking from the hands of my follower. "Do not close your eyes, sir," he said, "or you will never open them again."

It was a hard task making the effort, but it was done, and presently I had in my turn to keep him from succumbing to the cold. All this time the driver was uttering some grunting exclamations from beneath the snow, which my slight knowledge of the Tartar language did not allow me to comprehend; loud hoarse sounds and ejaculations blurting forth at intervals and breaking the stillness of the night, for the wind had fallen and a dead silence reigned around.

"What is he doing?" I inquired of my servant; "is he praying?"

"No, sir," was the reply; "he is only lamenting his fate, and swearing at the horses for having brought us into this plight."

So the night wore on, and those only who have laid on a sick bed, and heard the endless tick of the clock as the hands go round the dial, can tell how glad we were when the first faint streak of colour in the far-off east warned us that the day was breaking. We then pulled out the driver from beneath his cold white canopy, and found him, though very stiff, otherwise not much the worse for his night's lodging. He shook the snow from off his furs, and then stretching himself two or three times to see if his joints were all right, proceeded to mount one of the horses, and said that he would ride off to the next station for help. This he did, making his way as best he could to the road now distant from us nearly a mile, at times disappearing from our gaze as horse and rider struggled through the piled-up snowy ridges.

An hour sped by, and yet another, but there was no longer any danger in seeking sleep, and at mid-day

I was aroused by a friendly pressure from the hand of a farmer, who had been summoned to our assistance by the driver.

"Well, brother," said the jolly, round-faced old countryman; "cheer up, we have arrived in time, praise be to God!" "Now, then, children," to some of his labourers who had come with him, and who were provided with spades and shovels, "dig out the sleigh." This was soon done, a well-earned remuneration bestowed on the kind-hearted peasants, when with three fresh horses we soon regained the road, and an hour later the station.

It had been a slow journey, for we had taken twenty-one hours to go eighteen miles; however, we were fortunate in not having lost something else besides time. A little while after our arrival, having partaken of a strange culinary composition of Nazar's, made of rice, eggs, and chocolate, boiled in milk, over a spirit lamp—this strange mixture proving in our ravenous state the most savoury of dishes—I felt myself once more in working order and ready to start.

My bad luck still continued. The Fates were again unfavourable. On arriving at the next station I found congregated there four passengers, all prevented from travelling by a snow-storm. Among them was the courier with the mail from Orenburg to Tashkent, a short, thick-set, sturdy-looking fellow, with a revolver at his waist, and a determined dare-devil expression on his countenance, not the sort of fellow that any Kirghiz or Tartar marauders would be likely to get the better of in an encounter.

He told me that the storm was very great, it was useless attempting to go forward for the present, as if he were to do so he certainly would be benighted on the road, and very likely be frozen. The wind, according to him, was the main difficulty, for, cutting keenly against the horses' faces, it caused them so much pain that the poor beasts could not face it. This, he said, was the reason that travellers found themselves so constantly driving off the track.

Then came an officer and his young wife, who were returning to St. Petersburg from Tashkent. The lady looked little capable of resisting the rough life she would have to lead before reaching the railway at Sizeran. They had a comfortable close sleigh, arranged with every requisite for keeping the travellers protected from the elements, but in spite of this the lady, who unfortunately looked in a delicate state of health, had suffered a great deal in the journey.

Notwithstanding all the precautions which had been taken, she had found it impossible to keep her feet warm, the circulation in her extremities being sometimes quite checked by the cold wind which penetrated to the bones through carriage wraps and all.

Another benighted traveller was a doctor on his way to visit a patient who lived in a village about fifty miles further on the road. The sick man's residence was situated miles from a physician, and he had to send all the way to Orenburg for medical assistance. It appeared that he was suffering from a violent quinsy, or sore throat, an illness which is exceedingly rapid in its effects; the despatch for the doctor had been sent off eight days previous, and probably when the son of Esculapius arrived he would find that the invalid had either recovered entirely or had been buried in the family vault. The medical gentleman had come away without any caustic, and eagerly inquired if any of us had a medicine chest or could supply the deficiency.

My own travelling companions, the Cockle's pills and some bottles of cholera medicine, did not seem to be applicable in the case mentioned, though, if the sick man had been an Arab, I should have administered the former freely, and probably with success, as faith is worth any amount of physic and effects most marvellous cures.

Bleeding is still very much in vogue amidst the Russian practitioners, and one of the party suggested that a little blood-letting might be advisable, and lower the patient's inflammation.

The doctor shook his head, and immediately commenced a long professional dissertation, which he interlarded with various Latin words, in order to duly impress us with his classical education. He did not seem entirely to dislike the idea of the lancet, which I have but little doubt he eventually tried upon the unfortunate patient.

There was not much reticence amongst the party, each traveller being plied with different questions, and having to submit to a cross-examination as to who he was, from whence he came, where he was going to, and what was his business. In fact, the inquiries were of so exhaustive a character, the more particularly those made by the surgeon, that I had serious thoughts of telling him my age, income, and what I had for dinner the previous evening, in the hope of fully satisfying his curiosity.

The evening wore on, and one by one our party lay down to sleep or to find what rest they could obtain on the wooden planks of the floor, the lady being accommodated upon the sofa. In spite of the hardness of the boards we were all speedily plunged in the arms of Morpheus, the cold winds and exposure having taken more out of me than any other clime which I had hitherto experienced.

The burning rays of a tropical sun on an African Sahara dry up the sap of the human frame. A long camel journey fatigues the rider, but nothing like the pitiless cold and physical suffering which inevitably accompany a winter tour through Russia.

At long intervals travellers arrived from Orenburg, and then the repose of our party would be broken for a moment by the new comers, who strode in to take a share of the planks. There was no light in the room, and the fresh arrivals, in their endeavours to find a clear space on the floor, freely trod upon the body of the courier. Some strong language issued from the lips of the man with the letter-bags, for which he was rebuked by the son of Esculapius, who even at that hour of the night could not refrain from inflicting upon us a quotation.

CHAPTER XIV.

I DETERMINED to take advantage of the presence of the man with the mails, and said that I would continue the journey with him, hoping by this means the quicker to reach my destination. The courier had no objection, and, after a considerable delay in obtaining horses for our sleighs we started. There was an advantage in accompanying him, for he was well provided with shovels and spades to dig out his vehicle in the event of the horses straying from the path and stumbling into a snowdrift. The main difficulty I should have would be to keep up with him, this being owing to the superiority of the teams which are supplied for the post. However, I hoped to do this by the means of tea-money, an open sesame to the affections of Russian sleigh-drivers, and which I had hitherto found their most vulnerable point. Let it be known that you tip handsomely, and your Jehu will drive you along regardless of his master's interest, whilst the regulation ten versts an hour can often be converted into half as much again.

Alas! all my calculations were upset; once more I was doomed to disappointment. I began to think that there was some influence behind the scenes, purposely doing its best to retard me on my journey. The tinkle of the bell on the courier's sleigh resounded in my ears for the first half-hour or so, when I fell asleep.

On awaking a few moments later I found that the sounds were lost in the distance; my horses were travelling at a foot pace. The driver, who had descended from his seat, was flogging his poor beasts unmercifully, vainly endeavouring to get them into a trot.

"How far are we from the station behind us?" I inquired.

"Five versts" was the answer.

I looked at my watch. We had been one hour and a-half coming about three miles, and in spite of the sleighman's whip and imprecations, it seemed impossible that his weak team could drag us to the next stage.

It was no use going on, so I desired him to return immediately. On arriving at the station I sent for the inspector, and also for the book in which travellers inscribe any complaint they may wish to make.

I wrote in it that the courier and myself had been detained forty-five minutes, counting from the time when our horses had been first ordered, and that the animals which had been supplied me were so bad that they could not go out of a walk. I concluded my remarks by expressing a hope that the inspector would be punished for keeping such useless animals in his establishment.

Having written down my grievance, I read it out to the interested party, to the great satisfaction of some other travellers who, like myself, had suffered from his carelessness. The man now became seriously alarmed, and said that he had never been complained of before, that he would be ruined, and that if I would only pardon him on this occasion he would never err against another traveller.

"Please, little father, pardon," he cried; "and I will send you on with three beautiful horses, full of fire and bursting with corn."

"Will you promise to make up for the lost time and to catch the post at the next station ? If so, I will pardon you, but if not, you shall suffer for your carelessness."

The man caught at the chance, and I wrote down at the bottom of the page that I would forgive him if he fulfilled these conditions, which, much to my surprise, he succeeded in doing.

The country now improved very much in appearance. The low chain of mountains on my left was sometimes broken abruptly for a mile or so. Occasionally a single giant would rear itself up into space before us as if by its altitude to block the intervening gap. Various-coloured grasses could be seen through the fleecy snow. Golden-tinted and bright chestnut were the hues which predominated amidst the rising vegetation. Olive-coloured bramble, and sombre fir and pine forests, strongly contrasted with the pale carpet glistening beneath a mid-day sun. Spider-like webs of frozen dew were pendent from the branches. The tenuous icicles reflected through their transparent surface all the prismatic colours of a rainbow. Here a myriad threads of icy film spanned the frequent bushes. There, broken by a pitiless beam from the orb overhead, they hung in silky tresses, and floated in the rising breeze. Gnarled stumps and quaintly-shaped blocks of timber, half-hid from the gaze by their wintry raiment, might have been antediluvian giants of a former world, awakened to existence, and shaking off their snowy coverlet.

A considerable trade is carried on in the district between Orenburg and Orsk in shawls and neck-wrappers. These are made of gossamer-like webs of goats'-hair woven into the articles above-mentioned. They are marvellously light, a very large shawl, which can be put into an ordinary-size official envelope, not weighing more than a few ounces. What most surprises the traveller is the excessive warmness of these Oriental wraps, as well as the softness of their texture. Many of them are so delicately made that they can be passed through a finger-ring. Any one who has seen the extraordinary lightness and softness of this material can understand what the author of an Eastern tale had in his mind's eye when he invented the story of the fairy tent which could shelter an army, and was yet so light as to be hardly perceptible to the touch.

Amongst other kinds of shawls offered for sale at the various station-houses on the road, and where the good woman and her daughters entreat the traveller to purchase in so plausible and winning a manner that it is difficult to say nay, are wraps made of hares'-down. This is woven by the wives of the farmers and peasants in the neighbourhood into very warm shawls, and which are softer, if possible, than those made of goats'-hair, although they are not nearly so light.

The price of these articles of female attire is not by any means exorbitant. A good shawl can be obtained for from thirty to forty roubles. I feel convinced that if some of our London tradespeople were to send their travelling-agents to those parts, a very profitable return would be made on the capital invested; for the shawls in question would demand a ready sale in this country.

Just before reaching Podgornaya, a halting-place on the highway, the road became very precipitous. It was a dark night, though fortunately unaccompanied by wind; but a thick mist—which had upraised itself from the mass of vegetation which abounded throughout the district—made it extremely difficult for our driver to see the path before him. The road was bad, and in some places dangerous—now descending a steep decline, then taking a sudden bend, when a hairbreadth to right or left would have caused a general smash. At last we came to a spot where the slope was fearfully abrupt. At its steepest part our road branched off at right angles from the line in which we had been previously driving, and which terminated in a precipice. It was not quite the sort of spot that any one would have cared to drive over on a dark night. As for myself, I was unaware of the dangers of the route. They only became apparent when I was returning along the same track by daylight, and homeward bound from Khiva.

The two drivers had a long discussion before they would attempt the descent. When they at last commenced operations, it was with the greatest care, and one sleigh at a time, the two drivers stepping slowly backwards, and leading the sliding steeds of my vehicle, after which they returned for the sleigh with the post. A slip would have been fatal; but luckily the Fates were on our side, and let us pass in safety.

The weather became much warmer on approaching Orsk, and I began to flatter myself that the real cold of the journey was over, little anticipating what was still in store.

After crossing a few frozen streams, we entered the town, my driver crying out "Oura!"* at every moment to his horses, which, like himself, did not appear to be sorry that they had come to the end of the stage. The town is a clean-looking one. The houses are well built, and an air of comfort reigned around, delightful to behold after the rough work we had been going through for the last few days. The driver pulled up at a little inn known by the name of the Tzarskoe Selo. It was filled with farmers and peasants, many of them much the worse for liquor; and at a bar just within the portico a man was engaged in pouring out vodki, which was eagerly demanded by the customers.

The amount of this spirit, which is quite as strong as whiskey, that a Russian moujik can drink would be an interesting theme for Sir Wilfrid Lawson to dilate upon in one of his periodical dissertations on the advantages of temperance. If the teetotalers of England, like some of their missionary brethren, should ever think of making converts abroad, they would have a magnificent field for their labours in Russia. Often when driving through the streets I have been struck by the sight of some figure or other prostrate in the snow. "What is it?" I would ask; "is he dead?" "No; only drunk," would be the reply, followed by a laugh, as if it were a good joke to see a man who had made a beast of himself. It may be that in proportion to the population there are not more drunkards in the Tzar's dominions than in England, or rather Scotland but, at all events, to get drunk

* A Tartar word, from which, perhaps, our word "hurrah" comes. It signifies "beat."

lowers a man in the opinion of the public in our country. It is a feather in his cap in Russia.

Fortunately, there was a vacant room in the inn, and here I was at once supplied with the smallest of basins and a table napkin. In the meantime I despatched Nazar to the post to desire the inspector to send me three horses immediately. There was no time to lose, and I wanted to hurry forward that afternoon.

Presently my man returned with a joyous countenance, which betokened something disagreeable. In fact, in all countries where I have hitherto travelled, human nature, as typified in domestics, is much the same; they invariably look pleased when they have a piece of bad news to impart to their masters.

"What is it?" I asked. "Sleigh broken?"

"No, sir. No horses to be had; that is all. General Kauffmann went through early this morning and took them all. The inspector says you must wait till to-morrow, and that then he will have a team ready for you. It is nice and warm," continued Nazar, looking at the stove. "We will sleep here, little father; eat till we fill our clothes, and continue our journey to-morrow."

"Nazar," I replied, giving my countenance the sternest expression it could assume, "I command; you obey. We leave in an hour's time. Go and hire some horses as far as the next stage. If you find it impossible to obtain any at the station, try and get some from a private dealer; but horses I must have."

In a few minutes my servant returned with a still more joyful countenance than before. The inspector would not send any horses, and no one could be found in the town who was willing to let out his animals on hire.

There was nothing to be done but to search myself

Nazar had evidently made up his mind to sleep at
Orsk. However, I had made up mine to continue the
journey.

Leaving the inn, I hailed a passing sleigh, the
driver appearing to me to have a more intelligent
expression than his fellows. Getting into the vehicle,
I inquired if he knew of any one who had horses for
hire.

"Yes," was the answer. One of his relatives had
some. The house to which I was driven was shut up
No one was at home. I began to despair, and think
that I should have as much difficulty in obtaining
horses at Orsk as I had in procuring a servant at
Orenburg.

I now determined to try what gold, or rather silver,
would do, and said to the driver, " If you will take me
to any one who has horses for hire I will give you a
rouble for yourself."

"A whole rouble!" cried the man, with a broad
grin of delight. Jumping off his seat, he ran to
a little knot of Tartars, one of whom was bargaining with the others for a basket of frozen fish, and
began to ply them with questions. In a minute he
returned. " Let us go," he said; and with a "Burr"
(the sound which is used by Russians to urge on their
horses) and a loud crack with his lash, we drove
rapidly in another direction.

I had arrived at the outskirts of the town. We
stopped before a dirty-looking wooden cottage.

A tall man, dressed in a long coat reaching to his
heels, bright yellow trowsers, which were stuffed into a
pair of red leather boots, whilst an enormous black
sheepskin cap covered his head, came out and asked
my business. I said that I wanted three horses to go

to the next stage, and asked him what he would drive me there for, the regular postal tariff being about two roubles.

"One of noble birth," replied the fellow, "the roads are bad, but my horses will gallop the whole way. They are excellent horses; all the people in the town look at them, and envy me. They say how fat they are; look, how round. The Governor has not got any horses like mine in his stable. I spoil them; I cherish them; and they gallop like the wind; the people look, wonder, and admire. Come and see the dear little animals."

"I have no doubt about it. They are excellent horses," I replied; "but what will you take me for?"

"Let us say four roubles, your excellency, and give me one on account. One little whole silver rouble, for the sake of God let me put it in my pocket, and we will bless you."

"All right," was my answer. "Send the horses to the Tzarskoe Selo Inn immediately."

Presently the fellow rushed into my room, and, bowing to the ground, took off his cap with a grandiose air. Drawing out the money I had given him from some hidden recess in the neighbourhood of his skin, he thrust the rouble into my hand, and exclaimed, "Little father, my uncle owns one of the horses; he is very angry. He says that he was not consulted in the matter, and that he loves the animal like a brother. My uncle will not let his horse leave the stable for less than five roubles. What is to be done? I told him that I had agreed to take you, and even showed him the money; but he is hard-hearted and stern."

"Very well," I said; "bring round the horses."

In a few minutes the fellow returned and exclaimed, " One of noble birth, I am ashamed ! "

" Quite right," I said ; " you have every reason to be so.   But go on, is your uncle's horse dead ? "

" No, one of noble birth, not so bad as that ; but my brother is vexed.   He has a share in one of the animals, he will not let me drive him to the next station for less than six roubles," and the man putting on an expression in which cunning, avarice, and pretended sorrow were blended, stood on one leg, and added, " What shall we do ? "

I said, " You have a grandmother ? "

" Yes," he replied, much surprised.   " How did you know that ?   I have ; a very old grandmother."

" Well," I continued, " go and tell her that, fearing lest she should be annoyed if any accident were to happen during our journey—for you know misfortunes occur sometimes ; God sends them," I added, piously ("Yes, He does," interrupted the man; "we are simple people, your excellency;") "and not wishing to hurt the old lady's feelings, should the fore leg of your uncle's horse or the hind leg of your brother's suffer on the road, I have changed my mind, and shall not go with you to-day, but take post-horses to-morrow."

The man now became alarmed, thinking that he was about to lose his fare.   He rubbed his fore-head violently, and then exclaimed, " I will take your excellency for five roubles."

" But your brother ? "

" Never mind, he is an animal ; let us go."

" No," I answered.   " I shall wait—the post-horses are beautiful horses.   I am told that they gallop like the wind ; all the people in the town look at them, and the inspector loves them."

"Let us say four roubles, your excellency."

"But your uncle might beat you. I should not like you to be hurt."

"No," was the answer, "we will go;" and the knotty point being thus settled, we drove off much to the dissatisfaction of my little servant, Nazar—a blue-eyed siren in Orsk having, as the Orientals say, made roast meat of his heart, in spite of his being a married man.

CHAPTER XV.

THE aspect of the country now underwent an entire
change. We had left all traces of civilisation behind
us, and were regularly upon the steppes. Not the
steppes as they are described to us in the summer
months. Then hundreds of nomad tribes, like their
forefathers of old, migrate from place to place, with
their families, flocks, and herds. The dreary aspect
of this vast flat expanse is relieved by picturesque
kibitkas, or tents, and hundreds of horses, grazing on
the rich grass, are a source of considerable wealth to
the Kirghiz proprietors.

A large dining-table covered with naught but its
white cloth is not a cheery sight. To describe the
country for the next one hundred miles from Orsk, I
need only extend the table cover. For here, there,
and everywhere was a dazzling, glaring sheet of white,
as seen under the influence of a midday sun; then,
gradually softening down as the god of light sank
into the west, it faded into a vast melancholy-looking
colourless ocean. This was shrouded in some places

from the view by filmy clouds of mist and vapour. They rose in the evening air and shaded the wilderness around. A picture of desolation which wearied, by its utter loneliness, and at the same time appalled by its immensity; a circle of which the centre was everywhere, and the circumference nowhere. Such were the steppes as I drove through them at nightfall or in the early morn; and where, fatigued by want of sleep, my eye searched eagerly, but in vain, for a station.

On arriving at the halting-place, which was about twenty-seven versts from Orsk, Nazar came to me, and said, "I am very sleepy; I have not slept for three nights, and shall fall off if we continue the journey."

When I began to think of it, the poor fellow had a good deal of reason on his side. I could occasionally obtain a few moments' broken slumber, which was out of the question for him. I felt rather ashamed that in my selfishness I had overdriven a willing horse, and the fellow had shown first-class pluck when we had to pass the night out on the roadside. Saying that he ought to have told me before that he wanted rest, I sent him to lie down. He stretched his limbs alongside the stove, and in an instant was fast asleep.

The inspector was a good-tempered, fat old fellow, with red cheeks and an asthmatic cough. He had been a veterinary surgeon in a Cossack regiment, and consequently his services were much in request with the people at Orsk. He informed me that land could be bought on these flats for a rouble and a half a desyatin (2·7 acres); that a cow cost £3 2s. 6d.; a fat sheep, two years old, 12s. 6d.; and mutton or beef, a penny per pound. A capital horse could be purchased for three sovereigns, a camel for £7 10s., whilst flour cost 1s. 4d. the pood of 40 lbs. These were the prices at Orsk, but at times he said that provisions could be bought at a much lower rate, particularly if purchased from the Tartars themselves. The latter had suffered a great deal of late years from the cattle pest, and vaccinating the animals had been tried as an experiment, but, according to my informant, with but slight success.

The Kirghiz themselves have but little faith in doctors or vets. It is with great difficulty that the nomads can be persuaded to have their children vaccinated; the result is, that when small-pox breaks out amongst them it creates fearful havoc in the population. Putting this epidemic out of the question, the roving Tartars are a peculiarly healthy race. The absence of medical men does not seem to have affected their longevity. The disease they most suffer from is ophthalmia, which is brought on by the glare of the snow in winter, and by the dust and heat in the summer months.

After leaving Orsk, the podorojnaya or passport system came in force, and my pass and self underwent the most rigid scrutiny; the officials at the stations being very much alarmed lest any one should escape their vigilance and drive by the stations without having his papers examined.

I could not help asking the inspector, at a place where the examination was carried on in a very searching manner, if some horrible crime had not been committed in the neighbourhood, as it appeared to me that he was on the look out for a criminal.

" No," said the man ; " that is not the reason ; but we do not want any foreigners, particularly Englishmen, in these parts; our orders in this respect are very strict."

The cost of travelling was now reduced from four kopecks per horse to two and a half; however, we found that a traveller did not gain much by this reduction, as the amount paid for the podorojnaya very nearly made up for the difference. I now learned that the postal track was let out to some contractors, who receive a subsidy for carrying the post, and at the same time have to keep a certain number of horses for the convenience of passengers. The stations were filthily dirty, and the sofas in a disgusting state. Indeed, there were no arrangements made for washing, or for ablutions of any kind. It seems that the Russians are of opinion that soap and water are not required when travelling, and that the less washing done on these occasions the better.

On arriving at Karabootak, a small fort the Russians have built, 317 miles from Orsk, I found that the term fort was a misnomer. The place is not fortified in any sense so as to resist a disciplined force, although a few resolute men could doubtless hold it for a long time against any number of Kirghiz or Tartar horsemen.

I was obliged to halt for a time at this station. There was a snowstorm going on, whilst the wind howled and whistled about the house, driving before it in its course such clouds of flaky particles that no horse could face its onslaught. Later on, and when the wind had a little abated, I asked the inspector to give an order for three horses to be harnessed to my sleigh. But there were no animals in the stable, and we had to wait several hours before some could be procured. As a rule, however, there was but little delay, and the inspectors carried out their instructions to the letter.

Formerly, and even in European Russia, passengers were sometimes detained for days waiting for horses at the stations, the inspectors not troubling their heads about any traveller, unless he happened to be an officer. There is a story to the effect that a Frenchman, who had been kept waiting a long time for posthorses, and who could not induce the inspector to give him any, was much astonished by the behaviour of a Russian captain. The latter, on asking for a fresh team, was told that there were no animals in the stable. However, he at once procured a whip, and chastised the official, the result of the whipping being the instant discovery of some horses.

The Frenchman seized the idea, and taking his cane followed the example set him, which he found a most marvellous specific in the course of his travels through Russia.

Only a few years ago whipping was the order of the day; and, according to some accounts, the late Emperor Nicholas himself occasionally administered chastisement to his officers. But whipping in these days is out of the question, and so I had to remain kicking my heels about in the waiting-room, although in this instance I had a suspicion that the inspector had some horses in the stable.

After waiting for several hours I was informed that some horses had been procured. The snowstorm had somewhat lulled, but the wind was almost as high as ever, and the cold more intense than anything hitherto experienced. On leaving the station I had forgotten to put on my thick gloves, and took my seat in the sleigh, with each hand folded in the sleeve of its fellow, the fur pelisse in this way forming a sort of muff, and protecting my hands from the cold. The road was less jolty than usual, and the sleigh glided along, comparatively speaking, smoothly. The change of motion before long produced an effect; leaning back in the vehicle, I fell fast asleep.

In the course of my slumber my hands slipped from the warm fur covering in which they were inserted, resting themselves on the side of the sleigh, unprotected by any thick gloves, and exposed to the full power of the biting east wind. This, if impossible to withstand when stationary or on foot, was now doubly dangerous owing to the movement of the sleigh, which, going in an opposite direction, added considerably to the force with which the wind blew.

In a few minutes I awoke, a feeling of intense pain had seized my extremities; it seemed as if they had been plunged into some corrosive acid which was gradually eating the flesh from the bones.

I looked at my finger-nails; they were blue, the fingers and back part of my hands were of the same colour, whilst my wrists and the lower part of the arm were of a waxen hue. There was no doubt about it, I was frostbitten, and that in no slight degree; so calling to my servant, I made him rub the skin with some snow in hopes of restoring the vitality. This he did for several minutes, but all this time the same pain previously described was gradually ascending up my arms, whilst the lower portions of the limbs were lost to all sensation, dead to pain—dead to every sense of feeling—hanging quite listlessly by my side, Nazar in vain using all his energies so as to restore circulation.

" It is no good," he said, looking sorrowfully at me;

"we must get on as fast as possible to the station. How far off is it?" he inquired of the driver. "Seven miles," was the answer.

"Go as fast as you can," I cried.

The pain, which by that time had ascended to the glands under my arms, had become more acute than anything I had hitherto experienced. Apparently, extreme cold acts in two ways on the nervous system : sometimes, and more mercifully, by bringing on a slumber from which the victim never awakes, and at others by consuming him, as it were, over a slow fire, and limb by limb.

All this time the perspiration was pouring down my forehead, my body itself being as if on fire, the pain gradually ascending the parts attacked.

There are moments in a man's life when death itself would be a relief; it was about the day that an unfortunate criminal* would have to undergo the last dread sentence of the law, and I remember distinctly the thought occurring to my mind, as to whether the physical pain I was then undergoing was less than the mental agony of the poor wretch on the drop.

Would the distance that separated us from the station ever be traversed? Each mile seemed to me a league, and each league a day's journey. At last we arrived. Hurrying to the waiting-room, I met three Cossacks to whom I showed my hands. The soldiers led me into an outer room, and having taken off my coat and bared my arms, they plunged them up to the shoulder in a tub of ice and water. However, there was now no sensation whatever, and the limbs, which were of a blue colour, floated painlessly in the water.

Wainwright.

The elder of the Cossacks shook his head and said—
" Brother, it is a bad job, you will lose your hands."

" They will drop off," remarked another, " if we cannot get back the circulation."

" Have you any spirit with you ? " added a third.

Nazar on hearing this ran out and brought in a tin bottle containing naphtha for cooking purposes, upon which the Cossacks, taking my arms out of the icy water, proceeded to rub them with the strong spirit.

Rub, rub, rub, the skin peeled under their horny hands, and the spirit irritated the membrane below At last a faint sensation like tickling pervaded the elbow-joints, and I slightly flinched.

" Does it hurt ? " asked the elder of the Cossacks.

" A little."

" Capital, brothers," he continued, " rub as hard as you can ; " and after going on with the friction until the flesh was almost flayed, they suddenly plunged my arms again into the ice and water. I had not felt anything before, but this time, the pain was very acute.

" Good," said the Cossacks. " The more it hurts the better chance you have of saving your hands." And after a short time they let me take them out of the tub.

" You are fortunate, little father," said the elder of the Cossacks. " If it had not been for the spirit your hands would have dropped off, if you had not lost your arms as well."

Rough, kind-hearted fellows were these poor soldiers ; and when I forced on the elder of them a present for himself and comrades, the old soldier simply added, " Are we not all brothers when in misfortune ? Would you not have helped me if I had been in a like predicament ? "

I shook his hand heartily, and went to the waiting-room to rest on the sofa, as the physical shock just undergone had for the moment thoroughly prostrated me.   My arms also were sore and inflamed, the spirit having in some places penetrated the raw flesh; and it was several weeks before I thoroughly recovered from the effects of my carelessness.

CHAPTER XVI.

A FEW stations further on I met an officer who asked
very eagerly if I were going to Kashgar—he had
found out, by inquiry from the inspector, who I was—
and he afterwards assured me that there were thirty
English officers in the above-mentioned Khanate engaged in drilling the inhabitants. He said that my
compatriots had already organised a force of 10,000
men to resist the Russian advance, and declared that
this information had come from Yakoob Bek's envoys,
who had been sent from Kashgar to Tashkent, and
who had stated it to the Russians.

I assured my informant that there was no truth
whatever in the story, but with no effect; and he
seemed thoroughly impressed with the idea that I was
another agent of perfidious Albion, sent either to stir
up the Kokandians or aid the Kashgarians against the
designs of their Northern foe. I could not help remarking that if such were my designs it would have
been far easier for me to have gone from India to
Kashgar than to have come through Russia, and, as it

were, through the heart of the enemy's country; but even this argument had no effect. Tashkent, according to him, was a sort of Paradise, the climate was excellent, and the inhabitants actually boasted a theatre. He said that the city contained 5,000 Europeans and about 75,000 natives, besides the garrison. The commerce with Bokhara was rapidly increasing, and Tashkent becoming a great emporium for all merchandise to and from Central Asia.

According to my informant, the great desire of General Kauffmann, the Governor-General of the Province of Turkistan, was to establish a railway from European Russia to Tashkent. The road from Orenburg *via* Orsk, Kasala, and the town of Turkistan, had been surveyed, and was impracticable, owing to the nature of the soil. The line which would eventually unite the Capital with the East would most likely pass through Western Siberia, and before very long some decisive steps would be taken with the object of carrying this idea into execution.

As we were nearing Irghiz, another fortress on the Orenburg-Tashkent road, which is on a larger scale than the stronghold at Karabootak, although equally unserviceable, should it ever be attacked by a force belonging to a civilised power, Nazar suddenly exclaimed, "Wolf!" and, seizing my gun-case, commenced unstrapping it. But the animal showed no disposition to allow me to come to close quarters, and he slunk away as soon as he saw us, at a good jog-trot, not giving a chance for a shot.

After another long and uninteresting drive through the same sort of desert snow-covered country which I have previously attempted to describe, we came to Terekli, a station which divides the territory under

General Kauffmann's authority from the vast province which acknowledges the government of Kryjinovsky, the Governor-General at Orenburg. I was now 761½ versts, or nearly 500 miles, from Orenburg, and about to enter the Province of Turkistan, which extends from this point to a line not yet decided upon by the Russian geographers.

A colonel was in the waiting-room, and he had desired the inspector not to allow any travellers to enter this apartment, for the official refused to allow me to go there, and took me into a little den inhabited by himself.

Here the podorojnaya again underwent a most rigid examination. The inspector was very uncivil, saying if I wanted to rest I might stop in his room, but by no means enter the one set aside for travellers; and he then remarked that it was a gross piece of presumption on my part to think of associating with so exalted an individual as a Russian colonel.

The station-houses were much more comfortably arranged than those which I had seen in General Kryjinovsky's district. They were no longer con- structed of wood, which, by the way, was so infested with insects as to be a perpetual source of torment to the traveller, but of cement. The stoves, too, were better arranged, and the waiting-rooms furnished with divans covered with Oriental rugs, where we could rest, spared from the war hitherto waged on us by the insect tribe.

Nazar now came to me with a melancholy face. " The bottles are broken," he said. On looking I found that the contents of some bottles of strong pickles had become frozen into a solid mass of ice, and that in consequence the glass had been fractured   On a closer inspection, I found that the other bottles were in a similar state, and all of them had to be thrown away. The havoc made by the frost was the more remarkable as the articles in question had been carefully packed in cotton wool and in wooden cases, which in their turn had been thickly covered with hay.

The disregard shown for the passengers' necks by the Tartar sleigh-drivers in General Kauffmann's district was, if possible, even greater than in Kryjinovsky's province. Whenever the road allowed, the driver made his horses gallop the whole way, never once letting them trot. There was a notice put up in the waiting-rooms at each station to the effect that if a traveller should urge his driver to go more than the regulation pace, ten versts an hour, and in consequence any damage occur to the horses, that the traveller was to be fined forty roubles. I could not help thinking that in Russian Asia the authorities cared less for the travellers' lives than for horses, there being no punishment whatever for the drivers should they upset their fares. To put it more tersely, I could not harm a horse for less than forty roubles, whilst my driver might break my neck for nothing.

At another station Nazar, who had jumped off the sleigh to order a fresh team, ran back to inform me that there were no horses in the stables. It appeared on inquiry that the man who had contracted to supply the track with horses had been ruined. The animals, which under the most favourable circumstances never received much care during the winter, had been half-starved, some had died, and others been seized by the creditors in liquidation of their accounts. The consequence was that instead of being supplied with three fresh horses, their place was taken by three gigantic camels. I should have thought that one of these enormous quadrupeds would have sufficed to draw my tiny vehicle; but no! the order on the podorojnaya was to supply the bearer with three horses, and the number must be adhered to—such was the explanation given me by Nazar.

It was a strange sight to see these gigantic beasts harnessed by ropes to the little vehicle. I have tried many ways of locomotion in my life, from fire balloons to bicycles, from canoes and bullocks to cows, camels, and donkeys; whilst in the East the time-honoured sedan of our grandfathers has occasionally borne me and my fortunes, but never had I travelled in so comical a fashion.

A Tartar rode the centre camel. His head-gear would have called attention, if nothing else had, for he wore a large black hat, which reminded me of an inverted coal-scuttle, whilst a horn-like protuberance sticking out from its summit gave a diabolical appearance to his lobster-coloured visage. The hat, which was made of sheepskin, had the white wool inside, which formed a striking contrast to the flaming countenance of the excited Tartar. He had replaced the usual knout used for driving, by a whip armed with a thin cord lash, and he urged on his ungainly team more by the shrill sounds of his voice than by any attempt at flagellation, the Tartar seldom being able to get more than four miles an hour from the lazy brutes.

All of a sudden the camel in the centre quickly stopped, and its rider was precipitated head-over-heels on the snow. Luckily, it was soft falling; there were no bones broken, and in a minute or so he was again in the saddle, having changed the system of harnessing, and placed one of the camels as leader, whilst the other two were driven as wheelers. We got on very fairly for a little while, when the foremost of our train having received a rather sharper application of the lash than he deemed expedient, remonstrated with his rider by lying down. Coaxing and persuasion were now used; he was promised the warmest of stalls, the most delicious of water, if he would only get up. But this the beast absolutely declined to do, until the cold from the snow striking against his body induced him to rise from the ground.

We now went even slower than before. Our driver was afraid to use his lash for fear of another ebullition of temper on the part of the delinquent, and confined himself to cracking his whip in the air. The sounds of this proceeding presently reaching the ears of the leader, perhaps made him think that his companions were undergoing chastisement. Anyhow, it appeared to afford him some satisfaction, for quickening his stride he compelled his brethren behind to accelerate their pace, and after a long wearisome drive we eventually arrived at our destination.

The country now began to change its snowy aspect, and parti-coloured grasses of various hues dotted the steppes around. The Kirghiz had taken advantage of the more benignant weather, and hundreds of horses were here and there to be seen picking up what they could find. In fact it is extraordinary how any of these animals manage to exist through the winter months, as the nomads hardly ever feed them with corn, trusting to the slight vegetation which exists beneath the snow. Occasionally the poor beasts perish by thousands. A Tartar who is a rich man one week may find himself a beggar the next. This comes from the frequent snowstorms, when the thermometer sometimes descends to from 40 to 50 degrees below zero, Fahrenheit; but more often from some slight thaw taking place for perhaps a few hours. This is sufficient to ruin whole districts. The ground becomes covered with an impenetrable coating of ice, and the horses simply die of starvation, not being able to kick away the frozen substance, as they do the snow from the grass beneath their hoofs. No horses which I have ever seen are so hardy as these little animals, which are indigenous to the Kirghiz steppes; perhaps for the same reason that the Spartans of old excelled all other nations in physical strength, but with this difference, that nature doles out to the weakly colts the same fate which the Spartan parents apportioned to their sickly off-spring.

The Kirghiz never clothe their horses even in the coldest winter. They do not even take the trouble to water them, the snow eaten by the animals supplying this want. Towards the end of the winter months, the ribs of the poor beasts almost come through their sides; but once the snow disappears and the rich vegetation which replaces it in the early spring comes up, the animals gain flesh and strength, and are capable of performing marches which many people in this country would deem impossible, a ride of a hundred miles not being at all an uncommon occurrence in Tartary. Kirghiz horses are not generally well shaped, and cannot gallop very fast, but they can traverse enormous distances without water, forage, or halting. When the natives wish to perform any very long journey, they generally employ two horses; on one they carry a little water in a skin and some corn, whilst they ride the other, changing from time to time to ease the animals.

It is said that a Kirghiz chief once galloped with a Cossack escort (with two horses per man) 200 miles in twenty-four hours. The path extended for a considerable distance over a mountainous and rocky district. The animals, however, soon recovered the effects of the journey, although they were a little lame for the first few days.

An extraordinary march was made by Count Borkh to the Sam, in May, 1870. The object of his expedition was to explore the routes across the Ust Urt, and if possible to capture some Kirghiz aúls (villages), which were the head-quarters of some marauding bands from the town of Kungrad. The Russian officer determined to cross the northern Tchink, and by a forced march to surprise the tribes which nomadised on the Sam. Up to that time only small Cossack detachments had ever succeeded in penetrating to this locality. To explain the difficulties to be overcome, it must be observed that the Ust Urt plateau is bounded on all sides by a scarped cliff, known by the name of the Tchink. It is very steep, attaining in some places an elevation of from 400 to 600 feet. The tracks down its rugged sides are blocked up by enormous rocks and loose stones. Count Borkh resolved to march as lightly equipped as possible, and without baggage, as he wished to avoid meeting any parties of the nomad tribes on his road. His men carried three days' rations on their saddles, whilst the artillery took only as many rounds as the limber-box would contain. The expedition was made up of 150 Orenburg Cossacks, 60 mounted riflemen, and a gun, which was taken more by way of experiment than for any other reason, the authorities being anxious to know if artillery could be transported in that direction.

The troops at the outset met with serious obstacles in the passes over the northern Tchink; horses and men coming down every minute. The gun had to be dragged up the first pass by fifty dismounted Cossacks supplied with ropes. But, notwithstanding the difficulties experienced, the troops marched sixty miles, and did not halt till they had descended the following day to Kurgan Tchagai. Now commenced a long sterile sandy steppe. There was no forage underfoot, and no water save at considerable intervals, the wells being 180 feet deep. However, the little force again marched for sixty miles without a halt, when its leader was obliged to abandon the enterprise and retrace his steps, owing to the absolute dearth of provisions; the Kirghiz having received timely warning of his approach, and made off a few hours before the arrival of the party. The troops reached their quarters (Jebyske) on the sixth day, after a march of 266 miles over a desolate and arid country. The heat had been excessive, the thermometer sometimes reaching 117 degrees Fahrenheit during the day, whilst the nights were cold and frosty. The insufficiency of supplies had been so felt that the men on the fourth day of the expedition were obliged to kill and eat a Cossack's horse. There were no sick in the party, and only twelve horses, which had been ridden by the riflemen, were found to have suffered from sore backs. This being occasioned by the men not having properly adjusted their saddles before mounting. Similar rapidity characterised a raid made by Count Borkh in the summer of 1869 upon the aúl of the Kirghiz Amantai, a chief who nomadised at that time on the Teress-Akhana, a tributary of the Khobda.

Count Borkh, who was then constructing the Ak-

Tiube Fort, formed a flying column of 70 Orenburg Cossacks, and riding nearly 133 miles in two days, through a little-known country, reached Murtuk. Here intelligence was received that Amantai was nomadising with his kinsmen, the Chiklins. The ties of clanship are held in great esteem among the Kirghiz, and the whole success of the detachment depended upon its falling upon the Chiklins unawares.

The object of the detachment was favoured by the inclemency of the weather, which was such as is seldom experienced even in the steppes. Taking advantage of the darkness, Count Borkh ordered the Cossacks to tie up their sabres, cover their stirrup-irons, and put nose-bags over their horses' mouths, to prevent them neighing.

In utter darkness, and amid the howling of the storm, the Cossacks passed among the sleeping aúls. They were led by a trusty guide. Occasional flashes of lightning lit up, for a moment, their path.

At daybreak the detachment was far on its road. The leader perceived on the banks of a rivulet the traces of some Kirghiz, who had just quitted the spot. He trotted forward, and soon descried in a large ravine some aúls, among which was that of Amantai.

It was necessary to gallop at the enemy as quickly as possible, so as not to give the Kirghiz time to recover. Forbidding the Cossacks to fire, Count Borkh dashed at the aúls and commanded the astonished Kirghiz to surrender Amantai. He was at once given up.

Apprehending an attack on their return journey, the Cossacks formed a sort of movable square, and throwing out a chain of skirmishers around the herd which they had captured (about 900 head), prepared, in the event of attack, to dismount and fire over the saddle. The Kirghiz followed at a respectful distance, but observing the precautions which had been taken, commenced gradually to drop off. The detachment reached Ak-Tiube in six days, without any loss. It had marched 333 miles. Only two horses were lame.

From the incidents which I have cited, it will be at once seen that the Kirghiz horses yield to none in strength and endurance. A nation which is able to dispose of from 300,000 to 400,000 horsemen,* mounted upon steeds such as I have described, is a very formidable embodiment of military power. It must be remembered that the Cossacks are constituted no longer as irregular cavalry. They are being as highly trained as any troops in Russia. Great attention is paid to their shooting, and they are continually being instructed in dismounted service. The Russian cavalry bought its experience in the Crimea. Formerly it was the worst-led force in Europe; it is now well supplied with intelligent officers. In the next war in which Russia is engaged, her Cossacks will be found a very different foe from those undisciplined and badly-armed horsemen whom we encountered in the Crimea.

* A number which will each year increase, owing to the law of military conscription. It is said that this law is shortly to be applied to the Kirghiz.

CHAPTER XVII.

THE jolting imparted by the motion of the camels to the sleigh had been too much for the wooden framework. An inspector who gave me this information declared that it would be impossible for us to continue the journey save in another carriage.

Nazar, however, was of opinion that this statement on the part of the official was an interested one, and only made to induce me to hire one of his own vehicles. But as the chances appeared tolerably evenly balanced in favour of my sleigh reaching Kasala, or of my being left on the road—not a pleasant thing to look forward to, in the month of January, in the steppes—I determined to be on the safe side, and leave it behind, though with feelings of regret, as if I were parting with an old friend ; for it had carried myself and fortunes for more than a thousand miles.

The sleigh in which we now found ourselves was still more like a coffin than the one I had abandoned. In addition to being narrow, it was short. After once wedging myself in, there was no possibility of stretching my legs till I arrived at the next station.

There is in the Tower a singular instrument of

torture, invented by some diabolical genius of the
Middle Ages. It is called the "Scavenger's Daughter."
The victim who was wedded, as it was termed, to this
fiendish contrivance could not make the slightest movement, his limbs and body being compressed into the
smallest space. Of such a nature was the sleigh in
which I was now travelling. If Dante had ever
been placed in a similar predicament, he would undoubtedly have added yet another way of punishing
the ungodly to the long list of torments in his
" Inferno."

Our driver pulled up at a station called Soppak.
We were rapidly nearing Kasala. When we continued our journey, we passed by some small salt-lakes,
which were covered with thick ice. Far away in
the distance, and about forty versts from us, lay the
Sea of Aral. This, according to the inspector, was
also frozen for several versts from its shores, thus
rendering navigation impossible. A salt breeze was
blowing straight in our faces. It parched and dried up
the skin, and, in spite of the cold weather, produced
a state of feverishness. The tea which we drank
was not at all calculated to quench our thirst, as the only
water which could be procured had a brackish taste
and strong saline flavour. In fact, the whole country
in this district is impregnated with salt for miles
around, and undoubtedly at some not very remote
date has been covered by the sea.

The snow became less and less. At last the
horses could scarcely drag the vehicle over the thinly-
covered ground ; and when we stopped at a halting-
place about five stations from Kasala, it was necessary
to abandon the sleigh, and hire a carriage. Slowly
we rolled along the road, a rough and fatiguing one for

the half-starved horses, which were so weak from want of food that they could hardly put one leg before another. Presently another heavy snow-storm warned us that winter was still raging on in front.

The evening was well advanced. The last station but one had been reached, so I resolved to sleep there, and enter the town the following morning, not knowing where I should be able to find accommodation should we arrive at Kasala in the still hours of the night. There was no inspector in the station, for it was Christmas Day—not according to our English reckoning, for that had been passed at Orenburg, but the Russian anniversary of the same event, which is celebrated according to the Old Style, and takes place twelve days after our own. The official, finding it dull all alone, had given himself a holiday, and gone off to Fort Number One, there to eat, drink, and be merry.

I must say I was sorry not to have been able to arrive in time for the anniversary of this time-honoured festival, which is kept by the Russians with not one whit less pomp or feasting than in our own country. With them, as with us, it is customary for all the members of a family to assemble beneath one roof. Rich and poor relations unite together, the festive board is spread, and unusual hospitality prevails. Later on a Christmas tree laden with fruit and presents rejoices the souls of the more juvenile population. Pleasure, however, has its dark side, and vodki, like punch, cannot be drank with impunity. The appearance of the Russians the morning after the feast plainly tells its tale.

Russian girls frequently amuse themselves at this time of year by attempting to discover what sort of a husband will eventually lead them to the altar. A favourite manner of doing this is by so-called divination. The amorous female who is tired of a celibate life sits, in the mystic hours of the night, between two large mirrors. On each side she places a candle, and then eagerly watches until she can see twelve reflected lights. If the Fates are propitious, she ought also to discern the husband she desires portrayed in the glass before her. Another method of divination is to have supper laid for two. If the young lady is in luck, the apparition of the future husband will come and sit down beside her; but in order to secure success, the girl must not divulge to any one her intention of thus attempting to dive into futurity.

There is a story told in Russia to the effect that the daughter of a rich farmer was in love with a young lieutenant, and he, suspecting that she would probably have supper laid for two, climbed the wall of the garden, and, sitting down by her side, partook of the prepared banquet; the girl being under the impression that it was his apparition, and not the real Simon Pure. On leaving the room, the officer forgot his sword, which he had unbuckled before he sat down to supper. The girl, finding the weapon after his departure, hid it in the cupboard as a memento of the visit. Later on she married another suitor, and he, fancying that there was some rival who supplanted him in his wife's affection, and one day discovering the sword, was confirmed in his suspicions, and killed her in a fit of passion.

Sometimes the inquisitive husband-seeker will take a candle, and, melting the wax, pour it on the snow, after which she strives to discern in the hardened substance the likeness of him she seeks; whilst a very favourite

amusement at this season of the year, and when several
girls are congregated under the same roof, is to divine
by the aid of a cock. Each girl taking some corn,
makes a small heap on the floor, and there conceals a
ring. The chanticleer is then introduced, and is let
loose beside the corn. Presently he begins to peck at
the heaps of grain. At last one of the rings is exposed to
view, when its owner, according to the popular belief,
will outstrip her companions in the race for matrimony.

We left our quarters at daybreak. I had been informed that there was an inn at the fort, and determined
to drive there at once, and not to go to the regular postal
station at Kasala, so as to avoid losing any time.
As we neared our destination, the country on both
sides of the road was covered with sheets of ice.
The frozen water was an overflow from the Syr
Darya, or Jaxartes, which in the autumn had risen
far above its banks and inundated the country in the
neighbourhood. The air was bright and pure, and
my spirits rose with the idea that probably my sleigh-
travelling was over, and that now I was about to commence another phase in my journey—the march to
Khiva. From the information which I had been able
to gather on the road, it appeared that there was snow
on the ground all the way from Kasala to the newly-
annexed khanate. If so, it was all the better for my
journey, as we should have no difficulty about water.

We now drove into the little town of Kasala, otherwise known as Kasalinsk, or Fort Number One. The
inhabitants are composed of nomad Kirghiz, who pitch
their *kibitkas* or tents in the outskirts of the town, and
there pass the winter, migrating once more in the early
spring; of Russian and Tartar merchants, who live in
one-storied brick or cement-built houses; whilst Jews,

Greeks, Khivans, Tashkentians, Bokharans, and representatives of almost every country in Asia, are to be met with in the streets. Kasala is a place possessing considerable commercial importance in Central Asia, owing to its geographical position. All goods coming to Orenburg from Bokhara, Khiva, Tashkent, and Kokan have to pass it on the way. The entire population is about 5,000. At the time of my visit it was garrisoned by a local infantry force of 350 men, under a commandant, and a cavalry regiment of about 400 strong. In addition to this force, there were the sailors of the Aral fleet. This consisted of four small steamers, drawing but little water, and able to ascend the Amou Darya to within a few miles of Petro-Alexandrovsk, a Russian fort, built on Khivan soil. This territory has been recently annexed to the Russian Empire, in spite of Count Schouvaloff's assurance to her Majesty's late Government. The crews of these vessels augmented the garrison by about 750 men. There were a few nine and four-pounders, and a small detachment of artillery permanently stationed within the walls. There were also fourteen small guns, capable, however, of throwing a ten-pound shell. These had been taken out of the steamers, and were available should they be required.

The fort itself is in the shape of a half star. It is an earthwork, defended on the south by a bastioned front which extends to the banks of the Syr Darya, here about half a verst wide. The fort is surrounded by a dry ditch and a parapet about eight feet high and twelve thick, the ditch being about thirty feet broad and twelve deep. Within the structure there are barracks sufficiently large to contain 2,000 troops, and also warehouses filled with stores. These buildings are constructed of bricks and dried clay. The plan of the fortification is badly designed, and the place might be very easily taken; however, it answers the purpose for which it was intended, namely, to check the Kirghiz.

The hostelry to which we were bound was called the Inn of Morozoff. Morozoff being a speculative Russian who had built a small one-storied house and roughly furnished it, trusting to make his profits out of the officers of the garrison and the Russian merchants who were continually passing through Kasala.

On inquiring if I could have a room, the waiter, a man of Jewish type, informed me that the town was full, and that there would be no room vacant for several days. However, he gave us the name of an individual who kept a sort of lodging-house.

"It is very dirty," observed the waiter, "but I dare say you don't mind that," and he looked contemptuously at my sheepskin attire.

The man who addressed us was himself begrimed with dirt, and Morozoff's inn, in point of cleanliness, would have been surpassed by the pigstyes in many of our Leicestershire farms. However, there are comparisons in dirt. The proprietor of the lodging-house where I now betook myself was even more unwashed than the waiter above mentioned.

"Rooms?" said he; "no: we are here five and six in a room, and our passages are full too."

"Do you know of any other lodging-house?" I inquired.

"Lodging-house? no; go with God, brother"— with these words he slammed the door in my face, leaving Nazar and myself looking pensively at each other outside.

" He is the son of an animal !" exclaimed my faithful follower; " but it is cold here. One of noble birth, what shall we do ?"

An idea struck me. " Drive to the Jews' quarters," I said to the sleighman, thinking that perhaps amongst the tribes of Israel I might find quarters for the night.

Abraham, Isaac, and Jacob were now visited but in vain, and the Mohammedan inhabitants were equally impervious to an offer. The fact was, that a feast peculiar to the followers of the Prophet happened to fall on the same date as the Russian Christmas. People had come from every part of Asia to meet their friends and relatives. Unusual rejoicing was going on. The Russian making his heart gay with vodki, whilst the follower of Islam, after stuffing himself with pillaffs of rice and mutton, was seeking in the fumes of opium relief from the cares of this world, and a foretaste of the one to come ; a Mohammedan's paradise consisting of an unlimited seraglio, which costs nothing to keep, and where the female inhabitants require no guardians, do not quarrel or pull his beard, and are always young.

As it was impossible to find any lodgings in Kasala, I resolved to drive to the fort and see if the commandant could do anything for us. This officer received me very courteously, and at once sent his servant to search everywhere in the town for rooms. In the meantime he offered me an apartment in his own house. A large brass basin was brought in, and I now enjoyed the luxury of soap and water, which was well appreciated after a continuous journey for twelve days.

Foreigners cannot understand an Englishman's love of water, and look upon us as dirty for requiring so much washing. Russians consider a vapour bath once a week an *embarras de richesse* in so far as cleanliness is concerned, whilst the mere idea of any one having a cold bath every morning is beyond their comprehension, and another proof of the eccentricity appertaining to an insular character.

The room in which I found myself was furnished in the simplest manner, a bedstead and a few wooden chairs being all the furniture; however, it was clean, and free from insect life. Presently, the servant sent out by the commandant in search of lodgings returned. He had been everywhere in Kasala and there was not a room, or even the share of a room, to be had. I now learned that privacy is not considered at all essential in the steppes, where three or four officers will often share the same apartment.

CHAPTER XVIII.

THE Commandant pressed me to remain beneath his roof, at least until such time as I could find sleeping quarters. His wife now informed me that an English engineer officer * had resided beneath their roof the previous summer, and had subsequently accompanied a Russian scientific expedition as far as Petro-Alexandrovsk, the object of his journey being to survey the Oxus. The members of the expedition had, at the time my compatriot was with it, navigated the stream to the fort, but since his departure some Russian officers had ascended the river seventy versts beyond that part; indeed, the Commandant informed me that when a steamer then being built was finished, which would draw but little water and steam twenty versts per hour, it would be able to ascend the stream for a much greater distance, and perhaps to the source of the river. The chief obstacle hitherto experienced

* Major Wood.

had been the rapidity of the current, and as the engines on the vessels in commission were of little horse-power, it had been difficult to make headway against the stream.

Permission had been given to a merchant to build a fleet of fishing vessels for the Sea of Aral, which is said to abound with the finny tribe. This would doubtless be a great convenience, as in case of necessity these barges could be used to transport troops up the Oxus.

The distance from the Sea of Aral to European Russia is considerable. The Black and Caspian Seas abound with every kind of fish. It is to be feared that the enterprising individual who is about to construct this fleet of fishing barges will find his speculation anything but a lucrative one, although from a military point of view it will be extremely useful.

My hostess poured out some tea, and, handing me a cigarette, lit one for herself. This is not at all an exceptional proceeding in Russia, where the women smoke as much as the men. In the best society at St. Petersburg it is not at all an uncommon spectacle to see the married women and aged chaperones indulging in cigarettes. Fortunately the girls have not as yet taken to the habit.

The disturbances in Kokan, by all accounts, had been much exaggerated, and the Russian troops had not at any time been in danger. An officer who had passed through Kasala, on his road from Tashkent to St. Petersburg, had said "that his comrades and self were very surprised to find that they were such great heroes. This was all owing to the *Invalide* newspaper, for the Russian military journal had belauded the officers under Kauffmann to a ridiculous extent: but that it was well this organ had done so, as there would now be plenty of medals and decorations. If the paper would only continue its abuse of Yakoob Bek, it would very likely bring about a campaign in the summer against Kashgar, and that this was the wish of General Kauffmann, the Governor-General of Turkistan."

I now proceeded to Morozoff's hostelry to see what could be obtained for dinner, as I felt excessively hungry, the keen air of the steppes having produced a most healthy appetite. On asking the same domestic who had greeted me in the morning what there was to eat—

"Anything you ask for," was the immediate reply.

This, when submitted to investigation, proved to be slightly incorrect, for some cabbage soup and cold mutton were the sole contents of the larder.

"We have magnificent wine," observed the servant, producing a bottle of port as black as ink, and which appeared to be a concoction of Russian spirits, thickened with soot. "Delicious! taste it; our wine is famous all over the country."

The room in which I found myself was of an oblong shape, and without any furniture save a table and bench. A few sheepskins in a corner showed that the apartment was already taken. In reply to my inquiry I was informed that three merchants had slept there, but that they not being at home the waiter had taken possession of their room.

According to him, it was a delightful Christmas. More vodki had been drank the previous evening than had ever been known in the annals of Fort Number One. Universal drunkenness still prevailed, and the inhabitants in consequence were thoroughly enjoying themselves.

I ordered a sleigh, but had some difficulty in obtaining one, as there were only five of these vehicles in Kasala. I then drove to the house of Colonel Goloff, the District Governor. He was not at home, but engaged in paying visits to the families of the principal officials in the garrison, as it is the custom in Russia to call on your friends during the Christmas week, and offer them the congratulations of the season. His servant, however, told me that the Governor would soon return, so I resolved to await his arrival.

The house was a substantial and well-built edifice, but only one storey high, like almost every other building in Kasala. The two sentinels outside the building, and whom I could distinguish through the thick double-glass windows, every now and then took a short run backwards and forwards in front of their sentry-boxes, so as to keep up the circulation in their feet, the cold being very great.

A small entrance-hall afforded every convenience to the visitor for hanging up his fur pelisse and depositing his goloshes. Four large and lofty rooms opening one into the other formed the dwelling apartments of the family. There were fine parquet floors in each of these rooms. Some full length mirrors, with a few chairs and tables, constituted the entire furniture. Large stoves set in the walls were arranged so as to impart a genial warmth throughout the building, whilst three or four back rooms, used as offices and kitchen, looked out upon a small garden and stable which were behind the Colonel's residence.

Presently the rattle of a sleigh which stopped before the portico announced to me that the Governor had returned, and a minute later he entered the room.

He was a tall but somewhat corpulent man, evidently on the wrong side of fifty, and clad in a dark blue uniform. I introduced myself to him, and apologised for the liberty I had taken in calling.

He said that he had heard from the authorities at St. Petersburg that I was on my way, at the same time observing that he could not allow me to remain under the Commandant's roof. "His house is small," remarked the Governor; "besides that, he has a wife and children; here, I am all alone, my family has gone to Russia. You must come and stay with me."

"Nay, you must," he added, somewhat sharply, as I hesitated to intrude myself on his hospitality; so thanking him for the invitation, I drove back to the Commandant's quarters. It was with difficulty that I could persuade him to let me depart, and then it was only by saying that the Governor had expressed his wish, or rather orders, on this subject in such a peremptory manner that it was impossible for me to refuse.

On returning to the Governor's I found the reception-room filled with officers who had come to offer him the usual Christmas congratulations. He then told me that there would be an assembly at his house later on in the evening, when I should have the opportunity of seeing all the beauty and fashion of Kasala.

The apartments were thrown open and fairly lit. Shortly afterwards the ladies began to arrive, all of them being in high dress, and little coteries were speedily formed. Some settled down to play whist, regardless of the buzz of conversation around them.

Others promenaded about the rooms with the lady of their choice. Men and women all with cigarettes in their mouths, and filling the apartments with clouds of smoke. There was no stiffness anywhere, and everything was done to make a stranger feel thoroughly at home. General Kauffmann had passed through Kasala a few days previous, and had left a very pleasant impression upon the fairer part of the community, with whom the aged General was decidedly a favourite, and many remarks were made as to why he had gone to St. Petersburg.

One of the officers spoke Portuguese, having been some time at Lisbon. He had been attached to a Russian squadron which had sailed to America a few years ago, and he was now doing duty on board a vessel belonging to the Aral fleet. He informed me that his ship drew but little water, not more than from three to four feet, and that she could steam from Petro-Alexandrovsk to Tashkent; the great difficulty, however, was the scarcity of fuel, for they had to burn wood instead of coal. It was very difficult to carry a sufficient supply of this article, which was very bulky, for a long journey, whilst the expense to the Government was enormous.

The officers in the garrison were unanimous in envying the luck of their more fortunate comrades in Kokan, who had been engaged during the recent disturbances, and they bitterly complained of the slowness of promotion and the dreary existence at Kasala.

" Anything for a change," remarked one of them, a dashing little fellow with several medals, " we are bored to death here."

" Yes," added another, "when we fight you fellows

in India then we shall have some promotion; as to fighting with the Kokandians we might as well shoot pheasants; none of our seniors get killed."

"I don't think England will interfere with us about Kashgar," remarked an officer apparently much older than his comrades.

"Who knows, and who cares?" said another; "if we do fight we will shoot at each other in the morning, and liquor up together when there is a truce. Come along and have a drink," and with these words he led me into an adjoining room where some servants had just brought in what the Russians call Zakuski— caviare, salt-fish, little bits of bread and cheese, slices of highly-flavoured sausage, and spirits of every kind.

I was surprised to find that so few of the party could speak French; in fact there was hardly a lady present who could converse in this language, indeed, they did not blush when acknowledging their ignorance. It was quite a pleasure to meet with some people who were not ashamed of their own language. There is a general opinion in England that Russians are good linguists, because their own tongue is so difficult that all others become easy to them afterwards. This is an entire fallacy. The true reason why some Russians speak two or three foreign languages well, and with a perfect pronunciation, is the attention that is paid to the subject, the more particularly in Moscow and the capital. There the child has an English or French nurse as soon as he is able to speak, and he learns the foreign languages at the expense of his own, for the pronunciation first acquired is the one to which we generally adhere. By the time he is ten or eleven years old he often speaks French,

German, and English, whilst these languages are grammatically studied as he gets older.

Now in England we fall into the opposite extreme; we usually neglect the modern languages, and even omit the study of our natural tongue. We occupy the whole of our boy's scholastic and college career with the study of Latin and Greek, imagining that we are laying a good foundation for the lad to learn modern languages later on in life, and when he leaves college. But this is then a hopeless task; after twenty it is very exceptional to find any one who can tutor himself to a new pronunciation. Lads and men when leaving school or college have generally but little time for further education. The result is that we are as a nation the worst linguists in the world. As it is, our schools are kept up for the advantage of the masters, who having been trained themselves in a special branch of study, would be ruined if any other system ot education were insisted upon by the parents. The masters benefit, the boys suffer. If, at our schools, Latin and Greek were made to change places in relative importance with French and German, many lads on entering life would find that they had built a two-storied house, instead of having merely laid the foundation of an edifice which they will never have time to complete.

The evening wore on. Thicker and thicker grew the clouds of tobacco-smoke which escaped from the lips of the smokers. Some servants now brought in two magnificent sturgeon, which were placed on the supper-table. The host walked up to his different guests and invited them to partake. Tobacco did not affect the appetites of the party, and a bite and then a whiff would often be indulged in by some of the

guests. Wines of all kinds were placed on the table.
The clinking of champagne-glasses, as the guests
pledged their host, mingled frequently with the conversation.

"So you are going to Kashgar?" said a young
officer, who had been so kind as to point out to me the
different celebrities of the evening.

" No."

"Why do you not go there?" he continued; "you
would meet a quantity of English officers who are
teaching Yakoob Bek's men to fight."

" Do not talk politics," said another, his senior; "of
course we shall have to fight England some day;
but the English, although they fought against us in
the Crimea, were much better fellows than the
French."

Trays were now brought in with dishes containing
small beefsteaks and fried potatoes, which were replaced
at intervals of about half an hour by fresh courses.
But it was getting very late, and with difficulty I could
keep my eyes open. It was ten days since I had taken
off my clothes to sleep, and a sleigh journey over the
steppes takes a little out of any man's constitution.

Fortunately my host observed my inability to
keep awake, and volunteered to show me my sleeping
apartment.

"You have brought your bed-linen?" he remarked.
"But of course you have. You are too old a soldier
not to have done so," and with these words he shut a
door which separated me from the rest of the company.

I had fortunately, in anticipation of some such
event, brought an air mattress from England. It did
not weigh above two or three pounds, was easily
inflated, and very portable. This, being blown up

and placed on the floor, made a capital couch; whilst, as I had no sheets or blankets with me, I did what the Russians do under similar circumstances, and lay down with my pelisse as a blanket. The door of the apartment was thin. The partition-wall which separated my room from those occupied by the guests offered little impediment to the sound; but ringing laughter and jingling of glasses do not keep a man from sleeping if he is once really exhausted, and I speedily became lost to consciousness.

CHAPTER XIX.

THE following morning at ten, Nazar, coming into my room, informed me that Colonel Goloff was dressing, and that breakfast would soon be ready.

On asking for a basin, I was informed that it was not the custom to wash in the sleeping apartment, but that a regular room was set aside for this purpose. I was then taken into a sort of scullery, with a sink and large copper utensil. In the last-mentioned article was a supply of water. This, on pulling a string attached to a plug in the vessel, streamed out from an aperture in the side.

It was a primitive sort of arrangement, as I could only wash one hand at a time, and very cold, as there was no stove, whilst the icicles hung about the window-frames. Under these circumstances the morning ablutions became a tedious process, and rather a pain than a pleasure.

The Colonel now entered my room, and invited me to breakfast. The repast was of a frugal nature; it merely consisted of tea and dry bread, more substantial food being considered quite out of place at such an hour of the day; the habit the Russians have of eating supper in the early hours of the morning not being conducive to appetite.

My host then informed me that he had himself been five times to Petro-Alexandrovsk.

The Turkomans, he said, gave a great deal of trouble, as they crossed the Oxus, when the river was frozen, and made frequent raids upon the Kirghiz, carrying off their sheep and cattle. Indeed, on this account he thought that it would be better for me to have an escort of Cossacks; "for then," he added, "it can accompany you to our fort, and Colonel Ivanoff, the Chief of the Amou Darya district, will send you on to Khiva, which is about sixty miles from Petro-Alexandrovsk, with a fresh escort."

On asking what would happen to me if I were to visit the Khan's capital alone and unprotected—

"That would never do!" he said. "Why, the Khan would very likely order his executioner to gouge out your eyes, or would keep you in a hole in the ground for five or six days before he admitted you to an audience. The Khivans are very dangerous people."

I thanked him very heartily for the information, which, I dare say, was given in a friendly spirit. It was refreshing to find that the good Governor of Kasala valued my life so highly, and I shall always feel deeply indebted to him for his kindness.

He now promised to get me a guide; and, ringing a bell, desired the servant to send for a Kirghiz officer. The latter could communicate with his country-men, and tell them that I wanted to buy some horses, for the journey would have to be accomplished on horseback, and it was impossible to hire any animals in Kasala.

Camels would also be required, and a kibitka, or circular tent. As for provisions, the Colonel recommended me to take some *stchi*, cabbage soup, with meat cut up in it. This, he declared, was very portable, as it would become frozen, and keep for any amount of time, whilst it might easily be carried in iron stable-buckets. The principal difficulty for a traveller, in his opinion, was the forage; a sufficient supply of it must be taken for a fourteen days' journey, twelve pounds of barley per diem being the ordinary allowance for a horse. This would add enormously to the weight of baggage, as for three horses we should require thirty-six pounds of barley a day, or 504 pounds for the march. According to the Colonel, I need not burden the caravan by taking a supply of water, as in all probability there would be snow on the ground the whole way. However, I had better purchase some sacks, so that in the event of it appearing likely that any part of the route before us would be thinly covered with snow, we could put some in our sacks and thus carry it on the camels.

The cold would be my greatest enemy, as the winter we were then experiencing was the most severe he had ever known at Kasala, and several people had been frozen to death. When we had finished our breakfast, the Governor left me till dinner, which he said would be on the table about 2 P.M., and departed to go through his routine of duties, when I determined to walk through the town and look at the Kirghiz population.

I took Nazar with me to act as interpreter, in the event of my wishing to converse with any of the inhabitants who could not speak Russian. The little man was full of admiration at the splendour and luxury in the Governor's residence. He described to me in glowing terms the magnificent banquet he had partaken of the previous evening; his only fear being lest in some disguised form or other he had eaten of the unclean animal, for this is a sore point with the Tartars, as, indeed, with all other Mohammedan nations. The bazaar, he said, would not be open, on account of its being a feast day, and he had been to the Treasury to change some money and found that this establishment was also closed. Presently some Kirghiz men and women rode by, the latter sitting astride their horses, and managing their palfreys with the most consummate ease and grace.

We now met some Bokharans and Khivans, the marked Jewish type and swarthy faces of the former contrasting strongly with the Khivans, who were several shades lighter in complexion. Every one, man or woman, was enveloped in some kind of fur or other, and not a particle of their skin was left uncovered save just about the eyes.

A few Cossacks from the Ural, who were exiled from their far-off home, walked in little knots before their dwelling-houses, some discussing the chance of a pardon and a return to their families at Uralsk, others the hardship of a journey to Khivan territory, whither it was rumoured they were shortly to be sent. Many of these men appeared to be considerably past their prime, and the journey to Kasala must have been a very trying one for them. Their one idea was that the Emperor himself had not wished their offence to be punished in so stern a manner, and that the order for their banishment had been obtained through some source, which, unfavourable to the dissenters, had exaggerated the facts of the case to the Tzar.

The town of Kasala was kept in a very dirty state, and did not reflect credit on those authorities whose duty it was to see after such matters. Filth and ordure were strewn about the thoroughfare, and if it had not been for the extreme frost which kept everything congealed, the effect upon the atmosphere would have been anything but pleasant. Indeed, it is a wonder that more sickness does not ensue, the more particularly in the early spring. In houses where there is a certain pretension to wealth and comfort the refuse is never removed, and the retiring-rooms are left in a state which must be seen to be believed ; indeed, any attempt at description would inevitably disgust the reader. The result is that when the cold takes its departure and a thaw sets in, the houses become a hotbed of fever, whilst the death-rate amongst the population is often doubled.

On the outskirts of the town some Kirghiz had pitched their kibitkas. These tents are the homes of the nomad tribes, and are carried by them on camels from place to place. One of these abodes was adorned inside with thick carpets of various hues, and bright-coloured cushions, on which the inmates reposed. A small fire in the centre of the apartment gave out a thick white smoke, which wreathed itself round in serpent-like coils, till, gradually reaching the roof, it escaped through an aperture left for that purpose. Very pungent and trying to the eyes was this dense atmosphere—a wood, or rather sort of bramble, called saksaool, which is found in large quantities on the steppes, being used for fuel. The women in the tent appeared to have no fear of strangers, and did not cover up their faces, as is the custom amongst other Mohammedan races. They were evidently delighted at our visit, and, laying down fresh rugs on the ground, invited me to sit by their side. As a rule, there could not be much said for the beauty of their appearance; indeed, making every allowance for Mr. MacGahan's advocacy of the fair sex in Tartary, I cannot help thinking that the energetic correspondent is either extremely susceptible, or else very easily pleased, as a moon-faced, red-cheeked girl, the acme of perfection from a Kirghiz point of view, does not quite answer to my ideas of a beauty. Most of the women have good eyes and teeth, but the breadth of the face and the size of the mouth take off from these advantages; whilst the girls are not at all graceful, although on horseback they appear to perfection.

An elderly man, clad in a long brown dressing-gown thickly wadded to keep out the cold, was the proprietor of the kibitka. Pouring some water into a huge cauldron, which was suspended from a tripod over the fire, he proceeded to make the tea, whilst a young girl handed round some raisins and dried currants. The inmates were surprised when I told them that I was not a Russian, but had come from a land far away towards the setting sun.

"Anglitchanin, Englishman," said Nazar; and the party gravely repeated the word Anglitchanin. One of the men now inquired if I had brought my wife with me, and he was astonished on hearing that I was unprovided with a helpmate, the whole party being of the opinion that such an appendage was as necessary to a man's happiness as his horse or camel.

The Kirghiz have one great advantage over the other Mohammedan races. They have the oppor-

tunity of seeing the girls whom they wish to marry,
and of conversing with them before the bargain is
concluded with their parents—one hundred sheep
being the average price given for a young woman
Among those Tartars who have fixed residences, and
who do not migrate from place to place, this state
of things is not allowed. Here the man who wishes
to buy a wife has to run a considerable risk, for he
seldom has an opportunity of judging of her looks,
temper, or disposition. The girl always keeps her
face covered when in public, and is concealed from
the men as much as possible. The man's mother, or
some other female relative, occasionally acts as his
agent, and arranges so that her client may be hid
behind some cupboard in their house. They then
invite the girl to visit them, when the latter, thinking
herself alone, is induced to uncover her face. The
suitor now makes a mental calculation as to how
much she is worth. The bidding then commences,
the young lady's parents asking at first much more
than they will eventually take.

" She has sheep's eyes, and is lovely," says her
mother.

" Yes," replies the female relative, the wife-seeker's
advocate, " she has sheep's eyes, but is not moon-
faced, and has no hips whatever! Let us say 200
roubles."

And so the bidding goes on, until eventually, the
bargain being concluded, the ceremony, such as it is,
takes place, very few preliminaries being considered
necessary.

" Do you like Kasala ?" I inquired of the best-
looking of the girls.

" No," replied an aged female, not giving the

maid I addressed time to speak; "we all prefer the steppes." And with these words she glanced contemptuously at her daughter, who, as Nazar afterwards informed me, liked the slight civilisation that Kasala was able to afford better than the beauties of nature and the trackless wastes in Tartary.

On leaving the kibitka I proceeded to Morozoff's hostelry to call upon a young Russian officer, to whom I had been introduced the previous evening. I found my acquaintance at home. He inhabited a small room in company with another officer, who had been waiting for six weeks to join his regiment at Petro-Alexandrovsk, and who, to all appearance, did not much fancy the journey, as he was still at Kasala when I returned there six weeks later.

The room was fitted up very simply. The furniture consisted of two small bedsteads; some coloured French prints and photographs were suspended from the walls, whilst a few books and two strong wooden chairs completed the arrangements.

The officers were glad to see a visitor, and have an opportunity of talking about St. Petersburg. One of them at once produced some bottles of vodki, and was much surprised to find that I was not addicted to strong drinks. "You do not mean to say that the officers in your army do not get drunk?" he said. "Why, liquor is the only thing worth living for!" and he tossed off a tumbler of the pure spirit. The main difficulty, however, was to disabuse my friends' minds of the idea that I had been sent out by the English Government, and that the authorities at home paid for my expenses.

"And so you might have spent all your leave of absence in St. Petersburg, and yet only remained there ten days! How very strange!" said the elder of the two, evidently wondering how I could have stopped for so brief a time at this elysium in the eyes of a Russian officer.

This gentleman had been in the Guards, but, like many of his comrades, had outstripped his allowance and run into debt. In consequence of this he had been removed to an appointment at Kasala, which happened at that time to be vacant; and my young friend now found himself acting as a sort of police magistrate—rather a change from his former life at St. Petersburg. Existence in the fort, according to him, was fearfully dull—hardly any female society, and but little to do. Now at Khiva there was always the prospect of a war with the Turkomans, or some little excitement in the shape of a rebellion to suppress, and then men might have a chance of seeing service.

In fact, you cannot be with Russian officers in Central Asia for half an hour without remarking how they long for a war. It is very natural; and the wonder to my mind is why Russia has not extended herself still farther in Central Asia. If it had not been for the Emperor, who is, by all accounts, opposed to this rapid extension of his dominions, the Russians would already be on our Indian frontier. Nothing would be so popular with the officers in Central Asia, or indeed, for the matter of that, in European Russia also, as a war with England about India; and as the only public opinion which can be said to exist in the Tzar's empire is represented by the military class, which in a few years will absorb all the male population of the nation, we ought to be thoroughly prepared for any emergency. Indeed, should Russia be permitted to annex Kashgar, Balkh, and Merve, an invasion of India would be by no means so difficult or impossible as some people would have us believe. Russia, if her reserves were called out, would be able to dispose of 1,300,000 men. In the event of a campaign the 847,847 men in her active establishment could be reckoned upon as available for offensive purposes.

The Province of Turkistan is the one which most closely adjoins our Indian empire. Here, according to Russian data, there are 33,893 men. I use the term Russian data because we have no means of knowing whether these figures are accurate. At the present moment, the greater part of the forces in the Western Siberian, Orenburg, and Kazan districts might be concentrated in the neighbourhood of Tashkent and Samarcand, and no one in this country would be the wiser. We have no consular agents in any of the towns through which these troops would have to march on their road to Turkistan. No Englishmen are allowed to travel in Central Asia. Owing to the Russian newspapers being completely in the hands of the authorities, the information which is published may be purposely intended to mislead. If the Governor-General in Turkistan were forming large *étapes*, or depôts, of provisions and arms in Samarcand, Khiva, and Krasnovodsk, we should be equally ignorant, until awaking up one morning we might discover that instead of our having to fight an enemy 2,000 miles distant from his base of operations that a base had been formed within 350 miles of our Indian frontier, which was as well supplied with all the requisites for war as St. Petersburg or Moscow.

In the Caucasus there is a standing army of 151,161 men within easy water communication of Ashourade. Along the valley of the Attrek to Herat there are no natural obstacles to impede an advancing force; indeed, if the Afghans, tempted by the idea of looting the rich cities in the plains of India, were to join an invader, he might give us a little trouble.*

* The Russian empire is divided into fourteen military districts (besides the Province of the Don Cossacks). Most of these districts include several governments, which are specified below. The following table shows the number of soldiers in each district:—

DISTRICTS.	MEN.
1. *St. Petersburg*—This includes the governments of St. Petersburg, Novgorod, Pskof, Olonetz, Archangel, Esthonia ...	84,353
2. *Finland*	14,787
3. *Vilna*—Including Vilna, Kovno, Grodno, Vitebsk, Minsk, Mohilev, Livonia, and Courland	93,370
4. *Warsaw*—Including Warsaw, Kalisz, Kièlce, Lomsha, Radom, Lublin, Petrikau, Plock, Siedlec, Suwalki	113,686
5. *Kiev*—Includes Kiev, Podolia, Volhynia	58,816
6. *Odessa*—Includes Kherson, Ekaterinoslav, Tavrida, and Bessarabia	63,391
7. *Kharkof*—Includes Kursk, Oriel, Tchernigov, Poltava, Kharkof, and Voronetz	65,457
8. *Moscow*—Includes Moscow, Tver, Jaroslav, Vologda, Kostroma, Vladimir, Nijni-Novgorod, Smolensk, Kaluga, Riazan, and Tambov	85,024
9. *Kazan*—Includes Kazan, Perm, Viatka, Simbirsk, and Samara	34,300
10. *Caucasus*—Includes the provinces of Kuban, Terek, Daghestan, Zakhatali; the governments of Tiflis, Erivan, Baku, Stavropol, and Kutais	151,161
11. *Orenburg*—Orenburg and Ufa	14,680
12. *Western Siberia*	16,256
13. *Eastern Siberia*	18,673
14. *Turkistan*—Comprising the government of that name	33,893
Total number of men	847,847

CHAPTER XX.

On returning to the Governor's I found that gentleman awaiting me for dinner. In the course of conversation he said that the Kirghiz officer had sent round to inform his compatriots that I wished to purchase some horses, and that several animals would be brought for my inspection on the following morning.

The priest now came in—he was a man about thirty, of an unwashed appearance, and with long uncombed locks reaching half way down his back. On the Colonel's invitation, he sat down by my side. He was a married man. The Greek religion allows every Russian priest to marry; but if his wife dies, the reverend gentleman cannot marry again. This is not a bad rule for the women, as the husbands look after all their ailments with the greatest care. Our conversation was chiefly about horses, when I discovered that the visitor had one for sale, and that this was the object of his visit. The Kirghiz, he informed me, do not have their horses shod, except when about to travel over very rocky ground. In winter and in summer the active little animals traverse the deserts, the hoof itself affording ample protection, and a lame or unsound steed is with them a rarity, whilst a hundred miles in a day has frequently been accomplished by some of the Kirghiz horsemen.

I had arrived at Kasala at a bad time for a man who, like myself, wished to push forward immediately. The following morning on inquiring if any horses had been brought for my inspection, I was informed that the festival was not over. The Kirghiz were still engaged in stuffing themselves with rice and mutton, and in drinking sour mare's milk (koomyes). They could not be induced to leave their houses, even on the chance of selling a horse to a Christian. I thought that Nazar's services might be put into requisition, so I desired him to go into the town and proclaim to his co-religionists that I was prepared to give a good price provided that they could bring me some animals which would suit. Under other circumstances I should continue my journey along the sleigh road to Fort Perovsky, and buying horses at that spot, ride from there to Petro-Alexandrovsk, my idea being that if the Tartars at Kasala heard that I was going to leave the fort and purchase horses elsewhere, they would take a little more interest in the matter.

I also desired him to make arrangements about the preparation of some *stchi*, or cabbage soup, for the journey, and also to order forty pounds of bread, of which half was to be made as light as possible. The Russian bakers possess the secret of making bread which is not much heavier than rusks would be, if made of the same size as the loaves in question. This is a great advantage in the desert, for at times, when no firewood can be obtained, the ordinary bread becomes so hard frozen that it has to be chopped with an axe ;

whilst a knife is utterly useless against the granite-like substance into which the flour is converted. Indeed, on one occasion I broke my best knife when attempting to cut a loaf of frozen bread.

My real intentions were not in favour of continuing the journey to Perovsky, if this could possibly be avoided, for by doing so we should be nearer the Capital of Turkistan. St. Petersburg is now in direct electric communication with Tashkent, whilst I believe that the wire has been recently extended so far as Kokan. The distance is about 670 miles from Kasala to Tashkent. There is also a wire from St. Petersburg to Orsk, which is about 500 miles from Kasala; but any communication coming from St. Petersburg would be more likely to pass through the head-quarters of General Kauffmann than by another route. I was not desirous to approach nearer to Tashkent than was absolutely necessary, as, although I had obtained permission to travel in Russian Asia from General Milutin, the Minister of War, it was not impossible that he might change his mind—such in fact having been the opinion of my friends at St. Petersburg, who had advised me to lose no time on the road.

Nazar's message to his countrymen proved of the greatest use. My departure for Perovsky would have affected them in their most susceptible point—the pocket—and in spite of its being feast-time they proceeded in search of all the animals which could be obtained in Kasala.

Now, the Kirghiz are not like the Arabs in one respect, though similar to them in many others. The descendant of Ishmael will seldom sell his horses, no matter how much money you may offer for these animals; whilst the Tartars will sell everything they have for money. The result was they began to think that it might be a good occasion to palm off some of their lame animals and utterly worthless screws upon the innocent Christian; or, if I would not fall into the trap set for me by the Faithful, to take advantage of my inexperience with reference to the average price of horses in that part of the world, and sell me a good animal, but at three times its market value. However, the steppe coper is not unique in this respect, and he would not get much the best of a London dealer.

Forthwith there appeared a procession before the Governor's house. This was composed of excited natives, looking, many of them, like animated bundles of rags, so thickly were they enveloped in shreds and tatters. Each of these animated bundles was astride on some sort of quadruped—camels, horses, donkeys, all were brought on the scene, forming a comical picture, which will never be effaced from my memory. The horses were, for the most part, of the worst description; that is to say, so far as appearance was concerned. Their ribs in many instances almost protruded through the skin, the proprietors of the quadrupeds having apparently been engaged in solving the knotty point as to how near they could reduce them to a straw-a-day diet without their animals succumbing to the experiment.

Don Quixote's steed, the far-famed Rosinante, was by all accounts not the best-fed of animals. The poor brutes which can be seen each summer expiring beneath the horns of the bulls in the Plaza de Toros of Seville do not carry much flesh, but many of them would have been equine Daniel Lamberts if compared with the horses now brought for my inspection.

If ever there was a Banting system especially

devised for four-footed animals, that system had been carried out to its fullest extent. Some of the poor beasts were so weak that they could hardly move one leg before the other. Except for their excessive leanness they looked more like huge Newfoundland dogs than as connected with the equine race, and had been turned out in the depth of winter with no other covering save the thick coats which nature has given them.

The late Mr. Tattersall himself could not have eulogised any animals brought to the hammer more than did these red-faced, high cheek-boned, ferret-eyed Tartars their respective quadrupeds ; whilst each man commented on his neighbour's property in terms of scorn and derision. At last, after rejecting a number of jades which looked more fit to carry my boots than their wearer, I selected a little black horse. He was about fourteen hands in height, and I eventually became his owner, saddle and bridle into the bargain, for the sum of £5, this being considered a very high price at Kasala. The saddlery was of the most gaudy description, the saddle being made of highly-painted wood, richly decorated with gilding and enamel, whilst a small knob about six inches long, sticking up at the pommel, looked especially contrived for the impalement of the rider.

The following day the Kirghiz official, who had been desired to procure a guide, called upon me with a candidate for that office.

The latter was a tall, muscular-looking man, with a cunning and avaricious expression about the corners of his mouth whenever he indulged in a smile. His head attire consisted of a tall black sheepskin hat, of the sugar-loaf pattern; the thick wool around the lower part of it was so arranged as to protect his eyes against the glare of the snow. His neck was encircled by a dirty goat's-hair shawl, which had been once white, but was now almost of the same hue as his coarse black beard and moustache. A bright yellow dressing-gown, thickly wadded to protect the wearer from cold, was girt around his waist by a green sash. Yellow leather trousers were drawn over his lathy legs, whilst an enormous pair of boots, the toes of which were turned up and culminated in formidable-looking points—fearful weapons to deliver a kick with—protected his extremities. For arms he carried a short scimitar, which was buckled around his waist by a narrow leather strap. However, the sword was not of much use, as it had been little cared for, and was very rusty, whilst the steel of which the scimitar was manufactured was of an utterly worthless character.

He announced himself as ready to guide me to Petro-Alexandrovsk, the Russian fort, and his companion, the Kirghiz official, said that the man had acted as guide to the troops which marched upon Khiva during the expedition against that country, and that he could be thoroughly depended upon.

An agreement was soon made by which he was to provide me with some camels. He would also bring his own horse, whilst if I could not find at Kasala an animal worth buying for Nazar, the little man should be mounted upon a camel. The price the guide first demanded for his services was very exorbitant, being three times more than the ordinary tariff; however, after a little bargaining, he became more moderate in his demands. When everything had been arranged he proceeded in search of some camels, and I determined to start in thirty-six hours.

In the meantime Nazar had tied my recently-acquired purchase to a cart which stood in the Governor's orchard, and had gone in search of a shoeing smith. I did not know what sort of ground would have to be traversed once we were on the other side of Khiva, and if it were of a rocky nature, horseshoes would be indispensable.   Nose-bags and horse-rugs had also to be purchased, two rugs to be put under the saddle, whilst the third was to be strapped above it, and thus to interpose between the seat of the rider and the wooden framework of the saddle, this being the system adopted in the steppes, and with great success, as the horses hardly ever have sore backs.

The following day I called upon the Commandant to say good-bye and thank him for all his kindness. He informed me in the course of our conversation that the Russian troops which marched against Khiva* carried nothing but their arms and ammunition, their great-coats and knapsacks having been transported on camels.   Occasionally, he said, the men would accomplish fifty versts (thirty-three miles) in a day.   At times the heat was very great, and the troops were then only served out with tea and biscuits, as meat was supposed to have an injurious effect upon their marching powers.   The Kirghiz, he said, lived entirely upon milk during the hot weather, and only killed their sheep in the winter months, or when obliged by sheer necessity.   The nomad tribes could not exist without their flocks, which form their chief source of wealth, cattle being very scarce amongst them.   The Kirghiz, however, possessed plenty of horses, and a man's riches would not be estimated by the number of roubles he

---

* This expedition took place in the spring and summer months of 1873.

had, as in Russia, but by the quantity of horses and sheep in his possession.

"I am afraid you will have a terribly cold journey," said the old officer, as he shook hands with me and said farewell; "the thermometer was down to 32 degrees below zero (Reaumur) yesterday (40 degrees Fahrenheit), and indoors it was bad enough. We piled as much wood in the stove as it would hold, and sat in our furs all day long, but in spite of this the cold made itself felt."

The winter we were then experiencing was an exceptional one even for that part of the world, and when I returned to the Governor's house I found the Kirghiz, who were engaged in putting up a kibitka in the garden for me to look at, grumbling as much as the Russians at the cruelty of the elements.

CHAPTER XXI.

Water Route from Kasala to Petro-Alexandrovsk—The Irkibai Route—The Winter March Route—General Perovsky—His Expedition—Loss of Nine Thousand Camels—New Year's Day—Two out of Ten Cossacks Frozen to Death—Major Wood and the Survey of the Oxus—Struggling into the Saddle—Your Horse is Tough—Ophthalmia—Cotton Bales—The Moham-medans and the Deity—Fatalism—The Will of Allah.

THE water route to Petro-Alexandrovsk was closed to me by the frost, but it affords easy communication in summer with the Khivan khanate. Indeed, should the Russian Government ever permit Englishmen to travel in their Asiatic dominions, Khiva will probably become known to Mr. Cook, and on the list of his personally-conducted tours. However, besides the water route by the Jaxartes, Sea of Aral, and Oxus, there are several land routes used respectively in summer and winter.

One way of reaching Petro-Alexandrovsk is the track taken by the column which marched from Kasala on Khiva during the war. This route, striking slightly to the south-east, brings the traveller to the Irkibai ford, and then diverging to the south-west continues to Kiptchak. From there the traveller can proceed along the banks of the Amou Darya river to within a short distance of the fort. This is a very circuitous route, the great advantage it possesses being a sufficient supply of wells on the road to make it a practicable one during the summer months. The climate of the Kirghiz steppes being just as remarkable by its intense heat during June, July, and August, as by its extreme cold throughout the winter. Wyld's map of Khiva and the surrounding territories shows this line of march, which occupies about twenty-five days, very correctly.

Then there is another road which is known as the winter march road. It is a much shorter way from Kasala to Petro-Alexandrovsk, the Russian fort in Khivan territory. This road leads south by east to Balaktay. It then turns south and slightly south-west to Tan Sooloo, which is 124 miles from Kasala. Diverging to the west, it continues south to Kara-batoor, about 303 miles from Kasala. Finally passing Tadj Kazgan and Kilte Moonar, it goes straight to Petro-Alexandrovsk, a distance by march route of 371 miles from Fort Number One.

This road, however, is impracticable in summer, as there are scarcely any wells along it. Those which exist contain water so salt and brackish as to be only fit for camels, whilst human beings and horses can only drink it when reduced to extreme necessity. Along this route there are wells at Balaktay, 30 miles from Kasala; at Berd Kazgan, 66 miles further on, there is more water; the traveller then must journey for 81 miles to a place where there are some very brackish wells, and from thence it is 126 miles to Karabatoor, where first you find water fit for human consumption. After this there is a plentiful supply of water till you reach Petro-Alexandrovsk.

I enter thus minutely into details about this route, as it is not marked down in any English map that I have seen, and in the one in my possession it is not shown accurately, Karabatoor being represented as close to the Oxus, whereas in reality it is 67 miles from that river. I am not aware that the above-mentioned road has been travelled by any Englishman save myself; indeed, it is seldom used except by the Tartars or Cossacks on their way to and from Khiva, and when the snow, which covers the ground for ten weeks in the year, supplying the place of water, renders the journey possible.

It is a very arduous march, however, and one which requires a great many preparations beforehand, as everything has to be taken by the traveller in the shape of provisions for himself, barley for his horses, and occasionally fuel to burn in those places where saksaool, the firewood of the steppes, is not to be found. He must also not forget bags to carry snow, should it appear likely that for any long distance there will be a deficiency of this substitute for water. The result was, I found that for myself, whose only personal luggage consisted of a change of clothes, a few instruments, and my gun, and for my Tartar servant, I could not do with less than three camels and two horses.

It will be easy from these few details to imagine the preparations which General Perovsky had to make in the year 1839, when he attempted to take Khiva in the winter, and why he failed. Intense frost, heavy snowstorms, and want of provisions compelled him to retire when only half-way from Orenburg, having lost two-thirds of his men, nine thousand camels, and an immense quantity of horses, from illness, cold, and hunger—the expense of the expedition amounting to six and a half millions of roubles. The sum for those days appears a large one, but it is not so if we consider that the invading column consisted of three and a half battalions of infantry, two regiments of Ural, and four sotnias, or 750 Orenburg Cossacks, besides twenty-two guns and a rocket battery. In all of four thousand five hundred men, accompanied by a large intendance, and, in addition to horse transport, ten thousand camels, with two thousand Kirghiz drivers.

It may be thought that the Khivan enemy assisted in the destruction of the Russian expedition. But this was not the case; the greater part of Perovsky's forces never saw the foe, and there were only slight engagements with advanced parties, in each of which the Khan's troops were put to flight.

The cold on New Year's Day, eighteen hundred and seventy-six, Russian style, or the 12th of January according to our calendar, was the greatest I ever remember to have experienced. The sentries posted outside the Governor's and Commandant's houses were obliged to wear the thickest of goloshes stuffed with hay, and to keep running backwards and forwards the whole time they were on duty, to prevent their feet freezing. The instant any man left the house his moustache was frozen into a solid block of ice. If his nose were exposed to the wind for a minute or so it turned first blue and then white, whilst, as to touching anything in the shape of metal with the bare hand, you might as well have taken hold of a red-hot iron.

Everything was ready for a start. Three camels and a Turkoman driver were at the door laden with the kibitka, forage, &c. I had declined the offer of an escort.

Indeed, it would have been hard upon the poor Cossacks, giving them a long useless journey over the steppes, merely on account of the Turkomans; and it was as well I did so, as out of a party of ten soldiers at that time marching from Petro-Alexandrovsk, I was subsequently informed that two had been frozen to death and several others frostbitten, the uniform of a

Cossack not being nearly so proof against the onslaught of the elements as the thick furs, sheepskins, &c., which can be worn by a private individual.

The guide rode his own horse, one, if possible, a little thinner than mine. The little Tartar servant was seated on a huge corn sack, balanced on the other side by a bundle of firewood, and perched upon the tallest of the camels. He smiled lugubriously as he bade farewell to his numerous acquaintances, and turning to me said—

"Please God we shall not be frozen."

To which I devoutly replied—

"Inshallah."

In spite of some drawbacks to the road selected, such as our being obliged to use melted snow instead of water, and to carry more firewood than would be required along the other track, for me it possessed several advantages.

First of all I could get to Petro-Alexandrovsk in half the time employed if I took the Irkibai route, and secondly I should see a new track, or, at least, one which was not marked on Mr. Wyld's map of Khiva, whilst however much I might wish to visit Khiva in the summer, and sail across the Sea of Aral, circumstances over which I had no control would prevent my carrying this into execution.

For provisions I had supplied myself with stchi or cabbage soup, with large pieces of meat cut up in it. This, poured into two large iron stable buckets, had become hard frozen, and was thus easily carried slung on the back of a camel. Twenty pounds' weight of cooked meat was also taken, and a hatchet to chop up our frozen food, or to cut down brushwood for a fire. A cooking lamp with a supply of spirit to be used under the mess-tins, in the event of our fuel running short, made up the baggage.

Although I had hired the camels as far as Petro-Alexandrovsk, I had not the slightest intention of going there if it could be avoided. I had the permission of General Milutin, the Russian Minister of War, to travel in Russian Asia, and considered myself at liberty to change my direction at pleasure without consulting any officers subordinate to him in the Russian service.

However, the rumours which had reached my ears about Major Wood's journey made me very doubtful as to whether General Milutin might not change his mind, and I had a strong presentiment that I should never see Khiva if, like my compatriot, I once were to find myself in Fort Petro - Alexandrovsk. Indeed, as I subsequently learned from Major Wood's lips, he had never been permitted to go within sixty versts of the Khan's capital, and when he expressed a wish to Colonel Ivanoff, the Commandant of the garrison, to be allowed to see Khiva, that officer informed him that there was a strict order from General Kauffmann on this subject, and no such permission could be granted.

Since Major Wood's departure the river Oxus has been surveyed for a considerable distance beyond the fort. It is to be hoped that when a more extended survey takes place, the military authorities at St. Petersburg will ask Major Wood to participate in it. It is as important to Englishmen as to Russians to know how far the mighty stream is navigable. Another reason also induced me to ride to Khiva without going to Petro - Alexandrovsk. In the event of the Russian Commandant permitting me to enter the capital, which was highly improbable, I felt convinced that it would be with an escort, and then I should be taken about to see everything *couleur de rose*, or as the Russians would like me to see it, and not be permitted to take my time and wander free and unrestrained about the city. I was also curious to know whether the Khivan sovereign was as great a barbarian as the Russians made him out to be.

It was only after a great deal of struggling that I managed to get into the saddle. Although my horse was only fourteen hands high, my sheepskin clothes and other thick garments were very heavy, and could not have weighed less than fifty pounds. The stirrup-irons also, though huge of their kind, were barely large enough, as Nazar had covered them with felt, so as to prevent my feet freezing to the steel.

The little animal groaned as I gained my seat. The guide here made a remark to Nazar, and a wolfish expression passed over his countenance. It wore a hungry sort of look, and he glared at my horse in such a peculiar manner that it attracted my attention.

" What does he say, Nazar ? " I inquired.

" He says that your horse has very little fat, but that he is tough," was the reply.

" I hope so," I observed, "the poor beast has to carry me a long way, and he is very much over-weighted."

" No, sir, you do not understand me," continued my domestic. " He means that when your horse breaks down and we have to kill him, that he will be very tough food."

" What ! you do not intend to say that the fellow wants to eat my horse ? " I remarked indignantly.

" Oh, yes, the brute will never get to Petro-

Alexandrovsk, and then we will all have such a feast," and my little Tartar's eyes glistened as much as the guide's had done, as he gloated over the anticipated banquet, horseflesh being considered a great delicacy by the inhabitants of those regions.

We soon crossed the Syr Darya river, the Jaxartes of ancient history, which bathes the southern side of Fort Number One. A high road had been made over its frozen surface, which glistened beneath the rays of a midday sun like a vast sheet of burnished steel. The steamers belonging to the Aral fleet lay embedded in the ice, the black funnels and smoky appearance of the vessels contrasting strongly with the bright colours worn by the peasantry who strolled along the banks.

A few exiled Cossacks from Uralsk were grouped together busily engaged conversing with a Tartar, who had just arrived from Orenburg. They were trying to learn some tidings of the old folks at home; whilst two wild-looking Kirghiz were haggling with a knot of Khivans, the latter wishing to buy a sheep which the natives had for sale.

A little way from the town we came upon hundreds of cotton bales lying scattered along the path. No one was left in charge of them, and the huge bundles seemed at the disposal of any would-be thief. It appeared that they had been brought from Bokhara; the camel-drivers had gone on to Kasala to feast with their friends in that town, but would return when the festival was over, and then continue the journey to Orenburg. In the meantime their master's property was left in the steppe, this affording a striking proof of the happy-go-lucky disposition of the Tartar camel-drivers.

"Will not some of the cotton be stolen?" I inquired of Nazar.

"If God pleases," was the pious answer.

The Mohammedans invariably throw upon the Deity the responsibility for any mischance that may occur through their own negligence. The doctrine of *fatalism* thus covers a multitude of sins.

I subsequently discovered that the only way to impart a little circumspection to my careless camel-driver when, after smashing my boxes, he excused himself on the ground that the Almighty had been the cause of his disaster, was to administer to the delinquent a slight chastisement. This having been inflicted, I exclaimed, " Brother, it was the will of God. You must not complain; it was your destiny to break my property and mine to beat you. We neither of us could help it, praise be to Allah."

This method of dealing with my party had a capital effect upon them, and much more care was afterwards taken in loading and unloading the camels.

Kasala now lay far in our wake, and naught could be seen save an endless white expanse. A gale came on. The wind howled and whistled, billowing before it broad waves of snow. Our eyes began to run, and the eyeballs to ache; the constant glare and cutting breeze half blinded us as we rode. The horses waded heavily through the piled-up ridges. The poor beasts suffered like ourselves; their eyes were encrusted with frozen tears; and it was as much as we could do to urge them forward.

I had taken the precaution to bring some tinted spectacles from England in order to protect my eyes from this evil, which gives rise to many cases of ophthalmia amidst the nomad tribes, the dust and sun in the summer months being nearly as trying as the cutting winds and dazzling snow throughout the winter. However, my shades proved to be useless.   The side-springs were made of steel, and directly they touched my cheeks I felt as if they had been seared with a red-hot poker.   There was nothing to be done but to pull my cap well over my eyes, and look as best I could through the dark fur.   This somewhat shaded the glaring mirror at our feet, and relieved the aching pupils.

CHAPTER XXII.

Camels—Their Rate of March—How to divide the Marches—The Kibitka—
   Better be Cold than Blind—A Tartar Cook—The Turkoman's Appetite—
   A Khivan Caravan—The Main Road goes to Khiva, the Branch Road to
   the Fort—Drinking Tea with the Khivans—Sheltering the Camels.

AFTER marching for about five hours, the guide asked
me to halt the caravan. The sun was fast disappearing in the west. We had started late, and as it is
always as well to make a short journey on the first
day, in order to see how the saddles fit, and if the
luggage has been well adjusted on the camels, I
consented, but with the express stipulation that we
must strike our camp and start again at twelve that
night.

Camels will only feed in the daytime, and the best
plan is to march them as much as possible during the
night. They walk very slowly, and as a rule cannot go
more than two miles and a third an hour. This is the
average rate of a caravan; however, they walk a little
faster at night than during the day. It is always as
well to halt at sunset and start at midnight, unloading
the camels for about two hours in the day to feed.
By this means the traveller ought to get sixteen hours
per day steady work from his caravan, and march at
least thirty-seven miles.

All this time the Turkoman driver and guide were
engaged in putting up the kibitka; this was intended
to screen us from the bitterly cold wind which, coming

straight from the east, whistled across the desert, unchecked by mountain or forest.

The kibitkas* are very simple in their construction. I will endeavour briefly to describe them. Imagine a bundle of sticks, each five feet three inches in length, and an inch in diameter ; these are connected with each other by means of some cross sticks, through the ends of which holes are bored and leather thongs passed. This allows plenty of room for all the sticks to open out freely, they then form a complete circle about twelve feet in diameter and five feet three in height. They do not require any forcing into the ground, for the circular shape keeps them steady. When this is done a thick piece of *cashmar*, or cloth made of sheep's wool, is suspended from their tops, and reaches to the ground. This forms a shield through which the wind cannot pass. Another bundle of sticks is then produced. They are all fastened at one end to a small wooden cross about six inches long by four broad ; a man standing in the centre of the circle raises up this bundle in the air, the cross upwards, and hitches their other ends by means of little leather loops one by one on the different upright sticks which form the circular walls. The result is they all pull against each other, and are consequently self-supporting ; another piece of cloth is passed round the outside of this scaffolding, leaving a piece uncovered at the top to allow the smoke to escape. One stick is removed from the uprights which form the walls. This substitutes a door, and the kibitka is complete.

* Lieutenant Stumm, a German officer who accompanied the Russian expedition to Khiva, highly approved of these kibitkas for military purposes. He brought one back with him to show to the military authorities in Berlin.

A fire is now lit in the middle of the tent, some snow put in a kettle, which is suspended from a tripod of three sticks above the flames, and under the influence of a few glasses of scalding tea the wayfarer makes himself as comfortable as circumstances will admit.

However, the smoke from the damp wood filled the tent. It was of so pungent a character that we found it impossible to keep on the roof. Our eyes, which had suffered from the wind and glare, now smarted from the smoke. It was impossible to keep them open.

"The wood is damp," said the guide; "better be cold than be blind," and unhooking the upper framework of the kibitka he left only the walls standing.

It was a glorious evening, the stars as seen from the snow-covered desert were brighter and more dazzling than any I had hitherto witnessed. From time to time some glittering meteor would shoot across the heavens. A momentary track of vivid flame traced out its course through space. Showers of orbs of falling fire flashed for one moment and then disappeared from our view. Myriads of constellations and worlds above sparkled like gems in a priceless diadem. It was a magnificent pyrotechnic display, Nature being the sole actor in the spectacle. It was well worth a journey even to Central Asia.

In the meantime the guide, who took upon himself the office of *chef de cuisine*, was occupied with an iron pot, his special property. He was busily engaged throwing into this receptacle slices of meat which with difficulty he had hacked from a piece of frozen mutton. A few handfuls of rice were next added, and some hunches of mutton fat. This he extracted from a hiding-place in his clothes, and the culinary compound was speedily crackling over the red-hot embers of our fire.

It was not a very appetising spectacle, nor a dish that Baron Brisse would have been likely to add to any of his *menus*, but after a ride across the steppes in midwinter the traveller soon loses every other feeling in the absorbing one of hunger, and at that time I think I could have eaten my great grandfather if he had been properly roasted for the occasion.

Nazar's face assumed a most voracious aspect. Seizing a large wooden ladle he buried it in the cooking mass, then first of all filling his own mouth, with a look of supreme satisfaction he handed me the ladle.

The guide, baring his arm to the elbow, plunged his hand into the pot, and throwing about a quarter of a pound of its contents within his capacious jaws, bolted it at one swallow. His eyes nearly started out of his head with the effort. He smiled condescendingly, pointed to the viands, the result of his culinary skill, and, rubbing his stomach slowly, gave me to understand that the meat was done to a turn.

The Turkoman sat in a corner of the kibitka. He was taking some little square biscuits or cakes, made of flour, salt, and fat, from a small bag which had been attached to the saddle of his donkey. His countenance wore a melancholy expression, for the biscuits were frozen as hard as brickbats. From time to time he would lay one of the cakes upon the embers, and when it was thawed through, hand it to one of my party. "Yackshe" (good) he said to me, looking at the smoking mutton with a beseeching look, as much as to say, Let me, too, partake; when, notwithstanding the disapproving looks of Nazar and the guide, who wished to eat it all themselves, I desired him to squat down by their side.

It was a quaint sight, the two wild figures before me, with their bare arms thrust alternately into the pot, every now and then swearing and looking fiercely at the Turkoman, who, to make up for lost time, ate much more rapidly than they did. I myself was supplied with a large saucerful of rice and meat, which, in spite of the rough manner in which it had been prepared, proved a very savoury compound.

Whilst thus engaged, three Khivans rode up to us. One was a merchant, who had been to Orenburg. He had there disposed of his cotton bales, and was now returning to Khiva with a supply of Russian goods in the shape of knives, saucers, cups, and bright-coloured chintzes, such as find a ready sale in the Khan's territory.

He was a strong-built, sturdy fellow, and about five feet ten in height. A tall, cone-shaped black Astrakhan hat covered his head, whilst his body was clad in an orange-coloured dressing-gown, thickly quilted, and girt tightly around his loins with a long red sash. A heavy sheepskin mantle enveloped him from head to foot, and with his coal-black beard and piercing dark eyes, he would have been worth a large sum to an artist as a model.

For weapons, the Khivan had armed himself with a long single-barrelled gun. This was ornamented with damascene work, and had a large bell-shaped muzzle. The barrel was very thin, and I could not help thinking that the firearm, should it be discharged, would be much more dangerous to its owner than to his foe. A short richly-mounted sabre completed his offensive arsenal.

He was accompanied by two countrymen, his

servants. They kept a careful eye on their master's goods, and were similarly armed. The party would have made the fortune of any London stage manager who might have required some brigands for a piece, could they have been placed on the boards as I saw them then attired.

The merchant had twelve camels and four camel-drivers with him, besides five led horses. He himself rode a very nice-looking grey, which I afterwards tried to purchase, but no offer would tempt the owner to part with his animal.

He could speak a little Russian, having learnt that language when trading at Orenburg. On my offering him a glass of tea, he squatted down by the fire and proposed that we should continue the journey together, when our united caravans would run less risk if attacked by any band of marauding Kirghiz. He also informed me that the track on which we had that day been travelling led straight to Khiva, but that a little further on the road, at a place known by the Kirghiz as Tan Sooloo, there was a branch road which would take us to Petro-Alexandrovsk.

My guide, however, did not appear much struck with the new arrival, and here observed that we were not going to Khiva but to the Russian Fort, and that his orders were to take me to Petro-Alexandrovsk, whilst Nazar whispered in my ear that the Khivan and his followers would be dangerous companions, the more particularly as their party was, numerically speaking, far stronger than our own.

It was evident that neither my servant nor the guide much liked the proposed addition to our caravan, the real reason being that they thought the Khivans' appetite might perhaps surpass the Turkoman's, and should I extend my hospitality to the former as well as to the camel-driver, there would be little left for themselves to eat.

My mind was soon made up about the matter. I had learned one piece of important information. This was with reference to the road to Khiva. I determined, if the merchant could only be persuaded to march as rapidly as ourselves, to join his party.

On mentioning this to Nazar, he shook his head, and remarked that we should be at least twenty days reaching Khiva, even supposing that our guide would accompany us there, as the heavily-laden camels of the trader would never be able to keep up with our own. The thought then occurred to me that the amount of barley I had brought for the horses would only last fourteen days, and hearing from the Khivan's lips that he did not expect to reach his destination for at least three weeks, I gave up the idea.

After staying at our fireside for about half an hour, the merchant left, and in a short time sent a message by one of his servants asking me if I would honour him by drinking tea with himself and followers.

I found the party encamped in a small ravine, about a hundred yards from my own kibitka, and seated round a fire. They had sheltered themselves in the same way as ourselves, and, in addition, had raised up an embankment of snow in the direction of the wind, so as to be better protected from its gusts. The camel-drivers had unloaded their animals, and were engaged in shovelling away the snow, so as to leave a dry spot upon which the huge beasts could lie down. Should this not be done, and the camels rest on the snow, the heat of their bodies converts it into water, and the animals get cold in the stomach, an illness which generally proves fatal to them. The luggage and saddles were placed around the cleared spot so as to protect the camels from the wind, and I found that my Turkoman had joined the party, and that his three beasts were also within the enclosure.

The merchant, producing a pillow and piece of carpet, made me sit in the place of honour, nearest the fire. Presently he handed me a tin slop-basin, full of what he called tea, but which was the nastiest beverage it has ever been my bad luck to taste. It was not tea in our sense of the word, but a mixture which had a peculiar flavour of grease, salt, and tea-leaves. Swallowing my nausea as best I could in order to avoid offending my host, I drank off the nasty draught, and exclaimed, in the best Tartar I could master for the occasion, "Excellent!"

My host was much pleased at my appreciation of the beverage, and said, "Now I see that you are not a Russian" (Nazar having previously informed him that I was an Englishman). "Strange to say, Russians do not like my tea. Good tea comes from Hindostan. You will drink some more?"

Fortunately Nazar now came to my rescue. He called attention to the stars, said that it was late, and that we were going to start early; so shaking hands with my host, I escaped from his well-meant but decidedly disagreeable hospitality.

CHAPTER XXIII.

A Lazy Guide—A Cold Pig—Insubordination—How to awake Arabs—Hot Embers better than Cold Water—Power of Camels to Carry Burdens much Exaggerated—Quickest Road to a Tartar's Affections—Sores from Fróstbites.

I FOUND the guide lying at full length on an old piece of carpet, which he had placed by the fire. He showed no readiness to resign his place on my arrival. The little Tartar, however, soon removed him, for taking up the cooking-pot, which was by that time filled with ice and water, he poured a portion of the contents on the head of the delinquent. The latter started up, uttered some fearful language at this summary proceeding, which he did not seem to relish, then rolling the folds of his sheepskin tighter round his body, he threw himself down a few yards further off from the fire.

"We shall have trouble with him," said my faithful follower; "he says that we are not to start till to-morrow morning. I told him that you would strike the camp at midnight. He remarked in that case we should go alone, and that he would return to Kasala."

It was not pleasant at the outset of the expedition to find this insubordination in one of my party, and I felt that the only thing for me to do was to bring matters to a climax before the refractory spirit communicated itself to the camel-driver.

"We shall march at twelve," I observed; "call me

if I am not awake;" and buckling my sheepskin tightly around me, I soon fell fast asleep.

It is a curious fact that almost every one of us, if we really wish to awake at a certain hour, invariably do so, and the more frequently a little before the time. The result was that at half-past eleven I started up thinking that I had overslept myself, but as half an hour at least was required to saddle and load the camels, I determined to awake the guide.

Walking up to his side I shook him well; he slowly opened his eyes, but seeing me, emitted a grunt of displeasure, and turned over again. It is always difficult arousing this class of people, particularly when they have once made up their minds to sleep till morning.

In the deserts of Africa I used to have the greatest trouble with them, one old Sheik, who acted as head man to my party, being the most sleepy of mortals. However, I discovered a method of arousing him, which proved invariably efficacious. His attire was scanty and slightly indecent according to our ideas. It merely consisted of a large sheet; this he was wont to wind many times round his body, and sleep, thus protected from the winds, which are very cutting at night-time in the Sahara. No amount of kicking would then awake the old fellow, and I found that the best plan was to gradually roll him over and over until the piece of calico was unwound, and the aged gentleman began to feel the cold breeze against his nude body.

This invariably produced the desired effect, and, arising from the sand, he, in his turn, would visit the other camel-drivers, and perform on them the same operation. However, my Kirghiz guide and Turkoman camel-driver wore no such light apparel. Their sheepskin garments were tightly strapped around their waists, and of course prevented any such action on my part.

By way of a commencement I took down the walls of the kibitka, allowing the wind to exercise its full sway upon the bodies of the sleepers. I then trampled upon the embers of our fire. Nazar, who by this time had awoke, now came up, and solved the difficulty by putting some hot ashes on the guide's sheepskin. The fellow had been awake the whole of the time, and it was only his obstinacy which prevented him from getting up. In fact, no amount of blows would have stimulated the man half so much as the fear that his clothes should suffer.

He sprang to his feet, and, casting sundry imprecations upon Nazar's head, proceeded to arouse the Turkoman.

It was a strange, wild scene; the vast snow-covered steppe, lit up as brightly as if it were midday by a thousand constellations, which reflected themselves in the cold white sheet below. Not a cloud dimmed the majesty of the heavens; the wind had lulled, and no sounds broke the stillness of the night. The Khivan and his followers were buried in the arms of Morpheus. The merchant's head rested on his richly-ornamented saddle, whilst a sword was placed by him ready for instant action. The camel-drivers lay within the enclosure formed by their camels. My Turkoman had huddled himself up for warmth against the body of our largest quadruped; whilst his donkey, attracted by the warmth of the fire, had hobbled to the embers, and was sleeping side by side with the trader.

The Turkoman resented strongly the unceremonious manner in which he had been awakened; and he took hold of the haft of his knife, prepared to avenge this kind of treatment. However, the guide placed his hand upon the hilt of the rusty old weapon which was strapped to his side, and the camel-driver succumbed. With a half-suppressed curse he helped to pack our baggage.

There was now no more resistance. My men were thoroughly aroused, and a few minutes later our camels could be heard venting their indignation at being laden by deep, low growls, bursting out at intervals, as each beast thought that his own load was heavier than that of his fellow's.

There is a good deal of nonsense talked and written about the patience and long-suffering of these so-called ships of the desert. I should much like any individual who thus sings the virtues of these huge animals to ride a thousand miles on a camel, as the writer of these lines has done, and find his patient quadruped either running away, or else suddenly lying down without any forewarning motion. This latter camel eccentricity is most disagreeable, as the rider has his back-bone nearly dislocated, or otherwise feels as if his body had been split up by the unexpected concussion. The power of camels to carry burdens is also much exaggerated ; * and although a strong beast will carry 800 pounds day after day for a short journey, he very soon breaks down if you should increase the march.

I had reduced the weight carried by my own animals to 400 pounds per camel, and even with this

---

* A Russian officer, Captain Potto, remarks in his work, " Steppe Campaigns " : " The weight of a camel-load should be limited to 700 pounds. This load is generally diminished in the spring, when the camels are casting their coats, and increased when the roads are good, when there is plenty of forage, and when no great speed is required. Then the load may be increased to 800 and even 880 pounds, which is about the weight with our traders' caravans. On the other hand, the English calculate the normal load at 560 pounds, and the French and Arabs at from 800 to 960 pounds.

light load had great difficulty in making them march sixteen hours a day.

Nazar by this time had blown up the embers of the fire into a flame, and was ready with some large beakers of boiling tea. This beverage becomes an absolute necessity when riding across the steppes in mid-winter, and is far superior in heat-giving properties to any wines or spirits. In fact, a traveller would succumb to the cold on the latter when the former will save his life. The hot liquid soon put the Turkoman and guide in good humour; and the fond way in which they looked at my little servant when he handed them each a handful of sugar showed me that this difficulty was settled. The quickest road to a dog's affection is through his stomach, and a Tartar's sympathies lie very much in the same direction. My men had now learned that they must obey, and the guide, this having once been thoroughly impressed upon his stolid mind, became thoroughly amenable to discipline.

A considerable amount of time, however, had been lost, and it was 3 A.M. before we were in the saddle. The Turkoman knew the road, and started with Nazar and the caravan, whilst the guide and myself trotted forward at the slow, ambling pace peculiar to the animals of the steppes, and which some of them can keep up for twenty-four hours on an emergency. It is not quite so fast as a huntsman's average pace when returning with his hounds to the kennels, but a much more jolting one, as the Kirghiz horses are generally very rough. Indeed, I soon found this out to my cost, for the sores on my arms and elbows were only half healed over, the limbs not having recovered from the effects of the frostbites inflicted during my sleigh-journey. Not being able to change my clothes was an additional source of annoyance, for if I could only have bathed my arms, there would have been less suffering; but undressing in those climes would only have added fuel to the flame, and created fresh frostbites.

After about two hours' riding the guide suddenly stopped. He now proposed that we should wait until the caravan arrived, and hobbling our animals with a piece of cord made of horsehair, and which the Kirghiz use especially for this purpose, we threw ourselves down upon the snow and tried to sleep.

No fire could be made, as there were no brambles in the neighbourhood, and the cold, which was becoming very intense, penetrated through my sheepskin clothes.

It was impossible to go to sleep, the frost not being of that violent nature which utterly prostrates a man, although it was quite sufficient to make me feel very uncomfortable. However, the guide seemed to be impervious to the weather, whilst some loud snoring informed me that he was lost to consciousness.

There is a sort of dog-in-the-manger feeling which seizes many of us when we see another enjoying that of which we cannot ourselves partake, and the weakness of human nature is such that I felt very much inclined to awake the slumberer, and make him teach me a little of the Kirghiz language, instead of letting the fellow rest in peace. However, I resisted the temptation, and lighting a cigarette walked up and down, straining my eyes in the direction of our gradually approaching caravan. I was looking forward to the moment when we could once more trot onwards, the rough motion of the horse, frostbites and all, not being so hard to bear as this wearisome onslaught of the elements, which utterly prevented slumber.

CHAPTER XXIV.

THE sun now arose bright and glorious. All the colours of the rainbow lit up the sky. The wind had calmed. The cold became less searching. Presently my little caravan loomed in sight. Nazar was fast asleep, and stretched out at full length on the top of a gigantic camel. The little Tartar's legs dangled on each side of the saddle, whilst, for better security, he had strapped himself to a corn-sack.

The guide now retaliated upon the sleeper for the ducking the latter had inflicted upon him the previous evening; he seized the camel's nose, and made that peculiar hissing sound which all Tartars use to these animals to make them lie down. The big brute went down at once on his knees with a sudden jerk. My little servant awoke, greatly alarmed, thinking that his strap had broken, and that he had been precipitated to the ground.

In a few minutes we had put up the walls of the kibitka, a fire was blazing, and one of the buckets containing frozen cabbage soup was gradually becoming thawed over the flames. It was just 9 A.M. The caravan had marched six hours, we having, according to the guide, done seventeen miles. What had surprised me most during our morning's march was the extreme endurance of our horses. The guide frequently had been obliged to dismount and to clean out their nostrils, which were entirely stuffed up with icicles; but the little animals had ploughed their way steadily through the snow, which was in some places quite two feet deep. The one I rode, which in England would not have been considered able to carry my boots, was as fresh as possible after his march of seventeen miles. In spite of the weight on his back—quite twenty stone—he had never shown the least sign of fatigue.

"He is a wonderful horse," I said to the guide.

"Horse!" observed the latter, very contemptuously; "call him a horse! You should see my brother-in-law's horses at Kalenderhana, for they are beautiful animals, round and fat."

"Where is Kalenderhana?" I inquired.

"On this side of the Oxus," was the reply, "and on the main track."

"Not on the road to Petro-Alexandrovsk?" I observed.

"No, on the road to Khiva."

A thought suddenly occurred to me. Why not try and persuade the fellow to take me to Kalenderhana under the pretext of buying some horses from his brother-in-law? It was true that I should still be a good many miles from Khiva, but if the guide could only be induced to continue the journey as far as his brother-in-law's village, I might then find some other excuse to proceed onward, and enter the Khan's capital without having put my foot into the Russian fort.

"How far is Kalenderhana from Petro-Alexandrovsk?" I inquired.

"About forty miles."

"It is a pity your brother-in-law's kibitka is so far from Petro, for perhaps you are right about this animal. He is hardly up to my weight, or fit for so long a journey; however, as we are going to the fort, I shall buy some horses in that neighbourhood. I am told that the horses there are very beautiful, that they are round and fat, and they can gallop like wind."

I had said enough. It seemed to me that the best course to pursue would be to let the conversation drop as if I had no particular interest in the matter, and had made up my mind as to what I was about to do. Nazar I had gained over to my views. I had promised him a 100 rouble note the day we reached either Bokhara or Merve, *viâ* Khiva. The little Tartar was well aware that if we once entered Petro-Alexandrovsk, he had but little chance of earning his promised reward.

The guide could not have been persuaded to go to Khiva by a mere offer of money. If this had been suggested to him he would have become suspicious, and have made a mental calculation as to whether it would not have been better worth his while to obey the Governor at Kasala and receive a reward from him, for having brought me straight to the fort, and carried out his instructions to the letter. However, there is one element in a Kirghiz's mental composition that outweighs every ordinary pecuniary consideration, and that is his intense love for horse-dealing. No Yorkshire farmer is keener in this particular branch of commerce than these half-savage wanderers in the steppes of Tartary.

The Turkoman, who was superintending the *cuisine*, now announced that the soup was ready, and we were soon at work swallowing large spoonfuls of this favourite Russian dish. It was not an appetising mixture to look at; masses of thick grease floated on the top of the finely-grated cabbage, whilst a few sticks mixed with some pieces of meat which had been cut up in the soup showed that one of the fagots had fallen into the cauldron.

The camel-driver again distinguished himself as a trencher-man. On this occasion he ate the whole of a four-pound loaf. Occasionally he would bury his head in the soup vessel, and suck up the half-tepid liquor, much to the indignation of Nazar and the guide, the former remarking that this way of eating was not fair, at the same time offering the Turkoman a spoon. This the latter gratefully declined, and made my followers still more angry by saying that the soup tasted better if eaten in his manner.

The time sped by rapidly. On looking upwards, I found that the sun would soon be at his highest altitude, and that we had already been nearly three hours stationary. The horses had finished feeding; so, saddling the animals, we proceeded on our journey with the Khivan caravan, which had by this time caught us up.

The merchant now announced his intention of continuing the march in our company; at all events for that day, in spite of the extra weight carried by his camels.

He was very inquisitive about England and her manufactures, the more particularly as one of his relatives had visited Hindostan, and he himself had been several times to Bokhara and Balkh.

"When the railway is opened from Sizeran to Orenburg, I shall go to St. Petersburg," he observed;

"they tell me that it is like an enchantment, that it is like a fairy city."

" The women expose their faces," I remarked.

" Yes, that I have observed during my visits to Orenburg, and was at first surprised to see that their husbands did not mind it any more than do these barbarous Kirghiz." As he said these words he looked contemptuously at the guide, who was riding a little in advance of the party, engaged in singing a song descriptive of his love for mutton.

The Kirghiz poetry is filled with odes in the honour of sheep, the natives placing this animal on the highest pinnacle of their estimation—after their wives, and, indeed, sometimes before them. Sheep make up the entire riches of the nomad tribes. A Kirghiz lives upon their milk during the summer and autumn. At that time of the year he would consider it a great piece of extravagance to eat any meat. This is only done should any animal become ill and die, in which case there is a feast in the kibitka. However, if a guest arrives, nothing is too good for him, and hospitality is shown by slaying one of the flock.

It is then a red-letter day, and it is remembered long afterwards by the owner of the animal.

In winter, when there is nothing else upon which the Kirghiz can subsist, they are obliged occasionally to kill some of their sheep. They vary this diet by eating either a horse or a little camel's flesh, but only in case any of these last-named quadrupeds should meet with an accident or die a natural death in the neighbour-hood. A native's clothes are made entirely of sheep's wool manufactured into coarse homespun. When he wishes to buy a horse or a camel he gives so many sheep in exchange. When he wants a wife he pays for her in the same commodity, a good fat sheep being worth in those parts about four roubles, or eleven shillings of our money.

The Kirghiz have a custom of betrothing their sons to girls often several years before the latter have arrived at puberty. This is done by the parents of the interested parties, the father of the lad giving so many of the flock to the girl's parents. When the lady is old enough the bridegroom fetches her home to his habitation. Her father, if he be generous, returns to the young couple the same number of animals that he has previously received, with a few in addition as interest. But this is only among the more wealthy families; the heads of poorer establishments do not feel inclined to give back any of their sheep. They prefer being thought stingy to having nothing to subsist upon during the winter.

Sometimes the matrimonial arrangement is made by the would-be husband, who, going straight to the girl's parents, strikes a bargain with them for their daughter.

When all things are arranged he returns alone to his own kibitka, which is, perhaps, two or three hundred versts from the young lady's home. After waiting here a few days he goes back for his bride.

It is considered a sign of manhood that the bridegroom should—regardless of robbers and marauding parties—bring no companions when journeying towards the kibitka of his betrothed. The young lady herself sits inside the tent, and sings a ditty which has reference to her lover's bravery, to her own good looks, and to his good fortune, to sheep, and to the festivities about to ensue.

The women of the tribe squat on the ground and form a circle round the tent. If the bridegroom attempts to enter the bride's kibitka the jealous females rush forward and beat him with sticks, the most unfavoured and elderly of the unmarried women taking great delight in this performance. However, love generally prevails; the young man's back smarts, but he forces a passage into the kibitka. His beloved one now throws herself into his arms, and he soon finds a solace for his troubles. The young lady then presents him with some feathers, red silk, and cloves, this being the accustomed offering made by a Kirghiz maiden to her bridegroom to testify to him her purity and affection. The happy couple are now left alone, the women outside singing some native ditty, in which the joys of marriage are rather forcibly described.

Feasting then begins. Friends and relations come from all parts of the steppe, having brought horses and sheep as a contribution to the festival; indeed, without this it would be impossible for the host to give the entertainment, for he would be literally eaten out of house and home.

Sometimes a hundred sheep and forty or fifty horses are slain, the iron cauldron being kept all day long at boiling point. The Kirghiz stuff themselves to re-pletion, and afterwards carry away in their trousers, which they tie up at the knee, the meat they are unable to swallow at the time.

It is a peculiar pocket, the roast mutton in this manner coming closely in contact with the Kirghiz legs; but such little matters do not affect these half wild wanderers. When the feast is over the games begin. The animals which have not been killed are set apart as prizes, the young men wrestling with each other; no tripping is allowed, no dexterity comes into play, and the contest is decided by sheer strength.

After this there are horse races, the length of the course being from twenty to thirty miles, this distance being accomplished at the rate of from eighteen to twenty miles an hour. The successful rider sometimes receiving eight or nine horses as a prize.

Then the girls mount the swiftest horses which they can borrow from their friends or relations. One of the Amazons challenging the men to race against her gallops across the steppe. She is pursued by a horseman, who strives to place his hand round her waist. The girl all this time showers blows with her whip on the head of her admirer, and does her best to keep him at bay. If he does not succeed in his attempt, she will turn round upon him, and so belabour the unfortunate wight with her whip that he frequently falls off his horse. He is then an object of scorn and derision to all the assembled guests. But if, on the contrary, he succeeds in placing his hand on the girl's breast, she surrenders at once, and they ride away together amid the cheers and encouraging shouts of the company. It is not considered strict etiquette to follow, as chaperons in Tartary are not considered necessary.

The Turkomans sometimes decide the knotty point of who is to marry the prettiest girl in their tribe in the same primitive manner. On these occasions the whole tribe turns out, and the young lady, being allowed her choice of horses, gallops away from her suitors. They follow her. She avoids those whom she dislikes, and seeks to throw herself in the way of the object of her affections. The moment that she is caught she becomes the wife of her captor. Further ceremonies are dispensed with, and he takes her to his tent.

"What do you pay in your country for a wife?" asked the guide, when I had finished questioning him on these subjects.

"We pay nothing; we ask the girl, and if she says yes, and her parents do not refuse, we marry her."

"But, if the girl does not like you, if she hits you on the head with her whip, or gallops away when you ride up to her side, what do you do in that case?"

"Why, we do not marry her."

"But if you want to marry her very much; if you love her more than your best horse and all your sheep and camels put together?"

"We cannot marry her without her consent."

"And are the girls moon-faced?"

"Some of them."

The guide appeared to be lost in a fit of meditation very unusual amidst the Arabs of the steppes. Presently, removing his sheepskin hat, and rubbing his closely-shaven head, he said, "Will you take me with you to your country? It would be so nice; I should get a moon-faced wife, and all for nothing. Why, she would not cost so much as a sheep."

"But supposing she would not have you?"

"Not have me!" and the guide here looked at me in astonishment, which he emphasised in a manner peculiar to his countrymen, by using his fingers instead of a pocket-handkerchief. "Not have me! Well, I should give her a white wrapper, or a ring for her ears or her nose."

"And if she still refused you?"

"Why, I would give her a gold ornament for her head; and what girl is there who could resist such a present?"

CHAPTER XXV.

THE afternoon was now drawing to a close. By this time the guide and myself had ridden on considerably ahead of the Khivan and his party ; the merchant, who spoke a little Russian, having sometimes acted as interpreter between myself and my follower. I had previously desired Nazar to continue marching with the Turkoman and our three camels until they came up to us.

From time to time the guide would leave the track, and, galloping his horse on to any little rising ground in the neighbourhood, search for a convenient spot upon which to encamp. At last he selected a small ravine, sheltered from the wind by two low hills. There was a great deal of brushwood in the neighbourhood, and I then learned that this spot, even in the winter time, was a resort of the wandering tribes, as a certain amount of grass could always be found beneath the snow ; in fact, sufficient to keep life in their animals till the early spring. But now, for as far as we could see, there was no living soul besides ourselves in sight.

The cold had become more piercing than ever, the

felt which covered the stirrup-irons had worn off in places, and I had continually to remove my feet from the stirrup-irons in order to prevent their adhering to the steel.   We looked everywhere, but in vain, for the caravan ; so dismounting and hobbling our horses we began cutting down what brushwood we could find for a fire, a small axe purchased at Kasala, and which was hung from my saddle, proving very useful.   Fortunately the wood was not at all damp ; the guide had found some grass as dry as tinder, and in about five minutes we had made a fire.

An hour passed away, and then another, but no signs of the caravan.

My follower now began to be alarmed, and proposed that we should retrace our steps.

After about half an hour's ride we came upon the Khivan's encampment. It appeared that he had stopped at this place ; and as our Turkoman had declared that he did not know the way, Nazar had taken upon himself to halt and to unload the camels.

My feet by this time were suffering a good deal from the cold, but it would never have done to have given in to my lazy followers, or these delays might be repeated.   I instantly ordered them to saddle and load the camels.   A few grumbles could be heard, but the men obeyed, and I then returned with them to the spot my guide had originally chosen.

The lesson produced its effect, and the trouble given in reloading the caravan proved most efficacious, as on no subsequent occasion did the Turkoman attempt to halt until such time as he had come up with the guide and myself.

I was now fifty versts from Kasala, and as the camels had marched for sixteen hours with but a short halt the previous evening, I determined to remain till dawn, and then start. This time I had little difficulty in awaking my party; they were becoming disciplined, and the moment I shook the guide he arose and began to load the camels.

I had promised to buy a sheep if we met any Kirghiz on the road who would sell us one. This had greatly raised the spirits of my followers. The guide had improvised a song about the liberality of the Englishman who was about to give them a whole sheep, of which he was to have the liver and the most delicate morsels as his own portion.

Quantities of shrubs on both sides of the path, and extending right and left as far as the eye could reach, varied the sameness of the scene; bright-coloured grass and low brushwood in great abundance were interspersed with thick masses of stunted bramble-trees. Evidently we were approaching a locality frequented by beings like ourselves, for human footsteps could be plainly traced in the track leading to some black dots yet only dimly seen in the gradually breaking morn. Larger and larger they became, until at last a thick cloud of dark blue smoke issuing from the roof of these dark objects showed us that we were approaching the dwelling-place of some Kirghiz.

On descending a steep ravine we came upon what appeared to have been a sheep-pen, for the footprints of these animals could be here seen in great abundance, and an enclosure of piled-up logs showed where the sheep had but recently been confined. The guide now got off his horse and looked at me complacently. " Bah, bah," he said, and opening his mouth from ear to ear showed a row of white teeth which would have been the envy of many a London dame.

However, he did not wish to go forward at once to the kibitkas. We should not present the same majestic appearance alone and unaccompanied, as we should make a little later, and at the head of our caravan. In Russia the importance of a traveller is gauged by the value of his furs, in Asia by the number of his retinue. The guide was aware of this, and in spite of his longing for mutton he was enabled to restrain himself until such time as we could appear with proper dignity.

I myself was not sorry of the opportunity afforded me to obtain a little sleep. Continued travelling had thoroughly tired me out, and flinging myself down by the side of a huge bonfire of brambles I became instantly lost to consciousness. When I awoke the sun was descending towards the west, and Nazar coming up told me that the caravan had been waiting there two hours, but seeing that I was so fast asleep he had not wished to awake me.

Another half hour, and we rode up to the principal kibitka. It evidently belonged to a wealthy Kirghiz. The dwelling was three times the size of an ordinary kibitka. The walls were ornamented with straw plaiting of different colours, whilst an abundance of hay in an enclosure adjoining the dwelling showed that the proprietor was a prudent man and had laid in a supply of fodder for his horses.

A girl who was carrying a large sheet of ice to the tent came up to the guide, who asked her if there were any sheep for sale. This inquiry instantly produced a sensation in the kibitka, and the whole family came out to have a look at the Crœsus who actually wanted to buy a whole sheep.

The head of the kibitka was a man considerably

above the middle age. He must in his earlier days have been a splendid type of mankind, for even now his muscular neck, square shoulders, and enormous girth of chest, showed that he would be a dangerous opponent in a hand-to-hand struggle. He was followed by a woman suckling a child, and in rear of her, and taking a shy inquisitive glance at the new arrival from behind the door of the kibitka was the girl the guide had accosted on arrival.

She was an exception to the generality of Kirghiz women, who rarely exhibit any marked signs of beauty, and their high cheek-bones, bullet heads, and low foreheads are not often appreciated by the foreigner.

A moon-faced girl in a London ball-room would be added to the list of wall-flowers, though in a Tartar's estimation that class of beauty is the highest to which the fair sex can aspire. The ice-bearer, however, would have held her own, if pitted for good looks, against any European belle; and her complexion, two or three shades darker than that of her companions, made my thoughts wander several thousand miles in another direction, and I bethought me of far-off Seville, for the girl might have been a *gitana* (gipsy girl), from Triana, by the side of the Guadalquiver.

She was evidently from a southern clime, her small mouth and well-shaped nose—a relief from the pug proboscies which, for the most part, distinguish the Tartars—denoting a Persian origin. Very likely the daughter of a captive who, in years gone by, been carried off in a raid from the country on the other side of the Attrek, and found favour in the eyes of her master.

The old man volunteered to lead us to the sheepfold. Dismounting from our horses, we accompanied him in that direction. The pretty girl, who had recovered from her shyness, hurried forward to catch one of the flock for our inspection. She ran like a hare over the rough stumps and brushwood which studded the snow-covered ground, a large number of black-faced sheep scampering before her. At last she came up with one which, fatter than its companions, could not keep up with the flock. Suddenly stooping, she seized her victim by one foot, and with a rapid movement turned him over on his back.

A clear ringing laugh resounded from her lips. She turned round to us, and pointed triumphantly at the sheep; then drawing her hand across her neck, she went through in pantomime the operation of cutting his throat.

My guide was now in his element; he rushed forward, and bending down punched the unfortunate animal in the ribs, then looking up at me he made use of the one word, " Fat!"

A bargain was soon struck, the price being four roubles; and we returned to the kibitka to pay a visit to the proprietor, the girl going on in front with her arm round the neck of my recently-acquired purchase. The slight shadow of sentiment created in my mind at the first sight of her beautiful face became rapidly effaced as I saw how eager she was to play the part of a butcher.

On entering the tent I found that the ground was covered with thick carpets; a layer of hay having been put down between them and the ground. The carpets were of many colours, and on inquiry I learnt that they had been purchased from a merchant who had passed that way on his road to Kasala. A cushion was brought for me, and I was given the post of honour by the fire, which consisted of a few red embers piled up in a shallow basin of dried clay. The proprietor, squatting down opposite me, whilst the rest of his family, seated on their hams, their knees and chins touching, gazed curiously upon the newly-arrived stranger.

The children were so wrapped up in skins and furs that each child looked three times his natural size. They were amusing themselves by teasing the unfortunate sheep, which was tied up to the door of the kibitka. A single-barrelled gun—the barrel tied to the stock by a leathern thong—and two old swords were hung up in the corners of the tent. A few iron cooking-pans, a bright-coloured earthenware tea-pot, and some wooden spoons stood on a gaudily-painted wooden box; this contained the valuables of the proprietor.

A large brass pipe was near the fire. It resembled a Turkish so-called hubble-bubble, as the smoke had first of all to pass through some water which was contained in a receptacle below the bowl, whilst, instead of there being a long india-rubber tube through which to inhale the fumes, this was substituted by a wooden stem about two feet long, to the end of which was a horn mouthpiece. The tobacco smoked was very different to any I have seen in other countries. It was so strong that two or three whiffs were sufficient to prostrate for the moment any man not accustomed to its use.

The host, taking up his pipe, slowly inhaled the fumes, until after about half a minute he fell back upon his carpet, apparently stupefied by the effects of the tobacco. Indeed, I subsequently heard that all natives who much indulge in this kind of smoking are subject to heart disease, and a number of sickly Khivans were pointed out to me as victims to this habit.

We were informed that the snow on the desert in front of us was very deep in several places, and that we should have a great deal of difficulty in riding through some of the drifts. To the guide's inquiry whether there had been any bands of Turkomans in those parts, the answer was " No," that the country was comparatively speaking quiet, but that as the Oxus was frozen no one could tell whether some Turkoman party or other might not have crossed the river during the last few days.

There is a sort of desultory warfare, which is carried on at intervals between the Russians and some of the Turkoman tribes, the former shooting down the Bedouins of the steppes without any mercy whenever they catch them. Where might is right, a great deal can be done by this terrorizing system. However, it is as well to call things by their proper names. It would be more correct to say that the progress of Russia in the East is based upon the sword and the gibbet rather than upon Christianity and the Bible.

The guide now became impatient, and proposed that we should return to our tent, which had been pitched at about ten minutes' walk from the *aul* (Kirghiz settlement). He was a little alarmed lest I should invite his compatriots to the feast, in which case, as it is always the custom to help the guests first, and their appetites he gauged by his own, he thought that there would be little or nothing left for himself and Nazar. In the meantime the young lady—the *ci devant* object of my admiration—had cut the sheep's

throat, and a little while later the carcase was brought
to our encampment, the fair butcher receiving the skin
and head as a recompense for her trouble.

My followers were in their element. Huge lumps
of half-cooked meat and fat rapidly disappeared
down their throats, the feasting going on steadily
during several hours. At last nature could do no
more, all the belts had been let out to the last hole,
and Nazar, putting his head close to mine, eructated
loudly in my face, the Turkoman and the guide performing the same operation, but fortunately at a little
distance. This was done in honour of the entertainer, and in order to show their appreciation of the
repast. Indeed, to such an extent is this filthy habit
fashionable in Central Asia, that a Kirghiz who has
eaten nothing in his friend's house will do his best to
eructate outside, so that all the bystanders may say—

"See how he has been entertained! How he must
have feasted! His host has honoured him. He must
be a distinguished man!"

We continued our march at daybreak, and rode towards a spot known by the Kirghiz as Berd Kazgan,
where there was said to be a well of brackish water.
Our horses and camels had not drank since leaving
Kasala. They had only eaten snow, and although the
Kirghiz never give their herds of horses any water
during the winter months, but leave them to shift for
themselves, the animals suffer very much in consequence, and when they are doing hard work the owner
has to give them water at least every fourth day.

Our course now lay nearly due south. Occasionally
we came to places where the wind acting upon the
snow had blown it into all sorts of curious forms and
shapes. Sometimes in the misty gloom of awakening

day we seemed to be riding through endless cemeteries, the frozen patches resembling slabs or marble grave-stones, this apparently unbounded burial-ground ex-tending across the desert as far as the eye could reach.

As I was riding across the plain my horse stumbled slightly, when the guide remarked, " How thin the poor beast is ! If you could only see my brother-in-law's horses ! "

" Well," I replied, " it is rather out of the way to ride to Kalenderhana, but, to oblige you, I would not object to stretch a point and go there instead of to Petro-Alexandrovsk."

" What would the Commandant say ? " observed the guide. " He might punish me; perhaps I should be beaten."

" That is your business, not mine," I remarked; " but the horses are beautiful at the fort. We will go there."

" No," said the guide, "we will go to Kalenderhana, and then from my *aúl* to the fort. It will be a little way round—however that does not signify—we will not say a word to the Commandant, and you shall buy such a horse ! You will look with scorn at every other horse you may see, and people will say, ' What a for-tunate man.' "

We had now thoroughly outstripped the Khivan, being at least twelve hours ahead of his caravan. I was not sorry for this, as otherwise the sudden change in my route might have surprised him. We had left Ootch Ootkool, a spot marked on Wyld's map of Khiva, considerably to our rear, whilst the country was a succession of hill and dale; but much more undulating towards my bridle hand than in the direction of the setting sun.

Our course, as we neared a spot known by the Kirghiz as Tan Sooloo, was south-south-west. From this place to Tooz, our next halting-place, the distance was forty-five versts. On either side of the track there were deep hollows and ravines innumerable, whilst saksaool and brushwood became each moment more scarce. Apparently all this country had been at some remote period buried beneath the sea. Frequently we came across shells and other marine crustacea scattered in profusion along our path, whilst at Tooz we passed a small salt lake which lay about a hundred yards to the east of the track, and was frozen as hard as adamant.

Tooz signifies salt in the Tartar language, and the sand all about the lake is saturated with salt. Indeed, the traveller does not require any stronger testimony to this fact than the peculiar taste of his tea, for however carefully the snow is chosen it is sure to become mixed with a little sand, and the more you drink the thirstier you become. According to the guide there were two much larger sheets of salt water to the west, dividing the ground between ourselves and the Sea of Aral.

CHAPTER XXVI.

IT was a quaint spectacle to watch my little caravan as we rode away from our different encampments. First came the guide, clad in a long dressing-gown of crimson cloth, which he had exchanged for the more homely garment in which he commenced the journey. His robe, which was lined with sheepskin, was tightly girt round his loins with a broad blue sash; a tall, conical-shaped black hat surmounted his bronzed countenance. His sword dangled at his side, and he used the weapon sheathed as a whip to urge on his steed, now a little done up by this constant marching through the snow.

Then appeared a still more ludicrous figure—the Turkoman camel-driver. He rode a donkey he had purchased just before leaving Kasala; the long legs of the rider nearly touched the ground, whilst his figure was wrapped up in a tattered robe, that looked as if it might have formed part of an old Turkish carpet. His head was adorned with a white sheepskin hat of the coal-scuttle pattern. His feet, which had first been carefully wrapped up in many thicknesses of cloth, were inserted in a pair of enormous high boots. Around his arm was hitched the end of a rope; this was attached to a huge camel which strode behind the donkey.

On the top of the camel lay my Tartar servant, generally fast asleep, with arms and legs outstretched. A cord was bound round his waist, and attached to some corn-bags to keep him from rolling over. The other two camels stalked along in the rear, the whole cavalcade throwing weird and grotesque shadows on the pale carpet of snow, which exaggerated a thousand times in its reflections the motley appearance of my party.

We were approaching Jana Darya, the dried-up bed of a river which is lost in the sand. All the desert in this neighbourhood was once thickly inhabited; canals cut on all sides irrigated the now parched-up soil, and this not so long ago, for there are men alive who say that they have heard tell of the former richness of this district.

The grandfather of the present Khan of Khiva is said to have been the cause of this once fertile plain having been changed into an absolute waste, for, fearing that the Russians would make use of the Jana Darya and its communication with the Syr Darya as a means to advance upon Khiva, he had a dam built near the junction of the rivers. The Syr Darya then no longer supplied the Jana's channel; gradually the water dried up, and the inhabitants of this formerly rich district emigrated by thousands to the other side of the Oxus.

Later on, and after the Russians had built Fort Perovsky, the dam was destroyed, and the Jana Darya once more fertilised the district. However, the Jaxartes became then so shallow that the steamers in the Sea of Aral could with difficulty ascend to Tashkent. The old channel was once more blocked, and thousands of acres of once fertile territory are now a barren waste.

From Jana Darya we rode sixty versts, or forty miles, without a halt. I must say that I was astonished to see how well the Kirghiz horses stood the long journeys. We had now gone 300 miles, and my little animal, in spite of his skeleton-like appearance, carried me quite as well as the day he left Kasala, this, probably, being owing to the change in his food from grass to barley. We are apt to think very highly of English horses, and deservedly, so far as pace is concerned; but if it came to a question of endurance, I much doubt whether our large and well-fed horses could compete with the little half-starved Kirghiz animals. This is a subject which must be borne in mind in the event of future complications in the East.

Now the snow became scarcer along the track, and could only be found in thin patches, the sand being almost everywhere visible, and looking, beneath the influence of a glaring sun, like a sea of molten gold studded with silver isles. Presently the latter, in their turn, could no longer be seen; the snow had entirely disappeared from our gaze, and an unbounded ocean of sand lay behind us, before us, and all around.

It must not be thought that the cold had equally taken flight. The two days' march when the ground was exposed to view were the most trying of the journey. The mercury had descended to 30° below zero, and the wind was more biting than ever—in fact, we could not take off our gloves for an instant without the hands and fingers being instantly benumbed, and powerless to do their work. My followers had a great advantage in this respect, as their Eastern attire required no buttoning; whilst, if ever I unbuttoned my coat, my fingers lost their feeling, and the little Tartar's services had to be called into requisition to button it for me again.

Just before reaching a spot known to the Kirghiz as Kamstakak, we rode through a raised plain surrounded by sand-hills. It formed a vast natural amphitheatre, of a circular shape, with a diameter of quite five miles. In the centre of this plateau we came upon a freshwater pond, the result of the rain, which falls very heavily during the rainy season in the months of February, March, and April. A good supply of ice was chopped out with the axe, and some large pieces of the frozen water strapped to the saddle of one of the camels, for us to melt if required during our onward journey.

The country again showed signs of a return to vegetation. It was covered with thick brushwood. The shrubs were much larger; and the general appearance of the landscape betokened that we were approaching a more fertile soil. For the first time since I left Kasala, traces of game were to be found. Here and there a hare would dart across our path, whilst herds of *saigak*, as difficult to approach as the chamois, could be seen bounding away from us at the first sound of our approach. Pheasants were said to be plentiful in the neighbourhood, and occasionally we could see the birds running before us in the distance, seeking to hide themselves in the thick foliage.

Up to this time everything had gone smoothly with my party, and no one had shown any symptoms of illness; but this happy state of things was not destined to continue, for the camel-driver began to show decided signs of being done up. He had caught a fever some years before at Bokhara, and was subject to periodical attacks of this malady. He groaned a great deal, could not look at food, and on trying to mount his donkey fell backwards in the attempt. There was nothing for it but to strap him on to a camel and continue our march, the poor fellow writhing with pain at every movement of the animal. I offered him some quinine, but he had a horror of medicine, and said that he should not be well till he saw his moullah, or priest, when the latter could conjure the evil one out of him.

The Turkomans and other nomad races in the steppes often attribute a disease or illness to the devil, and think, like some nations of old, that they cannot be cured unless a holy man will exorcise the demon, and with him their malady. All that night the camel-driver groaned incessantly, and he showed such signs of prostration that I much feared we should never get him alive to the guide's *aúl*.

About twenty miles from the freshwater pond in the wilderness we came to a place known as Karakol. Here we saw, to the west of our route, what appeared to be a large lake. However, the guide said that it was an overflow from the Amou Darya. Close by the water there were a few Kirghiz kibitkas. The ground was cultivated in this neighbourhood, whilst corn and various grasses for cattle abounded throughout the district.

We now encountered a small party of Khivans. My guide gave them the customary salutation, "*Salam aaleikom ;*" however, they made no response. Their leader had observed by my dress that I was a foreigner. He looked fixedly at us, and recognised our guide as the one who had aided the Russians during their advance against the Khan's country. The Khivan stopped his horse, and called out to him, "There you are again, with dogs of unbelievers. I have little doubt but that you are an unbeliever yourself."

This was too much for the equanimity of my guide, who piqued himself upon his rigid observance of all Mohammedan rites.

Did he not wash his feet with snow the prescribed number of times a day in spite of the danger of having them frostbitten, and had he not once suffered in consequence ?

Did he not rub his hands with snow before eating ? and had he ever been known to put his left hand in the dish ? No ; I might be called a dog of an unbeliever, and that was very likely the case. Had he not seen me eat some sausages of that kind which, when at Kasala, he had been informed was made of the flesh of the unclean animal ? Was not one pot of the preserved meat which I had purchased at Orenburg, and of which he always refused to partake, also a composition of the same foul beast ?

The insult was too great to be borne, and he made a tremendous effort to draw his scimitar. This was a hopeless task, so rushing forward with his whip in the air he commenced the attack by smiting vigorous blows on a new Astrakhan cap which adorned the head of the Khivan. The latter retaliated by striking the guide on his crimson dressing-gown with a short camel stick. The damage done to their clothes was great, and the Khivan suddenly seizing the skirt of my guide's garment tore it up the back. The sound of the tear made my follower more furious than ever, for he was very proud of the robe in question, and was looking forward to displaying it to his brother-in-law at Kalenderhana.

The combatants became breathless with their exertions. The Khivan's companions surrounded the guide, and began to play with their knife-handles in a menacing manner. They were six men to two, as the guide and myself had outstripped our caravan by several versts. I now drew a pistol from its holster, and this action on my part immediately produced the desired effect. A revolver is a formidable weapon, and the band of Khivans had sufficient discrimination to recognise its use. Their party fell back a little, and one of them putting his knife down on the ground said something to me, which I understood meant, "It is not your business to interfere; let them settle it between themselves." To this I could not make any objection, when the opponents, seeing that they were to be the only combatants, left off wrestling together.

My guide, who was very much out of breath, now blew his nose with his fingers as a sign of contempt for his adversary, and squatted on his haunches on the ground. His foe, not to be outdone, performed the same feat with his nasal organ, and sat down opposite him. They then began a verbal battle, in which the reputations of their respective female relatives were much aspersed. This continued for about five minutes, when becoming tired with waiting I walked up to them and said "Aman" (peace); then taking hold of their wrists I forcibly made them shake hands. "*Salam aaleikom*" (peace be with you), at last said the guide. "*Aaleikom asalam*" (with you be peace), was the answer, and the combatants separated.

We now encountered a party of men and women who were engaged in unearthing a quantity of grass from a deep cutting in the ground. This grass had been mown in the previous autumn, and was thus pre-served until such time as the owner required it; the extreme cold, or perhaps the dryness of the air, keeping the grass as fresh as the day it was cut. Our road became less clearly defined, frequently making the most circuitous turns, and winding round in a northerly direction to turn once more due south. We passed by deep holes and chasms in the path. The chasms were caused by the heavy rainfall which occurs during the wet season. This would have made it dangerous travelling after nightfall if it had not been for the brightness of the moon and stars, which lit up the surrounding country and turned the night almost into day.

The camel-driver at last showed symptoms of re-covery; the fever had left him, but he was wretchedly weak, and could not sit on his donkey, Nazar riding that animal, having given up his own huge steed to the Turkoman. Presently we came across some Kirghiz tombs which were constructed of clay dried in the sun. Some of them rose from thirty to forty feet above the ground. These marked the resting-places of the richer Kirghiz, who, like Abraham and the forefathers of old, wandered from place to place with their flocks and herds, seldom however omitting to select a plot of ground and build a tomb to contain their ashes.

So, like the vanity of the human race, we too build tombs in order that some distinguished personages may be remembered, whilst posterity soon forgets the very name of the departed.

How many Egyptians are there that know who built the pyramids, and for whom they were constructed? How many Englishmen can tell us in whose honour some of the statues in the parks and squares of London were erected? The poorer Kirghiz, like the poor in other countries, have no such honours paid to their remains—no pillar or stone marks the spot where their bodies are turned to dust. "Where the tree falls, there let it lie." This old saying well applies to them: a hole is dug, a few shovelfuls of sand are thrown over their remains, and, save perhaps by their horses and camels, the children of the desert are soon forgotten.

The guide and I had by this time ridden a long way in front of our caravan. We determined to await its arrival. We were on the borders of Khivan territory. It was impossible to say how the inhabitants would receive us.

We lay down by the side of the road, and in a few minutes were fast asleep. Indeed, after several days of almost incessant travelling, I found myself continually dozing off on horseback, and then clutching convulsively at the pommel of my saddle, as the animal swerved and threw me off my balance. When we awoke, the guide was anxious to know whether the camels had passed us during the night. Looking down on the ground, he carefully inspected the various tracks—one of our camels having a peculiar mark upon a hind foot, which enabled my man to distinguish her tread from that of a million quadrupeds.

The vision of the Kirghiz is very extraordinary,

and my guide would often discern objects with the naked eye which I could barely distinguish with my glasses. His knowledge of locality was also very remarkable. Sometimes when no track could be seen, he would get off his horse and search for flowers or grass. If he could find any, he would then be able to judge by their appearance as to the district in which we were.

The Book of Nature was as familiar to this semi-savage Kirghiz as the Koran to his moullah. Presently pointing to a chain of mountains, which, rearing themselves up before us, extended east and west of our path, he observed that Kalenderhana was just behind them; then making a sound suggestive of a kiss, he informed me that he should not be sorry to see his wife.

The scenery became more striking as we approached this mountain barrier. Picturesque crags and large masses of sparkling quartz dazzled the eye with their glinting. Broken patches of frozen snow at intervals carpeted the sandy soil, and formed a mirror which flashed beneath the midday sun. Many streaks down the rugged sides of the heights around us showed where the rain, pouring down on their crests in the early spring, diverged in foaming torrents. Here, dashing with irresistible force through the narrow pass, they would furrow a road before them; there, emerging from the gradually widening defile, they would rush in a hundred different channels to swell the volumes of the mighty Oxus.

This mountainous ridge was called by the guide Kazan-Tor. My first impression was that the pass, which gives access to some fertile plains, would prove a formidable obstacle to an invading column. However, the chain of hills does not extend very far in an easterly direction. It comes to an abrupt termination about twenty-five miles from the track upon which I was travelling, and the flank can be easily turned. The defile is about a quarter of a mile broad, and about seven miles long, the ground having a strongly-marked auriferous nature; whilst, from the appearance of some of the rocks, I should say that a search for copper would not prove unremunerative to an engineer or his employers.

We emerged upon a vast plain, which was intersected by a quantity of water-courses, or canals. These, springing from the Amou Darya, are employed by the inhabitants of the adjacent villages for irrigating their fields during the summer.

CHAPTER XXVII.

PRESENTLY we came to some kibitkas which were evidently constructed as a permanency. Wide ditches were dug around them, and high wattled palisades, which in every instance encircled the dwellings, showed us that the inmates feared attack. Indeed, from this spot until we crossed the Oxus, each village was fortified in some such a manner. Formerly the Kirghiz and Turkomans lived in a continual state of war. The Kirghiz made marauding expeditions into their neighbours' territory, and carried off horses and cattle. Their foe, in his turn, frequently crossed the Oxus in armed bands of from fifty to sixty horsemen, plundered the Kirghiz kibitkas, and carried away the spoil. At the present moment, from Russian sources, we only hear of the marauding disposition of the Turkomans, and of the peaceful disposition of the Kirghiz. The Turkoman raids are purposely exaggerated, in the same way as previously the Khivans were maligned. This is done as an excuse for a subsequent advance upon Merve. The fact is, that if the Kirghiz carry off a Turkoman's cattle, no one hears of it. If, on the contrary, the latter crosses the Oxus by way of retaliation, it is made the subject for a tirade of abuse.

Indeed, if we were to believe some Russian statements, the Khivans have always been the aggressors. It is not generally known that the first attack on this Central Asian khanate was made by the subjects of the Tzar.

This occurred at the end of the sixteenth century. A band of Cossacks happened to capture some Persian merchants, and through them learnt of the existence of the rich territory of Khiva. Their cupidity was excited. They resolved to make a raid in that direction. The Cossacks rode across the Kirghiz steppe in light marching order, without having any baggage with them save that which could be carried on their saddles. After crossing the Oxus, they attacked the Khivan town Urgentch. The Khan and his forces were absent. Little resistance was made, and the town was destroyed, the Cossacks carrying off a thousand women, besides many carts laden with a rich booty. This extra baggage proved too much for them. They were overtaken and surrounded by the Khivans. The Russians had no water, but they fought for several days, quenching their thirst with the blood of the slain. Human nature, however, has its limits. At last, when nearly all the Cossacks had been killed, the remainder surrendered, and were brought back prisoners to the Khan.

The Cossacks did not recover very rapidly from this serious blow. After a time they once more marched upon Khiva in a band of five hundred strong, under the command of Ataman Nechai. The raid was made successfully; but when returning with their spoil the Cossacks were overtaken. The Khivans slew them to a man.

A third campaign was equally disastrous. The Cossacks lost their way. Instead of reaching Khiva, they found themselves by the shores of the Sea of Aral. The winter came on; frosts commenced, storms raged, provisions were exhausted. At first the Cossacks killed some of their number, and lived upon the dead bodies. Finally, they went to the Khivans, and voluntarily gave themselves up into slavery.

For the fourth time the Russians made war upon Khiva in the reign of Peter the Great. This monarch was fully aware of the advantages to be gained by taking possession of the country. The report that there was auriferous sand in the River Amou, and that the Khivans purposely concealed this circumstance for fear of bringing the Russians to the Khanate, also attracted the Tzar's attention. He determined to open out mercantile relations with India *via* Khiva.

Prince Bekovitch Tcherkassky was given the command of the expedition. Careful preparations had to be made previous to an advance. Points were selected by the shores of the Caspian, and forts built at Cape Tiuk-Karagan, and at the entrance to the Alexander and Balkan Bays (Fort St. George, Alexander, and Krasnovodsk*) so as to maintain communications with Astrakhan.

After securing his base in this manner on the eastern shore of the Caspian, Prince Bekovitch advanced across the Ust Urt into Khivan territory.

His detachment consisted of two companies of mounted infantry, one dragoon regiment, 2,500 Cossacks, with some Tartars and Kalmucks, in all of 3,300 men, and six guns. Three months' provisions were carried on camels and in carts drawn by horses. Bekovitch, after a two months' march, halted on the banks of the Oxus. He had then traversed 900 miles of sandy steppe, in the hottest season of the year, and when the only water that could be obtained had to be procured from wells dug at each halting-place. The Russian prince was attacked by the Khivans. He had drawn up his forces so as to protect his rear by the river, whilst his flanks were defended by a barricade formed of baggage wagons. After a fight which lasted three days the Khivans were repulsed. A truce was now declared, when the prince, thinking himself secure, was so idiotic as to divide his troops. The latter were at once attacked, and cut to pieces by their enemy.

Perovsky's expedition in 1839, which proved such a disastrous failure, I have already mentioned, and not much more was heard of Khiva until the year 1859, when a large Russian force, avowedly for the purpose of reconnoitring, was despatched to the east coast of the Caspian.

* Krasnovodsk by the latest accounts is to be the commencement of a line of postal stations between the Caspian and the Khivan town, Kune Urgendj. The new road will greatly facilitate the transport of troops and supplies to Khiva.

The Turkomans, who did not like this amicable survey of their country, attacked the expedition near Balkan Bay, and seized the Russian camel train and baggage. The commander was thus prevented making a map of the Balkan hills. However, he recommended the construction of a fort near Krasnovodsk Bay, under the pretext of opening out friendly relations with the Turkomans. He then sailed to Ashourade and to Hassan Kuli Bay,* where he bombarded a Turkoman settlement, and took Chikishlar.

The Russians commenced building a new fort at Krasnovodsk Bay in the autumn of 1869. A station was formed in 1870 at Tash Arvat-Kala, 103 miles from Krasnovodsk. Two military intermediate posts were also established, one on the shore of Michael Bay, at a place called Mikhailovsk, and another on the Aktam, at Mulla Kari. A connecting-link of communication was thus formed with the head-quarters at Krasnovodsk.

Chikishlar † was occupied in the month of November, 1871, and a fort erected there by Colonel Markosoff.

* A correspondent of the *Golos*, writing in 1871 from Baku, after a visit to all the military positions on the east coast of the Caspian, observes that " Hassan Kuli, Gomush Tepe, and the localities thereabouts, are now Turkomania *de jure*, and not *de facto*, as I was assured, in spite of my knowledge of political geography, that Persia begins now at the Attrek and not at the Kara-Su. The Yamud Turkomans, the owners of the country between the Attrek and the Kara-Su, are also not aware of this ; but in the loftier considerations of international rights, they are a people with whom it is not requisite to be on any ceremony."

† Venukof, in his military review, writing about Chikishlar, remarks, that "although the line of the east coast of the Caspian can be always easily defended, and therefore does not require one strong local central power, yet, that for the purpose of saving time in the execution of given orders, and for the purpose of uniformity of administrative and other action, in the eyes of the Turkomans it would be advisable to rest the control of affairs on the east coast of the Caspian in one chief officer, whose centre of administration should be in Chikishlar."

Ashourade was Persian territory.   However, this did not prevent its occupation by the Tzar's forces. The latter date Persia's recognition of their right to this station from the day when the late Shah came on board a Russian vessel, he having been told that in the Bay of Astrabad the water was not so rough as off other parts of the coast.

The Russians were now established at four points in and about Turkoman territory : in the island of Ashourade ; in the Mangyshlak Peninsula, by the Attrek ; and in Krasnovodsk Bay.

Everything was ready, and nothing wanted save some pretext for an advance upon Khiva.

A *casus belli* soon presented itself ; but in order to explain how matters were finally brought to a head, it will be necessary to return for a moment to the year 1869.

Amongst the nomad Kirghiz is a tribe known as the Adayefs.   When Fort Novo-Alexandrovsk was erected on the Mangyshlak Isthmus, the Russian Government felt that it was strong enough to tax this people.   The latter were in the habit of paying taxes to Khiva, but this did not avail them with the Tzar's officials, and a forced contribution of one rouble and fifty kopecks was levied from each kibitka, or tent. This was in 1850 ; but in 1869 a fresh system was introduced, and the taxes extorted from the Adayefs were raised 150 per cent.

This gave rise to great dissatisfaction, and in March, 1870, hostilities commenced between the Adayefs and the Russians.   The Khan of Khiva backed up the people whom he looked upon as his subjects.   He had been alarmed at the occupation of Krasnovodsk, and now finding that General Kauffmann was bent on war, despatched to him the following letter :—

"From the beginning of the world up to the present time there has never been an instance of one Sovereign, in order to reassure another, and for the well-being of the subjects of a foreign power, having erected a fort on the frontier, and having advanced his troops. Our Sovereign desires that the White Tzar, following the example of his fore-fathers, should not permit himself to be led away by the greatness of the Empire with which God has entrusted him, and should not seek to gain possession of the lands of other powers, which is opposed to the custom of great Sovereigns.

"If, on the contrary, trusting to the strength of his army, he desires to make war with us, let him remember that before the Creator of heaven and earth, before the great Judge of all earthly judges, all are equal—the strong and weak alike. To whom He will, to him He gives the victory. No one can succeed against the will and predestination of the All Highest."

In the meantime the Adayefs, who at the outset of their quarrel with the Russians had destroyed a convoy, and attacked Fort Alexandrovsk, had been completely overcome by a detachment of troops despatched from the Caucasus. Some Cossacks, who had been taken prisoners by the Kirghiz and brought to Khiva, were detained there by the Khan.

In the beginning of 1872 the latter sent two Embassies, one to the Viceroy of the Caucasus, and the other to the Emperor. In his letter to the Viceroy the Khan wrote as follows :—

"Harmony has existed between the two Governments. How then has it happened that during the last year your troops have landed at Cheleken, on the shores of the Bay of Khaurism, under the pretext of commercial objects, and that recently a small detachment of these troops was advancing towards the Sary Kamysh, which has of old belonged to us, but retired before reaching that point? Besides this, Russian troops have advanced from Tashkent and Ak Musjid (Perovsky) as far as the well of Min Bulak, which is situated within our hereditary dominions.

"We are ignorant whether the Grand Duke (the Viceroy) knows of these proceedings or not. Meanwhile, on our side, no such action has been taken as could violate friendly relations with you. Some Kirghiz had seized four or five of your people, but we took charge of them, and kept them in safety near ourselves. If you wish to maintain friendly relations with us, then conclude such conditions as will leave each of us satisfied with our former frontiers, and we will restore to you all your captives ; but if these captives are made to serve simply as a pretext for a war, of which the real object is the extension of your territories, the will of the powerful and holy One must determine what shall happen. A will which can be avoided by none."

The Embassy was not allowed to go to St. Petersburg. The envoys were informed that no communications would be held with them until the prisoners had been released. The Khan now despatched a mission to India. The authorities there, probably putting credence in the statement so often made by Russian officials that there was no wish to annex any of the Khan's territory, declined giving him assistance. They advised the sovereign to restore the Russian prisoners, and to make peace with the Russian Government.

The Russian Chancellor a short time afterwards heard of this refusal to aid Khiva. He remarked that this was in perfect harmony with the understanding which existed between the Imperial Government and that of her Majesty, and that it had given him great pleasure. It must undoubtedly have been highly pleasing to him. Now he knew that England had no intention to assist the Khan, and that the latter must in consequence unfailingly succumb to the forces under Kauffmann's orders.

The authorities in Great Britain were quite tranquillized as to any intention on the part of the Russian Government to annex Khiva. All their doubts on this subject had been put at rest by a statement made to Lord Granville by Count Schouvaloff, on the 8th of January, 1873. The words used by the latter were to this effect :—

With regard to the expedition to Khiva, it was true that it was decided upon for next spring. To give an idea of its character, it was sufficient to say that it would consist of *four and a half battalions.* Its object was to punish acts of brigandage, to recover fifty Russian prisoners, and to teach the Khan that such conduct on his part could not be continued with the impunity in which the moderation of Russia had led him to believe. Not only was it *far from the intention* of the Emperor *to take possession of Khiva*, but POSITIVE ORDERS had been prepared to prevent it, and directions given that the conditions imposed should be such as could not *in any way lead to a prolonged occupancy* of Khiva.

Count Schouvaloff repeated the surprise which the Emperor, entertaining such sentiments, felt at the uneasiness which, it was said, existed in England on the subject; and he gave Lord Granville most decided assurance that he might give POSITIVE ASSURANCES to Parliament on this matter.

The total force employed by General Kauffmann in his Khivan expeditiom consisted of 53 companies of infantry, 25 sotnias* of Cossacks, 54 guns, 6 mortars, 2 mitrailleuses, 5 rocket divisions, 19,200 camels, with a complement of about 14,000 men. Russian battalions appear to be of a very expansive character if fifty-three companies of infantry can be comprised in four and a half battalions. The strength laid down for a battalion is four companies of the

* A sotnia of Cossacks is about 150 horsemen.

line and one company of rifles. The war establishment of a battalion comprises 900 rank and file,
of whom sixty men are in reserve. Indeed, it would
appear that the Russian Commander-in-Chief had bor-
rowed a leaf out of the book of a sick patient. The
latter, when desired by his doctor to limit himself
to three glasses of wine a day, had some glasses
constructed which would contain a bottle. He thus
kept within the exact letter of his promise to the
medical gentleman.

The troops were divided into different columns.
They in their turn were divided into detachments—the
Tashkent column consisted of two detachments; of
the Djizzak, which marched from Tashkent, and of the
Kasalinsk from Fort Number One. The Orenburg,
Krasnovodsk, and Kenderli columns were to march
respectively from Embinsk along the shores of the
Sea of Aral, from Krasnovodsk, Chikishlar, and from
the Bay of Kenderli to the Aibougir Lake, travers-
ing the dreary wastes of the Ust Urt.

It seems strange that the water-communication from
Kasala by the Syr Darya, Sea of Aral, and Oxus was
not made use of during the invasion. Some vessels
belonging to the Aral fleet had sailed up the Oxus as
far as Kungrad, and there was nothing to prevent the
Russians attacking Khiva by water. This, indeed,
was strongly urged upon Kauffmann. But the General
is reported to have said that it must be a land expedition, as otherwise the sailors would share the rewards,
and that he wished all the decorations and honours to
fall to the lot of the army. Kauffmann was of opinion
that there ought to be only two detachments of troops

sent against the khanate, one formed of troops from the army of the Caucasus, which should march from Krasnovodsk to Khiva, and the other to march from Tashkent and be under his personal command.

Kauffmann's wishes in this respect were disregarded. Kryjinovsky, the Governor-General of Orenburg, urged upon the Government the dangers of such a plan. He observed that in the event of no troops being despatched from Orenburg, the Khivans and Turkomans might advance on the Kirghiz steppes, intercept communications on the postal road from Orsk to Tashkent, and possibly alarm the Ural and Oren-burg districts.

The troops from Orenburg had no difficulty in marching along the coast of the Sea of Aral to Kungrad. Here they were joined by the Kenderli detachment. Not being able to hear anything of General Kauffmann's column, they advanced upon Khiva, and captured the gate of that city. Intelligence was now received from Kauffmann that he had also arrived before Khiva, and that the city was about to surrender. However, the fire continued, and General Verevkin, who commanded the Orenburg column, took the city and citadel. This had scarcely been accomplished when the news was brought that Kauffmann had accepted the capitulation offered him by the chief inhabitants of the city, and that he was entering Khiva from another gate. The Khan had fled. However, after two days he returned, and was reinstated in his post; but was subjected to a council, or divan, formed for the most part of Russian officers.

The expedition from Krasnovodsk, under Colonel

Markosoff, proved a complete failure, owing to the want of water; and, after burying his cannon in the sand, the colonel ordered his troops to retire. The columns from the Caspian and Tashkent were practically of no use. The expedition from Orenburg, which had been despatched solely at the instigation of General Kryjinovsky, and with the reluctant consent of General Kauffmann, had beaten the enemy and taken Khiva.

A war indemnity of 2,200,000 roubles was imposed upon the Khivan sovereign. The news of his subjection spread like wildfire all over Central Asia. Russian influence became paramount in the khanates.

The so-called insolence of the Khan had been punished. His capital had been taken. He himself was in the hands of his foe. No sovereign's humiliation could have been more complete. Kauffmann had compelled him to drain the bitter cup to its dregs.

The object of the expedition was obtained. And now all there remained to do was to fulfil the promise of the Emperor, given to the English Government by Count Schouvaloff, Russian Ambassador in London. However, this was not done; there had been a misunderstanding, it was said, and the construction of a Russian fort was at once commenced on Khivan territory.

Shortly before this Prince Gortschakoff, writing to Kauffmann about the conditions of a treaty with Kokan, made use of the following language, which M. Terentyeff is so kind as to publish to the world in his work on England and Russia in the East:—

"You express your conviction, produced by experience, that in an intercourse with Asiatics the grand secret of success consists in unchanging veracity and firmness, combined with a decided attitude of peace. I, too, am the more firmly convinced of the correctness of this view, since it has invariably served as my guide in my political action and intercourse both in the east and west."

It is a pity that M. Terentyeff's work is not translated into the Tartar language. It would be refreshing to the Khan of Khiva to read of such a noble expression of feeling on the part of one of his foes. Fortunately the work has been translated into English. It will doubtless gratify the minds of those Members in the House of Commons who were under the impression that no part of Khivan territory was to be annexed to Russia.

A proportion of the war indemnity of 2,200,000 roubles was imposed upon a tribe of Turkomans, who had fought against the expedition from Orenburg. They were nominally Khivan subjects, and for a month after the conquest of Khiva they had been on friendly terms with the conquering officers, indeed, some Russian officers who had been sent out for the purpose of surveying, had remained for days and nights together in the Turkoman encampment.

There was no reason to believe that the Turkomans would break the truce. However, it would not do for the Tashkent column to return home without a little bloodshed. The glory of the war had been actually confined to the column from Orenburg. The officers from Tashkent had done nothing to merit promotion.

General Kauffmann now sent for the elders of the tribe, and declared that a part of the indemnity must be paid by them within a fortnight, and the remainder later on. At the same time the general detained some of the elders as hostages, until such time as the first instalment of the indemnity had been paid in to the Russian treasury.

But the Russian Commander-in-Chief was in a hurry. Instead of waiting the appointed time, he sent out a large detachment under General Golovatcheff to ascertain what chance there was of the payment being made.

This general, in order to discover the intentions of the Turkomans, gave an order to his soldiery not to spare either sex or age. Men, women, and children at the breast were slain with ruthless barbarity; houses with bedridden inmates were given up to the fiery element; women—ay, and prattling babes—were burned alive amidst the flames; hell was let loose in Turkomania. And this, the Russians would have us believe, was done to further Christianity and civilization. This is the sort of Christianity which some people wish to see established in Constantinople. Would they like this kind of civilization next our Indian frontier?

If the Turkomans had been treated differently they would have paid the tribute to the Russian general. But they are barbarous creatures, utterly unacquainted with that European civilization which characterizes Russian troops. They were so foolish as to be exceedingly angry. Indeed it is said that later on these poor ignorant Turkomans became utterly lost to all feelings of honour. They actually dared to attack General Golovatcheff's camp at Illyali; but they had no chance against the breechloaders of their foes, and were repulsed with great slaughter.

The Turkomans now abandoned the district. They were disinclined to listen to any terms of peace which might subsequently be offered them. However, they sent General Golovatcheff the following message:—

" We know how to respect peace, and shall keep it if you will have peace with us, but if you will not have it we shall fight, and we can fight well."

According to General Kryjinovsky, the Governor-General of Orenburg, the attack on the Turkomans was entirely uncalled for, and likely to lead to serious results. " It will now be necessary," he said, " for us to send expeditions against the Turkomans for many years to come. Their country will be a second Caucasus, and in the end we shall be obliged to take possession of it. This will undoubtedly lead to complications with England."

The remark of General Kryjinovsky has every chance of being realised. Colonel Ivanoff, the Commandant at Petro-Alexandrovsk, has found time to attack some bands of nomad Turkomans. On one occasion he made prisoners of two of these Arabs of the steppes. They had robbed, it was said, some Russian Kirghiz. In consequence of this the captive Turkomans were tried by court-martial and sentenced to death. The sentence was shortly afterwards put into execution.

The Turkomans on their side have captured a Russian soldier. They refuse to surrender him until such time as they receive a sum of money, perhaps to go to the widows of their fellow-countrymen. The man has not been tried by court-martial by the Turkomans, probably on account of their ignorance of military law. When they become more civilised they will doubtless follow the example set them by their Christian foe.

On the 24th of August, 1873, a treaty of peace,

which had been first of all approved by the Emperor, was made with Khiva. The khanate was reduced to a state of complete vassaldom. The delta and right bank of the Oxus were ceded to Russia. The Oxus was closed to all save Russian and Khivan vessels. Russian merchants were allowed perfect freedom of commerce in the khanate, with liberty to purchase and hold property. A Russian fortress was to be built four miles south of Shurahan, and in a garden belonging to an uncle of the Khan. All the territory situated between the former Bokharo-Khivan frontier, the right bank of the Amou Darya, from Gugertli to Meshekly, and the line passing from Meshekly to the point of junction of the former Bokharo-Khivan frontier with the frontier of the Russian Empire was taken from Khiva and annexed to the dominions of the Ameer of Bokhara.

A lifelong feud between Khiva and Bokhara will inevitably follow this redistribution of soil. After the Franco-Prussian War, if the Germans, instead of taking Alsace and Lorraine for themselves, had forced Belgium to accept these provinces, we could not have expected the French to have looked with friendly eyes upon the new proprietors. A spark would have been struck, certain at some future period to burst out into flame. This will happen between Bokhara and Khiva. It will not be difficult to get some one to stir the fire. The consequence will be the absolute incorporation of Bokhara and Khiva with the Russian Empire.

CHAPTER XXVIII.

SOME men and women running out of one of the
kibitkas and warmly greeting the guide, announced to
me that we had reached his home at Kalenderhana.
In a short time I found myself seated on a rug, an
object of curiosity to many of the inhabitants, who
had never before seen a man dressed in European
costume. Every part of my attire was in turn inspected
and commented upon, the women coming forward and
feeling the texture of my coat and trousers, the large
buttons being a source of great admiration.

The hostess was clad in a flowing white dressing-
gown, with a turban of the same colour, folded many
times around her small head. For a Kirghiz, she was
decidedly good-looking, and well worth the hundred
sheep her lord and master had paid for her. She was
delighted at his arrival, and two ruddy-faced little
children were seated upon their father's knee, and
playing with his beard and moustache. The brother-
in-law, a short, hump-backed fellow, who had been
informed that I wished to purchase a horse, was most
assiduous in his attentions. He seized a pillow
which an aged relative, his grandfather, had secured
for his own accommodation, and dragged it from

beneath this elderly gentleman, then pushing it behind
my back he patted me on the shoulder and said
that he had heard I wanted a horse. Well, he had
the most beautiful of the equine race; it had performed extraordinary feats, and was the wonder
of all the village. We would look at it, and then
I should see. Yes, what I should see! and pouring
me out some tea, he absolutely put four lumps of
sugar in my glass, to the astonishment of the other
inmates, who were aghast at such reckless extravagance. I replied, in a careless manner, that his horse
was doubtlessly a beautiful one, but that at Petro
there were lovely animals. If we went to the fort
I should very likely buy one there ; but if we
were not to go to Petro but to Khiva, that then I
would purchase his animal, and pay for it in the
Khan's capital. This having been duly interpreted by
Nazar, an animated conversation took place amongst
the members of the family, the guide being somewhat
reluctant, and his brother-in-law and other relatives
eager to contest all his arguments. He had already
brought me off the route to Petro; he would very likely
get punished for that. Why not go to Khiva ? And
Nazar suggested that then we would not visit the
fort at all, but would continue our journey to Bokhara.
I now inquired if we could procure some camels to take
us as far as that city. This was a fortunate remark, as
it appeared that another of the guide's relatives had
camels for hire. Eager that I should employ his
animals, he exhausted all his eloquence upon my
follower to persuade him to go to Bokhara. The
domestic pressure put upon the guide was too much
for him. Turning to Nazar, he agreed to go on
with us to Bokhara, where, he said, we could hire

fresh camels and return to Kasala, *viâ* Samarcand and Tashkent, thus avoiding altogether Fort Petro-Alexandrovsk.

My faithful follower now whispered in my ear, "We are to have a great feast to-night. The guide's brother-in-law has a horse which is not very well. The animal is to be killed directly, and we are to eat him." Later on, an enormous cauldron was suspended from a tripod across the fire. A heap of fagots was piled upon the embers, and a dense smoke filled the tent. Large pieces of the unfortunate quadruped were now thrown into the pot by the guide's wife, who officiated as cook. The host and the rest of the party superintended the operations with the greatest interest.

"Will there be anything else to eat?" I inquired.

"No," was the answer of my surprised Tartar. "What more would you have? We might eat two sheep at a time; but a horse—no. There will, perhaps, be enough left for breakfast, praise be to God for His bounty!" and the little man, opening his mouth from ear to ear, licked his lips in anticipation of the banquet.

A piece of raw cotton floating in some greasy substance, which was contained in a large iron ladle, threw a lurid light over the red faces of the hungry Kirghiz, eager to commence the banquet.

The dark smoke from the rude lamp was curling itself in spiral columns amidst the dense grey clouds which ascended from the burning pile. From time to time some relative of the family, lifting up the thick cloth that served as a door, entered the dwelling. The sudden draft would then upheave the thick atmosphere, and forcing it through the aperture, reveal the boundless canopy of the heavens, the sky studded with a million gems, whilst the queen of night, like a globe of metallic silver, cast her pale shadow through the half-raised rug or curtain.

My hostess was rocking a recently-born child with one hand, and stirring some rice which was boiling in an adjacent kettle with the other. My guide and Tartar servant were washing their hands and feet in the snow at the threshold. The brother-in-law was for the hundredth time informing me that his horse was a horse, and that all the rest of the equine race were mules in comparison, when the woman announced that the meat was done to a turn, and that all things were ready for the feast.

A portion of the steed and some rice were given to me in a slop-basin. The rest of the party, calling upon Allah to bless the entertainment, squatted round the cauldron, and thrust their hands into its seething contents, which speedily vanished down their throats. A conjurer, or fire-king at a village fair, might have swallowed swords or flames, pokers or daggers, but he would have had no chance whatever if pitted to eat horse against my guide's brother-in-law. I thought, when for the second time the cauldron had been emptied, that this would have sufficed. But no, for each man strove to outdo his neighbour. Belts and broad sashes were loosed from around the loins, and Nazar, who had made up his mind that he ought to eat for his master as well as himself, was actually swelling before my eyes, and becoming wheezy in his utterances.

Over-eating would seem to paralyse a man's speech almost as much as excess in alcohol, and the hoarse breathed-out tones of the Kirghiz men jarred on the ear in comparison with the clear voices of the females, who, not daring to eat at the same time as their lords and masters, stood round and helped them to the most savoury pieces.

At times the guide, by way of honouring me in the person of Nazar, would take a greasy piece of meat from the iron kettle. Then, holding the luscious morsel up at arm's length, so that all might perceive his intention, he would slowly insert it in Nazar's mouth; the latter gulping down the half-raw flesh without any attempt at mastication, in order to show how highly he appreciated the compliment.

I hoped that this would wind up the entertainment, but the feasters were far from having any such intention. The sounds of gorging going on steadily throughout the night and early morning announced to me that my follower would very likely be wrong in his conjecture, and that ere breakfast-time all the horse would have disappeared.

Long narrow wooden carts, each with high wheels, were all the morning bringing grass into the village for the horses of the inhabitants. A few high trees here and there, the first that we had seen since leaving Kasala, afforded a pleasing change to the vision, tired of gazing over snow and low brushwood, whilst a large supply of hay in an enclosure hard by the kibitka, showed that my guide had armed himself against the danger of a sudden thaw.

He now informed me that I could not go to the town of Khiva without first having the Khan's permission, and said that a letter must be written to that sovereign and sent before us, asking his leave for my followers and self to enter the city. This piece of information rather startled me. I had been under the impression that all I had to do was to ride to the town, encamp outside the walls, and ride in each day, so as to inspect everything worth seeing. However, according to the guide, not even this could be done without the Khan's permission.

I was puzzled, not knowing in what language to address him. My servant could not write in Tartar, and I was afraid that if I despatched a letter written in Arabic, some unintentional omission of the due amount of courteous expressions which one is bound to use when writing to a sovereign might offend this Khivan potentate.

Nazar at last proposed that I should inquire for some moullah who could write a letter in the Tartar language. On asking the guide, he at once sent for a learned man, who, he said, could write beautiful things, so soft and sweet that they were like the sounds of sheep bleating in the distance.

Presently the scribe arrived. He was a tall, angular-looking man, one shoulder being much higher than the other, whilst his dressing-gown bore signs of its having been originally made for a much shorter individual than himself. His long arms protruded through the sleeves, showing several inches of shirtless skin. He entered the kibitka with an air of great importance, whilst the party rose at his approach, much awed at the arrival of a person who had as much there, as the guide observed, pointing to his own head, as was in the united occiputs of all the people in the village.

The moullah carried an inkstand made of bullock's-horn. The ink was of the thickest possible description. A wooden stopper at each end of the horn formed the top and bottom of the inkstand. He unfolded a sheet of paper, and, squatting down by my side, pulled out one of the plugs from the horn bottle, at the same time producing a long style made of cane, which served him in lieu of a pen.

A dead silence reigned around. All the inmates of the kibitka were appalled by the preparations of the moullah. Writing a letter was no everyday occurrence in that village; and the man who was able to make a piece of paper speak—the common definition of writing amidst savage nations—was looked upon as a prodigy of learning.

The guide, however, did not appear so awed as the rest of his relatives. Had he not been to Kasala and seen the clerks write? "Why, some of the Russian soldiers could do as much!" and saying this in a muttered tone to Nazar, he undid a small parcel, and taking out some coarse snuff, put a quantity on the back of his hand, which he sniffed up his nostrils with an air of the greatest delectation.

"What shall I say?" inquired the moullah. "What is your tchin (rank)?"

"No particular rank," I observed. "You can leave that out."

"No," said the moullah; "we must have some tchin. Are you a polkovnik (a colonel)?"

"No, only a kapitan (captain)."

The moullah here picked his ear with his pen, and, turning to Nazar, said something.

"What is it?" I inquired.

"Why, kapitan will not do. They look down upon kapitans at Khiva. The word is like the Tartar word Kabtan, and gives no idea of rank to a Khivan. Better say polkovnik."

In the meantime the moullah had written a most flowery epistle. Nazar said it was beautiful, and all the

rest of the party greatly admired the composition.
However, the word polkovnik was still inserted, and
the moullah was so pleased with the letter that he
would not erase the expression.   Giving the fellow
some silver, I determined to write to the Khan myself,
and in the Russian language, as I had learned from the
guide that there were two or three Tartars in the city
who acted as interpreters.   I wrote as follows :—

   "An English gentleman who is travelling through Central Asia
requests the permission of his Majesty the Khan to visit his celebrated capital."

   " That will not do," said Nazar, dolefully ; "there
is no tchin.   Why do not you call yourself polkovnik ?
We shall not be received with due importance."   And
the little man sat down on the carpet with an indignant
air, as if to say, " See how you have humbled me !"

   A young fellow was found to go forward with
the missive.   It was arranged that he should start
at once with the letter, whilst the caravan and myself
would follow on later in the day.

   In the meantime the horse had been sent for.
Presently he arrived, escorted by the whole village,
everybody being eager to sing his praises save those
who had animals of their own for sale.   One old man
sought to attract my attention by shaking his head
violently, and frowning at the horse when he thought
that his owner was not looking ; but the aged gentleman assumed the pleasantest of smiles should any one
save myself catch his eye.

   " He has a beast of his own for sale," said Nazar.
" Look there ;" and he pointed to a brute which was
lame all round, and which looked only fit for the
knacker's yard.   Neither of the animals would suit,

the one belonging to the guide's brother-in-law being blind in one eye. This the unblushing Kirghiz said was of no consequence at all, for in his opinion one eye was just as good as two; however, he remarked, that if we would continue our journey to another kibitka, about five versts distance, he could then show me some horses with two eyes.

"Yes, with two eyes!" said all the rest of the party, gravely wagging their heads, as if such a complement of vision in one horse was a most remarkable fact in natural history. Our road now lay south-west, and in the direction of the town of Oogentch, which is distant about twenty-three versts from Kalenderhana. The country appeared to be highly cultivated, canals innumerable cutting the fields at right angles to each other, and arranged so as to supply the district with water from the Oxus. Corn is grown in great abundance in this neighbourhood, and also *jougouroo*, a species of grain which the Kirghiz and Khivans give their horses instead of barley.

Presently we came to another *aúl*, which was also the property of the guide's brother-in-law. I had begun to hate that man even more than Weller senior could have hated his mother-in-law. I did not want to buy any of the fellow's horses; I felt convinced that if he were to sell me one it would be a screw, or have some defect which I should only discover after the purchase was completed. But there was no help for it. It was one of those disagreeable things which had to be done, that is to say, if I wished to see Khiva; and the guide had already shown a little impatience at my not having bought the one-eyed brute shown me at the last kibitka.

This time a grey horse was brought out for

inspection. The lad who rode him, cracking his whip, rode straight at a ditch about ten feet wide, and got his animal over all right. The animal had two eyes, which was also a consideration, so I said that I would buy him and pay for my purchase in Khiva. But no, this proposal did not meet with the brother-in-law's approval. He knit his brows, and remarked to Nazar that I might be honest or I might be a rogue, " God only knew." If I took the horse, why perhaps the money would not be sent back, and he would lose the animal. People had stolen horses before, and would steal them again.

I here became a little indignant, and informed him that horse-stealing was not such a common occurrence in my country as in his, and that if I wished to steal a horse I should not steal a useless brute like the one I was about to purchase; that the guide knew who I was, and that if I might have the animal the money should be paid in Khiva. This the brother-in-law would not hear of for a moment, apparently fearing that if the money once came into the possession of the guide that there was little chance of the latter returning it to him. Finally matters were compromised, I agreeing to pay half the amount down and send the other half back with the messenger who had been despatched with my letter to the Khan. A saddle and bridle were also bought, and Nazar, descending from his huge camel, mounted the new purchase.

CHAPTER XXIX.

Now we crossed a little stream about twenty yards
wide, known by the name of the Oozek. It was
said to be a tributary of the Oxus. A rough bridge
made of cross-poles, sticks, and dried clay afforded
a means of crossing the water; for the banks were too
steep to admit of a descent to the frozen surface.
Finally, after riding along a narrow path planted on
both sides with high reeds, we arrived upon the banks
of the Amou Darya, and I gazed on that world-
renowned stream which in my boyish days it had been
my dream to visit.

The mighty Oxus—the Oxus of Alexander—lay
at my feet, its banks bound together by a bridge
of transparent ice, which, here at least half a mile
broad, is the boundary line separating the subjects of
the Khan from those who pay tribute to the Tzar.

Each Khivan has to pay an annual tax of eleven
roubles for his house to the Khan, whilst the inhabitants on the right bank of the river pay four roubles
per kibitka to the Russian authorities. The Khivans,
however, who live in town, pay no taxes, and the
sovereign obtains the greater part of his revenues from
crown lands, and from a duty of two and a half per

cent. on the value of all goods which are imported or exported from his dominions. But this source of income is now curtailed, as the Khan has become a vassal of the Emperor, and Russian goods pay no duty whatever.

Before crossing the Oxus we dismounted for a short time at a kibitka hard by the river. It was in former years a station-house where custom duties were levied on all goods brought from Russia. A few Khivans were warming their hands over a wood fire ; hey had come from Oogentch, and were going to trade n Shurahan, a town near Petro-Alexandrovsk, and which formerly belonged to the Khan, but has now been seized by the Russians. The merchants were fine-looking fellows, with a very different type of countenance to the Tartars and Kirghiz, the dark complexions and large eyes of the Khivans being the very opposite to the broad, barge-shaped faces, ruddy cheeks, and little eyes of the Tartars.

One of the traders recognised my fresh horse, and laughed as he pointed him out to his companions.

"What is it?" I inquired of Nazar.

"They only say that he is a slug, and stumbles," observed the latter. "He nearly fell with me as we were coming here. Please God I do not break my neck before we reach Khiva."

We met quantities of arbas—two-wheeled native carts—each of them drawn by one horse, as we rode across the river. A caravan, with camels belonging to the merchant in the station, was also traversing the frozen stream, which, as hard as a turnpike road, would have safely borne a battery of eighteen pounders.

The Khivans whom we met were for the most part dressed in long, red dressing-gowns, which reached down to their heels. These garments were made of a mixture of silk and cotton stuff, whilst they were thickly wadded with a species of quilting to defend the wearers from the cold. Tall, black lambskin hats, taller even than a Foot-guardsman's bearskin, covered their heads, and each man carried, strapped to his saddle, a long single-barrelled gun, with a short, highly-ornamented stock. The saddles, which were made of wood, were highly ornamented with gold, enamel, and turquoise stones. The bridles and steel appurtenances were clean and well appointed, in this respect affording a striking contrast to the slovenly equipment of the Tartars. The horses, too, were of a different breed, being much larger animals than those which I had seen on the steppes—the Khivan horses averaging about fifteen hands, whilst a good many which I met could not have been less than sixteen.

Every man whom we encountered in our path never failed to salute us with the regular Arab salutation, "*Salam aaleikom,*" each of us in turn responding "*Aaleikom salam;*" and the varied tones of the way-farers, as two large caravans passed each other, broke upon the ear almost like a response in the Litany, and carried my thoughts like a flash of lightning to very different scenes in my island home.

The shades of night were falling fast, and the guide, riding up, informed me that it would be better not to continue our march to Oogentch, but to halt at one of the many houses which were now to be met with at every turn. On my assenting to his proposal, he began to look about and to carefully inspect each abode which we passed.

"What is he doing?" I inquired of Nazar.

"He is trying to find a house where the owner is well off, and can give us plenty to eat," was the answer. "It is no good stopping for the night at any beggar's house, and getting starved in consequence."

The guide's search was finally rewarded, and he pulled up by the side of a large, substantial-looking, square building, built of dried clay. High wooden gates, strongly clamped with iron, gave access to the dwelling. The guide rapped with his whip-handle against the door. An old man, bent nearly double with age, tottered out and asked our business.

"We want your hospitality for the night," was the answer. When, as if this were the most natural thing in the world, the old fellow called out to his servants. Several of them ran forward, and, taking hold of my horse, aided me to dismount.

It now turned out that what I had at first taken for a house was merely a square courtyard, consisting of four high walls, whilst the edifice itself, built of the same material as the enclosure, was erected inside the gates. A similar entrance, on a smaller scale, led to some stables, which, in their turn, gave access to that part of the building which was inhabited by the family. Another door, however, on the opposite side of the dwelling, led to the harem and more private apartments. My host gave an order that our horses and camels were to be well fed; and seeing that Nazar was in the act of taking some barley from the sacks on our camels, made a sign for him to desist.

"Have I not corn?" he remarked. "Are not you my guests?" and calling his servants he desired them to look after our animals as if they were his own.

I now found myself in a lofty room, which was

reserved for great occasions, and for strangers like myself. One end of the apartment was covered with thick carpets. This was the place of honour for the visitors; in the centre of the room, and where there were no rugs, was a small square hearth. This was filled with some charcoal embers, which were surrounded by a coping of about three inches in height, forming a species of fender. On the coping stood a copper vessel of the same shape as many of the so-called Pompeian ewers. The vessel was richly chased, and constructed with a long swan-like neck, so that the attendant might the more conveniently pour water over the hands of his master's guests before they commenced their repast. On the other side of the hearth there was a square hole about three feet deep. Two steps led down to it, the cavity being adorned with variegated tiles. This was the place for ablutions, and thus arranged so as to keep the water from wetting the other parts of the apartment.

Two narrow slits, each about two feet long by six inches wide, supplied the place of windows, and some open wooden trellis-work served as shutters, there being no glass, which is hardly ever used in these parts. A few pegs in the wall on which we could hang our clothes supplied the place of a wardrobe. The floor on the opposite side of the room to that reserved for myself was covered with coarse cloth, and arranged for my retinue.

Presently the host appeared. He bore in his hand a large earthenware dish full of rice and mutton, whilst his servants brought baskets filled with bread and hard-boiled eggs. Some milk was now produced in an earthenware pitcher, and an enormous melon, which weighed quite twenty-five pounds, was carried in on a tray.   All the dishes were placed at my feet ; I being seated on the carpets, my head supported by a richly-coloured silk cushion which had been specially brought by my entertainer.   When all the viands had been thus set round me, the host, bowing to the ground, asked permission to retire; then walking backwards a few steps he sat down beside Nazar and the guide, who were gazing greedily upon the dishes, a striking change to the rough fare which we had lived upon for the previous thirteen days.

I made a sign for the owner of the house to approach and sit down by my side.   With an air of great humility, he complied with my request, the host on such occasions thinking it his duty to play the part of a servant to his guest.

I was much surprised at the size and flavour of the fruit, which was as fresh as on the day when it had been first picked.   The climate is so dry that all the Khivans have to do to preserve their melons is to hang them up in a temperature about two degrees above freezing point; for should the frost ever attack them they lose all their flavour and are useless for the table.   The melons here have a fame which is celebrated all over the East.   In former years they were sent as far as Pekin for the Emperor of China's table. Some of them attain forty pounds in weight, whilst the taste is so delicious that any one only accustomed to this fruit in Europe would scarcely recognise its relationship with the delicate and highly-perfumed melons of Khiva.*

---

* I subsequently procured some melon-seeds from a Russian officer, and brought them back from Khiva.   They did not turn out well in this country.   The seeds given to me might have been bad ; or perhaps the English soil did not suit them.

The host, when he got over his first diffidence, asked many questions about the countries through which I had passed. He had the idea that to go to England his direction would be eastward from Khiva. Geographical knowledge in the Khan's dominions is very limited, and Hindostan and England are continually blended together under the same head.

"So you have been thirteen days coming here from Kasala!" he exclaimed. "Praise be to God who has allowed you to pass the desert in safety. Have you camels in your country?"

"No," I replied, "but we have trains composed of *arbas* (carriages), with iron wheels; they run upon long strips of iron, which are laid upon the ground for the wheels to roll over."

"Do the horses drag them very fast?" he asked.

"We do not use live horses, but we make a horse of iron and fill him with water, and put fire under the water. The water boils, and turns into steam. The steam is very powerful, it rushes out of the horse's stomach, and turns large wheels which we give him instead of legs. The wheels revolve over the iron lines which we have previously laid down, and the horse, which we call an engine, moves very quickly, dragging the *arbas* behind him; they are made of wood and iron, and have four wheels, not two, like your *arbas* in Khiva. The pace is so great that if your Khan had an iron horse and a railway he could go to Kasala in one day."

"It is a miracle!" said the Khivan, as Nazar translated to him my little speech, my servant himself, who had never seen a railway, being a little incredulous as to the possibility of going five hundred versts in twenty-four hours. The guide, who sat on the opposite side of the fire, and was engaged in washing his feet over the cavity in the floor, now remarked "that his brother-in-law had the best horses in the steppes, but that they could not do the distance in less than ten days. Then how could a horse that was made of iron, and with wheels instead of legs, do it in one? If it could, we were conjurors, like the man he had once seen swallow a sword at Kasala. But who knew! He had heard something about it at the Fort," and he looked down contemptuously at the host's servants, who had assembled to gaze upon the new arrivals, and who were not travelled men like himself—a man who has been to Kasala and back being considered a great traveller by the Khivans.

Nazar did not want to be outdone in this way by the guide. He now said—

"They have wires which speak in Russia. This I have seen myself; they are fastened to the top of high poles, and the wires extend over miles of country. Any man in Sizeran who may wish to say something to a friend in Orenburg, goes to one end of the wire, they turn a handle, and it makes a noise at the other end in Orenburg; the moullah there understands what the wire says, and you can talk almost as fast as if you were actually speaking to your friend."

"I have heard something about this," said our host. "There was a merchant who passed through here two years ago, and he told me about it. He said that one of these speaking wires reached all the way from St. Petersburg to Tashkent, and that the White Tzar could speak with his soldiers at Tashkent. He also said that they were going to make a speaking wire to Petro-Alexandrovsk, and that then we could know everything that was happening at Kasala, and the price of cotton at Orenburg, without having to send a letter."

The evening was far advanced, and the host, seeing that I was very drowsy, retired, when Nazar, the guide, and camel-driver, drawing the piece of cloth close to the embers, stretched themselves out at full length, and soon fell asleep.

On the morrow I was puzzled to know how to reward my host for his hospitality. However, on inquiring, I was informed that the custom in those parts was for the guest to make a present to his host, and that the best thing would be for me to give as many roubles as I thought just. This is the system universally adopted throughout Central Asia, in the places where there are no caravanserais, or regular hostelries for the travellers. The Khivans are thus enabled to carry out the injunctions of their prophet to the letter, and to lavish hospitality on their guest, being sure that on his departure they will be well remunerated for their trouble.

CHAPTER XXX.

WE were about four versts from Oogentch, the first town the traveller arrives at in Khivan territory, if going from Kalenderhana to the capital. There was a singular dearth of rising ground throughout the route. If it had not been for the hundreds of dykes which traversed the country on every side, I should have imagined myself back upon the steppes. The snow, too, which had almost disappeared as we passed through the defile in the Kazan-Tor of mountains, now lay thick and flaky on the ground, whilst the cold, in spite of the latitude to which we had attained, was as intense as ever.

Large gardens, enclosed by high walls, were dotted about the landscape. Square-built houses similar to the one in which I had passed the night became more frequent as we gradually neared the town. Indeed, if the Khivans had only been supplied with arms and a good leader, it would have been difficult for the Russians to have entered Oogentch. Every walled garden could have been turned into a citadel, and a few resolute men with breechloaders might have caused great destruction in the invaders' ranks.

The merchants in Oogentch seemed to do a considerable trade with the people of the surrounding districts. The road was every now and then blocked up by hundreds of carts, all bringing corn and various kinds of grass to the market. Numerous camels laden with goods from other parts of the khanate had been formed into one vast caravan which extended for more than a mile, and was slowly filing into the town. The latter was defended by a ditch and high wall made of dried clay, now much out of repair. Masses of its *débris* had in many places choked up the surrounding trench.

The people gazed curiously at me as we rode through the narrow streets, my sheepskin attire not being a customary one in those parts, and some of the inhabitants, stopping the guide, inquired if I were a Russian.

" No," was the answer—" an Englishman."

The announcement of my nationality produced an evident revulsion of feeling in the Khivans, who did not appear to bear much goodwill towards their conquerors.

The bazaar through which we rode was held in a narrow street. This was partly covered over with rafters and straw, probably in order to protect the passers-by from the rays of the sun during the summer months. Grapes, dried fruits, and melons were for sale in many of the stalls; these last were niches or recesses in the walls, and no windows or shutters of any kind separated these primitive shops from the thoroughfare. In the centre of each recess sat the proprietor, surrounded by his wares, and generally engaged in warming his hands

over a charcoal pan, which, mounted on a tripod stand,
stood before him.   Farther on, men were to be seen
hammering into different shapes sheets of copper
brought from Russia, and manufacturing water-bottles
and pipes.   All sorts of bright-coloured calico stuffs
were offered for sale, and found ready purchasers.
Thick skeins of silk of various hues, and spun in
the country, were readily exchanged for Russian paper-
money, which passes in Oogentch as well as the native
currency.   Women continually flitted past us in the
street, taking sly glances at the strangers through
the corner of their veils, the fair sex in Khiva not
having their faces uncovered, as is the custom amidst
the Kirghiz, but obeying strictly the rules laid down
for their guidance by the prophet.

As I expected to arrive at the capital either that
afternoon or the following day, and wished to make
my entrance into the city clean shaved, and not with
a beard of thirteen days' growth, I asked Nazar to
make inquiries whether a barber could be found in the
neighbourhood.   The news that the Englishman wanted
to be shaved was soon spread through the town.
A boy volunteered to show me the way to the
barber's shop.   We were followed there by a crowd of
certainly from three to four hundred people.   It was
the more remarkable to them, as the report had been
spread that the stranger would have his chin shaved
and not his head, the Khivans keeping their heads as
devoid of hair as a block of marble.

" Have your head shaved, sir," said Nazar ; " it
will look so nice—just like mine ; " and, lifting off a
green skull-cap, he showed me his bullet-like poll.

If I had been quite certain that my hair would have
grown again, in all probability I should have followed

my man's example; but not wishing to return to London with my head *à la* Nazar, I declined the proposal.

On arriving at the shop, we dismounted, and sat down in the recess by the barber's side. The crowd had now greatly increased, and was each moment becoming more dense, the whole town having by this time become aware that an Englishman was within the walls, and that he was about to be shaved. Moullahs, camel-drivers, and merchants jostled the one with the other to obtain a good view. Their bronzed faces glanced and peered through the fur of their Astrakhan hats, and the idea occurred to me that, if the barber were fanatically disposed, he might think that it would be doing a good deed in the eyes of Allah and of his own countrymen, if he were forthwith to cut the throat of the unbeliever.

There was not a single Russian in Oogentch, and no authorities save the moullahs, or priests, who, in all probability, would be more fanatically disposed than even the rest of the population.

The remark made by the District Governor at Kasala now flashed across my mind—" If you go to Khiva without an escort, the Khan will very likely have your eyes taken out, or order you to be placed in a dungeon."

However, nothing was to be gained by crying over spilt milk—the die was cast; I was in Khivan territory, and what was far more to the point, in the hands of the barber, who was busily engaged in rubbing a thin strip of steel on a whetstone, the former article supplying the place of a razor, a handle being considered an unnecessary luxury. The street in front of the shop was now completely blocked up by the crowd.

The people behind, who were not able to see as well as they could wish, called out to their friends who hid the performance from their view, and made them sit down, so that all might be able to enjoy the spectacle. If their curiosity was excited, mine was equally aroused. It was a strange scene, the crowd of eager faces, all staring intently into the recess; even some women, in spite of the prohibitory law, had stopped for a moment and were looking at the performance with unmixed astonishment. If I had been in the hands of an executioner, and about to have my throat cut, this would not have been half so interesting to them; for was I not having my chin shaved? "What will he do next?" asked one of the more curious of his neighbour. "Perhaps have his moustache shaved," was the reply; "but who knows? These infidels have strange customs;" and the excitement grew to boiling pitch.

My little Tartar began to be rather alarmed; he had not anticipated such a gathering, and he murmured in my ear, "Please God you do not get your throat cut! They might cut mine too. Allah preserve us, and bring us out of this scrape! Have your head shaved, it will please them."

At that moment the barber had put the dirty thumb of his left hand into my mouth, and was brandishing the razor in the air; no soap being used, as water was considered quite sufficient. Even under the most favourable circumstances, with a well-lathered chin and the sharpest of razors, being shaved, if one's beard luxuriates in a two weeks' growth, is not a pleasant process, but at Oogentch it was a highly painful operation. The razor, at each movement of the barber's wrist, tore out those hairs in my beard which it was too blunt to cut. The people were delighted. They were not prepared for this feature in the entertainment, and they roared with laughter as I slightly winced. Later on the crowd became still more hilarious, and its enjoyment of the proceedings was greatly increased, for the awkward barber, who was confused at the presence of so large a number of spectators, became a little nervous, trembled, and gashed my cheek.

The operation was at last over. I was preparing to leave the shop, when a merchant came forward, and, addressing me in Russian, asked me to breakfast with him. On my entering the recess where his wares were exposed for sale, he removed a curtain which hung in an obscure corner, and, stooping, led the way through a low covered way into a good-sized room. This was the apartment used by his family. His wife was seated there, engaged in performing some culinary operations over a charcoal fire. Her face was uncovered, as she did not expect any visitors, and, with a rapid movement of her thick white shawl, she entirely concealed her features. She was not by any means a beauty, and her personal attractions not such as to overcome a traveller. However, thinking it best to keep us out of temptation, she left the room, and entered the harem, which was divided by a thick fold of cloth from the apartment in which we found ourselves.

A dish composed of small pieces of roast pheasant served up with a slightly acid sauce, and surrounded by a huge pile of rice, was now brought in, followed by fried fish much resembling gudgeon. Whilst I was eating, the host plied me with questions about the countries through which I had travelled. He was ignorant that any water communication existed between Great Britain and India, and thought that the ordinary route from England to that empire lay through China. He was aware, however, that England was not the same country as India, thus showing more geographical knowledge than was possessed by his compatriot at our sleeping quarters of the previous evening.

My host had been for some time in Tashkent, where he had learned Russian. He had also been to Bokhara, and had spoken with several merchants who had gone with caravans to Cabul and Lahore. He was the more curious at meeting me as he said that he had never seen an Englishman, and was very anxious to know whether there was any chance of a war between Great Britain and Russia. This, he observed, was looked upon in Tashkent as certain soon to happen, the Russian inhabitants of that city talking about India as of a mine of wealth, from which they would be able to replenish their empty purses.

"How will they march to India?" I inquired. "There are high mountains which block the way, and besides this, if they were to come, how do you know that we should let them get back again?"

"There are many roads," he answered. "Merchants go from Bokhara to Cabul in sixteen days in the summer months; then there is the road through Merve and Herat, which is now stopped by the Turkomans, but which the Russians are going to open, and at the same time to build a fort at Merve. You have fine soldiers in India," he continued; "but we are told that the natives of India do not like you, and will look upon the Russians as deliverers."

"How do you like the Russians?" I inquired.

"Pretty well; they buy my goods when I am at Tashkent, and leave alone small people like myself. If

I were rich it would be another matter, but then I could bribe. Money will go a long way with the colonels, and even the generals do not always keep their palms shut."

"Were you in Khiva when the country was taken?" I asked.

"No; I was then at Tashkent, and we thought that the Russians would never get here. It was fearful," he added, "so much bloodshed; so many friends killed; women and children too; such cruelties. War is a dreadful thing."

"Perhaps we shall meet some time or other in India," I remarked, "and then I will return your hospitality."

"That is to say, if the Russians let you," replied the man; "but when they are in Hindostan there will not be much left for yourselves, or the natives either, for the matter of that; the officers here know how to squeeze money out of a stone."

Nazar now came in. He informed us that the horses were ready, and that the guide was waiting for me to continue the journey; so pressing a few roubles on my entertainer, I mounted and rode off towards the capital. On emerging once more into the country, I found that the road was separated on each side from the adjacent lands by low walls of dried clay, each about four feet in height, and the neighbouring fields were divided from each other by ditches, which marked the boundaries of the respective properties. About nine versts from Oogentch we crossed a canal known by the name of the Shabbatat. This was surmounted by a bridge constructed in the clumsiest manner of upright beams driven into the mud below, and cross planks with earth thrown on them to form the road.

There was no wall or parapet on either side to prevent the passenger from falling into the stream, which was at least twelve feet below. With a frightened horse or drunken coachman it was not the sort of place that a nervous man would like to cross on a dark night.

The road was now no longer enclosed, and we rode through a sandy track of seemingly uncultivated ground till we arrived at a cemetery. Here the tombs were made of dried clay, and formed in strange and fantastic shapes to suit the caprice or taste of the dead one's relatives. Banners or large white flags, mounted on poles ten or twelve feet high, floated in the breeze over several of the sepulchres, and marked the burial-place of some fallen hero or other famous for his valour and prowess, whilst mounds of earth, unadorned save by the rising vegetation, were the last resting-places of his humbler followers. A small dwelling hard by this dead men's home was tenanted by an aged moullah, whose office it was to look after the cemetery, and offer up prayers for the departed. A lad now approached us, and offering me some dried fruits and tea, invited us to dismount and share their hospitality.

Later on I walked round the tombs, accompanied by the old moullah, who told of the fearful scenes enacted during the enemy's advance on his country; and on being informed that I was not a Russian, he heaped deep curses on the invaders. "They say that we began the war," muttered the old man; "and it was they who imprisoned our merchants at Kasala in order to provoke the Khan; but our day is gone by, and the infidels remain our masters."

After riding about seven versts further, we crossed another canal called the Kazabat. Night was coming on, and as there were no signs of the messenger I had sent forward to Khiva, we halted at a village called Shamahoolhoor. Here it was not even necessary for the guide to ask for hospitality. A fine-looking man, with a cheery frank expression on his nut-brown face, came out of a substantially built house, and asked us to honour his roof by resting beneath it till the morrow. He was apparently better off than the owner of the dwelling where we had stopped the previous evening. The room set apart for guests, though furnished in the same style as our quarters of the night before, was much larger, and the carpets, &c., of better quality.

Our host was a sportsman, and kept several hawks. These birds are much used in the chase by the Khivans. They are flown at hares or *saigaks*, a species of antelope. The hawk, hovering above its prey's head, strikes him between the eyes, and the animal becoming bewildered does not know which way to turn, and falls an easy victim to the hounds.

" Do you not hunt in this way in your country ? " asked the host.

" No ; we hunt foxes, but only with hounds, and follow ourselves on horseback."

" Are your horses like our own ? " he inquired.

" No ; they are stouter built as a rule, have better shoulders, and are stronger animals ; but though they can gallop faster than your horses for a short distance, I do not think they can last so long."

" Which do you like best, your horse or your wife ? " inquired the man.

" That depends upon the woman," I replied ; and the guide, here joining in the conversation, said in England they do not buy or sell their wives, and that I was not a married man.

" What ! you have not got a wife ? "

" No ; how could I travel if I had one ? "

" Why, you might leave her behind, and lock her up, as our merchants do with their wives when they go on a journey."

" In my country the women are never locked up."

" What a marvel ! " said the man ; " and how can you trust them ?   Is it not dangerous to expose them to so much temptation ? They are poor weak creatures, and easily led.   But if one of them is unfaithful to her husband, what does he do ? "

" He goes to our moullah, whom we call a judge, and obtains a divorce, and marries some one else."

" What ! you mean to say he does not cut the woman's throat ? "

" No ; he would very likely be hanged himself if he did."

" What a country ! " said the host ; " we manage things better in Khiva."

The guide was much astonished on hearing the price of horses in England.   " And what do the poor people do ? " he inquired.

" Why, walk."

" Walk ? "

" Yes, walk "—this appearing to the man such an extraordinary statement that he could hardly credit it.

Later on I took out my breechloader from its case, as the weapon had become very rusty during the march, and began to clean it.   The host scrutinised the gun very carefully, and was delighted at the rapidity with which it could be loaded.

" Ah ! " he said, with a sigh, " if we had only been armed with some of your guns, the Russians would never have got here ; the Khan's arms were useless in comparison." With these words my host showed me his own gun, which had a barrel at least five feet long, and a rest to stick in the ground so as to steady the aim. "It is a nice weapon, too," he added, "though not like yours, for mine takes five minutes to load, and quite a minute to fire; indeed, before I can shoot once, the Russians with their rifles can kill twenty men. Our Khan has now no soldiers; the Russians will not let him have any."

CHAPTER XXXI.

THE next morning we encountered on the road the
messenger whom I had despatched with my letter to
the Khan. He was accompanied by two Khivan noble-
men. One of them courteously saluted us. He then
said that his Majesty had received my letter, and had
sent him forward to escort me into the city, and to say
that I was welcome to his capital.

We were now fast nearing Khiva, which could be
just discerned in the distance, but was hid to a certain
extent from our view by a narrow belt of tall, graceful
trees. However, some richly-painted minarets and high
domes of coloured tiles could be seen towering above
the leafy groves. Orchards, surrounded by walls eight
and ten feet high, continually met the gaze. Avenues
of mulberry-trees studded the landscape in all directions.

The two Khivans rode first; I followed, having put
on my black fur pelisse instead of the sheepskin garment, so as to present a more respectable appearance
on entering the city. Nazar, who was mounted on

the horse that stumbled, brought up the rear. He had desired the camel-driver to follow in the distance with the messenger and the caravan, my servant being of opinion that the number of our animals was not sufficient to deeply impress the Khivans with my importance, and that on this occasion it would be better to ride in without any caravan than with the small one I possessed. We now entered the city, which is of an oblong form, and surrounded by two walls; the outer one is about fifty feet high; its basement is constructed of baked bricks, the upper part being built of dried clay. This forms the first line of defence, and completely encircles the town, which is about a quarter of a mile within the wall. Four high wooden gates, clamped with iron, barred the approach from the north, south, east, and west, whilst the walls themselves were in many places out of repair.

The town itself is surrounded by a second wall, not quite so high as the one just described, and with a dry ditch, which is now half filled with ruined *débris*. The slope which leads from the wall to the trench had been used as a cemetery, and hundreds of sepulchres and tombs were scattered along some undulating ground just without the city. The space between the first and second walls is used as a market-place, where cattle, horses, sheep, and camels are sold, and where a number of carts were standing, filled with corn and grass.

Here an ominous-looking cross-beam had been erected, towering high above the heads of the people with its bare, gaunt poles.

This was the gallows on which all people convicted of theft are executed; murderers being put to death in a different manner, having their throats cut from ear to ear in the same way that sheep are killed.

This punishment is carried out by the side of a large hole in the ground, not far from the principal street in the centre of the town. But I must here remark that the many cruelties stated to have been perpetrated by the present Khan previous to the capture of his city did not take place. Indeed, they only existed in the fertile Muscovite imagination, which was eager to find an excuse for the appropriation of a neighbour's property. On the contrary, capital punishment was only inflicted when the laws had been infringed; and there is no instance of the Khan having arbitrarily put any one to death.

The two walls above mentioned appear to have made up the defences of the city, which was also armed with sixteen guns. These, however, proved practically useless against the Russians, as the garrison only fired solid shot, not being provided with shell. The Khan seemed to have made no use whatever of the many enclosed gardens in the vicinity of the city during the Russian advance, as, if he had, and firmly contested each yard of soil, I much doubt whether the Tzar's troops could have ever entered the city.

It is difficult to estimate the population of an Oriental city by simply riding round its walls; so many houses are uninhabited, and others again are densely packed with inhabitants. However, I should say as a mere guess that there are about 35,000 human beings within the walls of Khiva. The streets are broad and clean, whilst the houses belonging to the richer inhabitants are built of highly-polished bricks and coloured tiles, which lend a cheerful aspect to the otherwise somewhat sombre colour of the surroundings. There are nine schools; the largest, which contains 130 pupils, was built by the father of the present Khan. These buildings are all constructed with high, coloured domes, and are ornamented with frescoes and arabesque work. The bright aspect of the cupolas first attract a stranger's attention on his nearing the city.

Presently we rode through a bazaar similar to the one at Oogentch, thin rafters and straw uniting the tops of the houses in the street, and forming a sort of roof to protect the stall-keepers and their customers from the rays of a summer sun. We were followed by crowds of people ; and as some of the more inquisitive approached too closely, the Khivans who accompanied me, raising their whips in the air, freely belaboured the shoulders of the multitude, thus securing a little space. After riding through a great number of streets, and taking the most circuitous course—probably in order to duly impress me with an idea of the importance of the town—we arrived before my companion's house. Several servants ran forward and took hold of the horses. The Khivan dismounted, and bowing obsequiously, led the way through a high door-way constructed of solid timber. We next entered a square open court, with carved stone pillars supporting a balcony which looked down upon a marble fountain, or basin, the general appearance of the court being that of a patio in some nobleman's house in Cordova or Seville. A door of a similar construction to the one already described, though somewhat lower, gave access to a long narrow room, a raised dais at each end being covered with handsome rugs. There were no windows, glass being a luxury which has only recently found its way to the capital. The apartment received its light from an aperture at the side, which was slightly concealed by some trellis-work, and from a space left uncovered in the ceiling, which was adorned with arabesque figures. The two doors which led from the court were each of them handsomely carved, and in the middle of the room was a hearth filled with charcoal embers. My host, beckoning to me to take the post of honour by the fire, retired a few paces and folded his arms across his chest, then assuming a deprecatory air, he asked my permission to sit down.

Grapes, melons, and other fruit, fresh as on the day when first picked, were brought in on a large tray and laid at my feet, whilst the host himself, bringing in a Russian teapot and cup, poured out some of the boiling liquid and placed it by my side; I all this time was seated on a rug, with my legs crossed under me, in anything but a comfortable position.

He then inquired if I had any commands for him, as the Khan had given an order that everything I might require was instantly to be supplied. On my expressing a wish to have a bath, a servant was at once despatched to give the necessary orders to the keeper of the establishment. In an hour's time Nazar informed me that the bath was ready, and that we should have to ride there, as it was in a house in the centre of the town. The host now led the way, Nazar bringing up the rear, carrying some soap in one hand, and a hairbrush in the other, the latter a source of great astonishment to the Khivans, who, having no hair of their own, could not understand the use of such an article.

The bathing establishment consisted of three large rooms with vaulted roofs. Several divans made of dried clay were arranged around the walls of the first apartment, and covered with rugs and cushions. On one of these sat the keeper of the bath. He at once arose, and beckoning to me to sit down beside him, produced a pipe. There is an old saying that when you are in Rome you must do as Rome does. I took two or three whiffs, and was nearly choked in consequence. Some sherbet was now poured out, and an attendant helped me to undress, when feeling the belt which contained all my gold, he asked what it was. It is no use showing Asiatics that you suspect them of possible dishonesty, and the result of my experience has been to prove that you can do more by apparently confiding in them than by any other method. I merely remarked, "Money," and asking him to take care of it whilst I went into the hot room, I gave him the belt. The man bowed down, and pointing to his head, conveyed to my mind that his life would answer for the money. He then led the way into a second apartment. Here there was a charcoal furnace, and on the fire a quantity of large stones which were at a white heat. He threw three or four pailfuls of cold water on the stones ; the liquid was in an instant converted into steam, and volumes of dense vapour filled the apartment. Hotter and hotter it grew, the atmosphere being so thick that the attendant was invisible. After steaming for about half an hour, he came to my side, and led me to a large reservoir filled with water and floating ice. Seizing a bucket, he soused me from head to foot. The process was over ; there was no shampooing or bone-kneading, as in similar establishments in Turkey, and I was conducted back to the dressing-room.

Here many of the principal inhabitants had assembled, in order to have a look at the stranger who, although a Christian, still liked washing. One of them, an old moullah, could speak a little Arabic. He had twice performed the pilgrimage to Mecca. He remembered Captain Abbott's visit to Khiva, forty years ago, and was under the impression that I, like that officer, had come to the Khivan capital from India and Herat.

" He was such a nice gentleman," observed the moullah, alluding to Abbott. " He was a medicine-man too, and cured several sick people. We heard afterwards that he had been killed by the Russians. Was that the case?" And on being informed that Captain Abbott had returned in safety to England, the old man gave praise to God.

" Your compatriot was with us about the time that the Russians were attempting to reach Khiva," continued the moullah. " People here then thought that an army from Hindostan was coming to help us. But we did not require any assistance; the winter killed the dogs by thousands. Praise be to God!" And this expression, which is the same in Tartar as in Arabic, was devoutly repeated by the rest of the company.

" How did the Russians succeed in taking Khiva?" I inquired.

" They came in the summer. Allah did not fight for us."

" It has been said," I remarked, " that your people had poisoned some of the wells in the desert. Was this the case?"

The old man turned red with indignation.

" Poison the wells which God has given us!" he said; " no, never; for that would be a sin in His eyes."

Nazar by this time had returned with the horses; so, shaking hands with the principal people, who arose at my departure, I rode away, followed by the blessings of the old priest, the latter, from the fact of my speaking Arabic, looking upon me as not quite a

Mohammedan, but as certainly a very distinguished moullah in my own country.

Later on in the afternoon I received a visit from no less a person than the Khans treasurer. He was a tall, fat man, of about forty years of age, and with a forbidding expression on his countenance. He was extremely anxious to learn my business, and to know if I had been sent to Khiva by my Government, and was much surprised that the Russians had not stopped me on the route.

" You have not been to Fort Petro-Alexandrovsk?" he observed.

" No," I replied.

" Ah ! that accounts for it," he continued, with a sarcastic laugh. " They do not much love you English people, though, by all accounts, you are now on speaking terms, and not at war."

" Do you think this state of things will last long ? " I inquired.

The man grinned, and, stretching out his arm, pointed eastward.

" They are pushing onward," he added. " You will have an opportunity of shaking hands with your friends before long. Four years ago we were quite as far from Russia as you are at the present time ; and you have not many white men in India."

" Quite sufficient to give Russia a good beating," I remarked ; when, asking at what time it would be convenient for me to pay my respects to the Khan, the following afternoon was fixed for an audience, and the treasurer left me.

A succession of visitors came pouring in during the evening, the arrival of an Englishman in Khiva being looked upon as an extraordinary occurrence. I have often pitied distinguished foreigners who, when visiting London, are taken, amongst other sights, to the Zoological Gardens on a Sunday. The *habitués* of the Gardens stare at the unfortunate stranger as if he were a choice specimen of the gorilla or chimpanzee which has been imported from some recently discovered region. The lions and monkeys are deserted for the new arrival, and his every gesture is scanned as if he were not made of flesh, blood, and bone, like an ordinary mortal, and had nothing in common with the rest of humanity.

This was my own position.

My manner of eating with a knife and fork much astonished some of the visitors. One of them, coming up, tried to imitate the proceeding, the consequence being that he ran the fork into his cheek. This greatly amused the rest of the party.

Nazar and the guide did not at all object to the intrusion on my privacy.

" It is their custom," said my little Tartar, at the same time expectorating on the floor ; " they are poor barbarous people, and do not know any better. They want to honour you," he added, " and this is their way of doing it. If you were a Russian there would not be half so much curiosity displayed."

The evening wore on, and taking an inkstand out of my writing-case, I tried to write a letter. However, this proved a difficult task. The ink, which was frozen into a solid lump, had smashed the bottle. The cold still remained as great as ever ; though now it was impossible for me to register it, owing to my thermometer having been broken during the journey. The small charcoal hearth in my room gave out but little warmth, and the draught through the apertures in the roof and walls was so great that it was impossible to undress. There was nothing for it but to wrap myself in my fur pelisse, and thus attired lie down on my air mattress. The latter was a source of the greatest astonishment to the Khivans, who were delighted when I explained how it could be used on an emergency as a raft. "We could cross the Amou on it," observed one of them. "And it is light and soft," added another, lifting it up between his finger and thumb. "The Russians have not such things," chimed in a third, who had once been inside Fort Petro-Alexandrovsk.

CHAPTER XXXII.

IN the morning my host again appeared, accompanied by several servants bearing sweetmeats and fruits, the invariable preludes to a breakfast at Khiva, whilst a frozen block of milk was also sent me, and some butter which was as hard as a billiard-ball. Nazar was all this time engaged in brushing a black shooting-jacket, the only garment I possessed except my regular riding attire. However, I had brought one white shirt, thinking that I might possibly have an interview with some Central Asian magnate or other. Greatly to my surprise, the article in question was not much the worse for the journey.

Whilst these preparations were going on, the host kept plying Nazar with questions as to my *tchin* (rank), and as to whether I had any orders or not, the Russian officers who had visited Khiva having been covered with decorations. A successful review or parade at St. Petersburg often enables an officer to obtain an order, whilst, with us, one would only be given for services in the field. Indeed, I remember once seeing a Russian official with his breast so covered with decorations, that, struck with astonishment, I asked in what sanguinary actions he had distinguished himself. The man whom I addressed smiled. " He has seldom been under fire," was the reply," but he is useful to the State, as, through his agents, he knows everything that goes on in Russia."

" You have no orders ? " inquired Nazar.

" No."

" Well, I have told them that you have a great many, but that you have not brought them with you for fear of their being stolen. If you had only a few crosses to attach to your coat it would look so well. The people, too, would think so much more of me ; " and my little Tartar servant swelled out his chest, as much as to say, " I am a person of considerable importance, though you do not seem to see it."

I was a good deal annoyed with Nazar for having thus imposed upon my host, and instantly desired him to state that in my country officers only received decorations for military services in the field. In consequence of this there were not so many worn as in the Russian army ; whilst as to my rank, I was a captain, travelling at my own expense and for my own pleasure, and not in any way as an agent of the British Government.

In the afternoon two officials arrived from the Khan's palace, with an escort of six men on horseback and four on foot. The elder of the two dignitaries said that his Majesty was waiting to receive me, and my horse being brought round, I mounted, and accompanied the Khivan to the palace. The six men on horseback led the way, then I came between the two officials. Nazar brought up the rear with some attendants on foot. They freely lashed the crowd with their whips whenever any of the spectators approached our horses too closely.

The news that the Khan was about to receive me had spread rapidly through the town. The streets were lined with curious individuals all eager to see the Englishman. Perhaps in no part of the world is India more talked of than in the Central Asian khanates. The stories of our wealth and power which have reached Khiva through Afghan and Bokharan sources have grown like a snowball in its onward course. The riches described in the garden discovered by Aladdin would pale if compared with the fabled treasures of Hindostan.

After riding through several narrow streets, where, in some instances, the housetops were thronged with people desirous of looking at our procession, we emerged on a small flat piece of ground which was not built over, and which formed a sort of open square. Here a deep hole was pointed out to me as the spot where criminals who had been found guilty of murder have had their throats cut from ear to ear.

The Khan's palace is a large building, ornamented with pillars and domes, which, covered with bright-coloured tiles, flash in the sun, and attract the attention of the stranger approaching Khiva. A guard of thirty or forty men armed with scimitars stood at the palace gates. We next passed into a small courtyard. The Khan's guards were all attired in long flowing silk robes of various patterns, bright-coloured sashes being girt around their waists, and tall fur hats surmounting their bronzed countenances. The courtyard was surrounded by a low pile of buildings, which are the offices of the palace, and was filled with attendants and menials of the court. Good-looking boys of an effeminate appearance, with long hair streaming down their shoulders, and dressed a little like the women, lounged about, and seemed to have nothing in particular to do.

A door at the further end of the court gave access to a low passage, and, after passing through some dirty corridors, where I had occasionally to stoop in order to avoid knocking my head against the ceiling, we came to a large, square-shaped room. Here the treasurer was seated, with three moullahs, who were squatted by his side, whilst several attendants crouched in humble attitudes at the opposite end of the apartment. The treasurer and his companions were busily engaged in counting some rolls of rouble-notes and a heap of silver coin, which had been received from the Khan's subjects, and were now to be sent to Petro-Alexandrovsk as part of the tribute to the Tzar.

The great man now made a sign to some of his attendants. A large wooden box, bearing signs of having been manufactured in Russia, was pushed a little from the wall, and offered to me as a seat. Nazar was accommodated amongst the dependants at the other end of the room. After the usual salaams had been made, the functionary continued his task, leaving me in ignorance as to what was to be the next part of the programme, Nazar squatting himself down as far as possible from one of the attendants, who was armed with a scimitar, and whom he suspected of being the executioner.

After I had been kept waiting for about a quarter of an hour, a messenger entered the room and informed the treasurer that the Khan was disengaged, and ready to receive me. We now entered a long corridor,

which led to an inner courtyard. Here we found the
reception-hall, a large tent or kibitka, of a dome-like
shape. The treasurer, lifting up a fold of thick cloth,
motioned to me to enter. On doing so I found
myself face to face with the celebrated Khan, who was
reclining against some pillows or cushions, and seated
on a handsome Persian rug, warming his feet by a
circular hearth filled with burning charcoal. He raised
his hand to his forehead as I stood before him, a salute
which I returned by touching my cap. He then made
a sign for me to sit down by his side.

Before I relate our conversation, it may not be
uninteresting if I describe the sovereign. He is taller
than the average of his subjects, being quite five feet
ten in height, and is strongly built. His face is of a
broad massive type, he has a low, square forehead, large
dark eyes, a short straight nose, with dilated nostrils,
and a coal-black beard and moustache. An enormous mouth, with irregular but white teeth, and a
chin somewhat concealed by his beard, and not at all in
character with the otherwise determined appearance of
his face, must complete the picture.

He did not look more than eight-and-twenty, and
had a pleasant genial smile, and a merry twinkle in
his eye, very unusual amongst Orientals; in fact, a
Spanish expression would describe him better than any
English one I can think of. He is *muy sinpatico.* I
must say I was greatly surprised, after all that has
been written in Russian newspapers about the cruelties and other iniquities perpetrated by this Khivan
potentate, to find the original such a cheery sort of
fellow.

His countenance was of a very different type to his
treasurer's. The hang-dog expression of the latter

made me bilious to look at him, and it is said that he
carries to great lengths those peculiar vices and depraved
habits to which Orientals are so often addicted. The
Khan was dressed in a similar sort of costume to that
generally worn by his subjects, but it was made of
much richer materials, and a jewelled sword was
lying by his seat. His head was covered by a tall
black Astrakhan hat, of a sugar-loaf shape, and on my
seeing that all the officials who were in the room at the
same time as myself kept on their fur hats, I did the
same.

The sovereign, turning to an attendant, gave an
order in a low tone, when tea was instantly brought,
and handed to me in a small porcelain tea-cup. A
conversation with the Khan was now commenced, and
carried on through Nazar and a Kirghiz interpreter
who spoke Russian, and occasionally by means of a
moullah, who was acquainted with Arabic, and had
spent some time in Egypt. The Khan, when he wished
to say anything which was not intended for the ears of
the other attendants, murmured his questions to this
official, who would then translate them to me.

The first question asked was how far England is
from Russia, and whether Englishmen and Germans are
of the same nation? thus showing rather a deficiency
in geographical knowledge.

Fortunately I had Wyld's map of the countries
lying between England and India in my pocket, and
producing it, I unfolded the map before him.

He at once asked where India was.

I pointed to it.

" No," he said, " India is there," pointing to the
south-east.

He was seated facing the south, and could not

understand that it was necessary to read the map to the reverse hand.

As I was not quite certain where the north was, I desired Nazar to give me my compass, which he wore round his neck. When he handed it to me I observed the countenances of the Khan's followers assume an expression of alarm, and they looked as if they thought that it was an infernal machine, and might go off. However, the sovereign himself instantly recognised the use of the instrument, and said that he had two which had been given him some time previous by a traveller.

I now adjusted the map to the north, and showed him all the different places he mentioned, at the same time pointing with my finger to the direction in which he would have to ride if he should wish to visit them.

He was under the impression that Afghanistan belonged to England, and was greatly struck with the size of India, and the small space that Great Britain takes up on the map. "China, where the tea comes from, belongs to you, also?" he inquired, evidently thinking that England has the same relations with the Celestial Empire as Russia with Kokan.

The Khan then putting his hand on Hindostan on the map, observed that India was large, but not so large as Russia, which required nearly two hands to cover it.

I here remarked that extent of territory does not make up the strength of a nation, and that India contained nearly three times as many inhabitants as were in the whole of the Russian Empire, whilst her Majesty ruled over such a large extent of territory which was not shown in the map, that the sun never sets throughout her dominions.

He then asked if it were true that the son of our Queen had lately married the daughter of the Tzar, as the Russians had told him so, and had said that it was a proof of the friendship which existed between England and Russia, and of the interests they had in common, which would eventually lead to the two empires touching in the East.

He was also very anxious to know whether Englishmen loved the Russians as much as the Russians said they did ; "for if I am to believe what I hear from other sources," he continued, "the more particularly through the Bokharans, there is not much love lost between the two countries, and the people in India are not at all eager to have their *dear friends* as such near neighbours."

He then said, " You had a war with Russia some years ago, and were the allies of the Sultan. This made a great stir in Central Asia, and we were very glad to hear the news, as we thought you would defend us in the same manner if we were attacked. There was another Khan, however, who helped you at that time, and from all accounts you took some Russian territory. Now," continued the speaker, " I want to know if it is true that the Khan, who was your friend at that time, has been since defeated by another power, and that the Russians then laughed at you, and said that you were weak and could not fight without your friend, after which they re-took all the country they had previously lost."

To this I replied that there had been no territory taken, and that as to our fearing Russia, or any other power, this was a statement as ridiculous as false ; that England had beaten Russia before, and could easily do so again, but that we were a peaceable nation, and never wished to interfere with our neighbours so long as they did not interfere with us.

"That is all very well," said the Khan; and after being silent for a few seconds, he suddenly observed, "Why did not England help me when I sent a mission to Lord Northbrook?"

To this I replied that being only a traveller, and not in the secrets of the Government, I could not possibly know all that passed in the political world.

"Well," observed the sovereign, "the Russians will now advance to Kashgar, then to Bokhara and Balkh, and so on to Merve and Herat; you will have to fight some day whether your Government likes it or not. I am informed that India is very rich," he added, "and that Russia has got plenty of soldiers, but little with which to pay them. I am paying for some of them now," he continued, looking with a sad smile at his treasurer.

The Khan next said, "We Mohammedans used to think that England was our friend because she helped the Sultan, but you have let the Russians take Tashkent, conquer me, and make her way into Kokan. What shall you do about Kashgar?" he suddenly inquired; "shall you defend Kashgar or not?"

Here I remarked that I was very sorry the Russians had been allowed to get to Khiva, as this might easily have been prevented, but that I could not give him an answer, as I was utterly ignorant of the policy of the Government.

"You do not have a Khan," he asked, "at the head of affairs?"

"No," I replied, "a Queen, and her Majesty is advised as to her policy by her ministers, who for the time being are supposed to represent the opinion of the country."

" And does that opinion change ? " he inquired.

" Very frequently," I resumed ; "and since your country was conquered we have had a fresh Government, whose policy is diametrically opposite to that held by the previous one ; and in a few years' time we shall have another change, for in our country, as the people advance in knowledge and wealth, they require fresh laws and privileges. The result of this is they choose a different set of people to represent them ; the sovereign, however, remains always immutable. She can make no mistake ; all the responsibility of government rests with the Ministry, who in their turn are selected from the majority of the representatives."

" Can your Queen have a subject's head cut off ? " asked the Khan.

" No, not without a trial before our judges—they answer to your moullahs—and then if the prisoner has committed murder, he is nearly sure to be sentenced to death, and hanged."

" Then she never has their throats cut ? "

" No."

" Hindostan is a very wonderful country," continued the Khan ; "the envoy I sent there a few years ago has told me of your railroads and telegraphs ; but the Russians have railroads too."

" Yes," I replied ; "we lent them money, and our engineers have helped to make them."

" Do the Russians pay you for this ? " he inquired.

" Yes ; so far they have behaved very honourably."

" Are there not Jews in your country like some of the Jews at Bokhara ? "

"One of the richest men in England is a Jew."

"The Russians do not take away the money from the Jews?"

"No."

The Khan here said a few words to his treasurer, and then remarked, "Why do they take money from me, then? The Russians love money very much." As he said this he shook his head sorrowfully at the treasurer, and the latter, assuming a most mournful expression, ejaculated, "Hum!" purring out this monosyllable in a doleful strain; the word "hum" having been constantly used during our conversation both by the sovereign and his nobles.

The Khan now by a low bow made me aware that the interview was over.

"I have given orders for you to be shown everything you may wish to see in my city," he observed; when saying good-bye, and thanking him for his kindness, I returned to my quarters. The people bowed down before the *cortége* as we rode back through the streets, for the news had spread that my reception had been a very gracious one.

CHAPTER XXXIII.

THE present Khan is the eleventh in succession of
the same family. He commenced his reign ten years
ago, at the death of the previous sovereign, the
khanate descending from father to son, and not to the
eldest male relative, as is the case amidst some other
Mohammedan nations. The monarch receives the
crown lands and gardens intact. With the rest of the
nation, the property at a father's death is divided equally
amongst his sons, thus doing away with the possibility
of any one possessing a large extent of the soil.

The actual Khan, after paying his annual tribute to
the Tzar, has 100,000 roubles, or about £14,000 a
year, left for himself. He has no army to maintain,
and some of the Turkoman tribes are recommencing
to pay him taxes. This they do for fear lest otherwise it might be made a pretext for a Russian advance
into their country.

The following day I rode out to visit the sovereign's
gardens, which are about three versts from the town.
He has five ; each of them is from four to five acres in

extent; they are surrounded by high walls, built of dried clay, with solid buttresses at the corners. Two large wooden gates at the entrance of the enclosure were opened by the gardener, a little swarthy man, clad in a dressing-gown of many colours, and with a long iron hoe on his shoulder. I was accompanied by the son of my host, and Nazar, when the former saying that I had the Khan's permission, the gardener stepped aside, and allowed us to enter.

The garden was remarkably well kept, and the horticultural arrangements much better than I expected to find so far from Europe. Here were to be seen long avenues of fruit-trees, carefully cut and trimmed. There men were engaged in preparing the soil, which would be thickly studded with melons in the ensuing spring. Apple, pear, and cherry-trees abounded, whilst in the centre of the ground high scaffoldings, covered with trellis-work, showed where, in summer, the vines are trained. Under their grateful shade, cool walks are formed to protect the Khan and his ladies from the burning sun.

He has a small summer palace in this garden, to which he resorts, and where he holds his court in June and July. Trenches for the purpose of irrigation are cut in all directions about the grounds, whilst frequent mulberry-trees, terminating in thick clusters of the same, are interspersed throughout the garden.

The scene must be a striking one when the Khan, surrounded by his court and officers of state, administers justice. For this takes place in the open, on a raised stone dais, which is ascended by a low flight of steps. There the delinquents are brought, and, if they do not at once confess their guilt to their lord and master, he orders them to be taken to the moullah, a learned man,

whose business it is to investigate into all such matters
The latter produces a copy of the Koran, and desires
the suspected individual to swear his innocence; if
this is done, and there are no eye-witnesses to prove the
man's guilt, he is allowed to go free. Should he perjure
himself, the Khivans believe that the vengeance of
Allah will speedily overtake him, and that the retribu-
tion will then be much greater than any punishment
which man's justice could inflict.

"But," I inquired, "are there never some wretches
amongst you who will risk the wrath of Allah, and,
perjuring themselves, be released to commit other
crimes?"

"No," was the answer. "The fear of God's vengeance is happily too great to admit of such wickedness."

"But, supposing that there are witnesses who can
prove that the person committed the crime, and he
still denies it; what do you do then?"

"Why, we beat him with rods, put salt in his mouth,
and expose him to the burning rays of the sun, until
at last he confesses, and then is punished for his
breach of the law."

After riding through the gardens which lie on the
southern side of the city, and are on the road to Merve,
we returned to Khiva, and visited the prison—a low
building on the left of the court, which forms the
entrance to the Khan's palace. Here I found two
prisoners, their feet fastened in wooden stocks, whilst
heavy iron chains encircled their necks and bodies.
They were accused of having assaulted a woman, and
two females were witnesses of the act; but as the
prisoners would not confess, they were to be kept in
confinement till they acknowledged their guilt.

On leaving the gaol, I rode to the principal school,

and found it a series of little low rooms or open niches, which enclosed a courtyard. A large fountain or basin for water had been constructed in the centre of the open space, the corners of the court being surmounted by some high domes and minarets of coloured tiles similar to those in the Khan's palace. A moullah superintends each school, and under his supervision there is a staff of other teachers. The subjects taught are reading, writing, and the Koran, pages of which are committed to memory by the pupils. The teacher squats beside the hearth in the middle of the room, whilst the boys sit around him, and learn from his lips verses of their scripture. The parents pay for their children's tuition in corn, a certain number of measures being given to the instructor in return for his labours. A crowd followed us about, and some of the people were much surprised, seeing that I wrote from left to right, instead of from right to left, as I jotted down my notes in a pocket-book.

A succession of visitors awaited us on returning to our quarters, several moullahs, who had been to Egypt and Mecca, calling to pay their respects to the Englishman, who, like themselves, spoke Arabic.

In the meantime Nazar was making preparations for a start to Bokhara. Bread had been ordered, or rather a peculiar sort of little round cake, which substitutes the so-called staff of life at Khiva. The guide had promised to accompany us, and the camel-driver was thoroughly prepared to accompany me to the end of the world so long as I gave him plenty to eat. I determined to remain one day longer, and then leave for Bokhara. This would be a twelve days' march from Khiva. From Bokhara I could go on to Merve and Meshed, where we should be in Persian territory.

I should much have liked to have remained some days longer at Khiva, but time was important. It was the 27th of January, and I was obliged to be back with my regiment on the 14th of April. However, *L'homme propose, mais, Dieu dispose;* and the truth of this celebrated old French saying was prominently brought before me the next morning, for on returning from an early ride through the market, where a great sale of camels and horses was taking place, I found two strangers in my apartment. One of them, producing a letter, handed it to me, saying that he had been sent to Khiva by order of the Commandant at Petro-Alexandrovsk.

On opening the enclosure I found a letter written in Russian on one side of the paper, and in French on the other

Its contents were to the following effect : that the Commandant had received a telegram, *viâ* Tashkent, and that I must go to the fort to receive the communication.

I was greatly surprised to find that any one took so much interest in me as to despatch a telegram so many thousand miles, and put himself to the expense of having the message forwarded from Tashkent, where the telegraph ends, to Khiva, a distance of nine hundred miles, by couriers with relays of horses. It must have cost a large sum of money sending that telegram, and I began to be a little alarmed, thinking that perhaps I should be asked to pay for it.

Again, what could have occurred of such great importance as to induce any one to telegraph? Could it be that General Milutin, the Russian Minister of War, had just remembered that I had called four times at his house, and that he had not been able to give me an interview, but that he was now prepared to grant one?

There was another solution which might also have been correct, and the thought suddenly occurred that perhaps Count Schouvaloff's brother, to whom the thoughtful* ambassador in London had so kindly given me a letter of introduction, had by this time arrived at St. Petersburg, and wished to show me some hospitality.

Anyhow, there was the letter, and I must go to Petro-Alexandrovsk to receive the telegram. It was not a pleasant thought, after having gone so far, to have possibly to return to European Russia over the snow-covered steppes. It is a hard journey even for the Tartars, this fourteen days' march, with the cold at 20° and 30° below zero, and no shelter to be met with on the road. The Tartar and Khivan merchants occasionally, it is true, make the journey in mid-winter, but invariably wait till the spring for their return to Orenburg.

I had accomplished the really hard part of my journey, and every degree marched in the direction of Merve would have led me to a warmer clime. How-ever, there was nothing to be done save to go to Petro-Alexandrovsk, and, then, if the despatch were of such a nature as to oblige me to return, to retrace my steps.

The messenger who had brought the letter was eager for my immediate return to the fort. This, I said, was out of the question till the next day, as I wished to make some purchases in the town, and must also pay a farewell visit to the Khan previous to my departure.

A little later I rode to the bazaar, accompanied by Nazar and the guide, the latter not being at all pleased at our having to go to Petro-Alexandrovsk. He was very uneasy in his own mind about the

* See page 15.

consequences which might occur to him for having brought me to Khiva.

One of the men sent with the Commandant's letter was now continually in our wake, and I subsequently learned that a strict order had been sent to the Khan to have our party followed and taken to the fort, in the event of my having left the city.

On arriving at the bazaar we were instantly surrounded by merchants, all eager to dispose of their wares. On selecting the most respectable-looking man I could see, he led me into a large room at the back of his shop. Here, after he had offered us some dried fruit and tea, as indispensable to a Khivan tradesman when bargaining with a customer as coffee to a shopkeeper in Cairo, he proceeded to a large wooden box which stood in a corner of the apartment, and unlocked it with an enormous key which hung from his girdle. The key, as it turned in the lock, gave out a peculiar hissing sound, owing to some hidden mechanism in the interior.

"Do you want something for a young or for an old woman?" asked the merchant—Nazar having previously informed him that I wished to buy some female ornaments.

"If you want it for a young wife, look how beautiful this is—she would look lovely with it;" and he handed me a large gold ring, curiously set with small pearls and turquoises.

"This would be too large for her finger," I remarked.

"Yes," replied the man; "but not for her nose. This is for her nose."

"Lovely!" said the guide. "My brother-in-law's wife has one its very counterpart; buy it."

"Sir," said Nazar, "no girl could resist you if you offered her such a present."

The whole party were much surprised when I informed them that in England we only put rings in the noses of the unclean animal.

The jewellery for sale was of a tawdry description; however, eventually I discovered a curiously-worked gold ornament, with long pendants of coral and other stones. After a great deal of haggling, Nazar succeeded in obtaining it for me at one-third of the price originally asked; the Khivan jewellers having very elastic consciences, in spite of the Prophet's injunction, that no true believer is to deceive the stranger within his gates.

On returning to my quarters I found the treasurer awaiting my arrival. He had heard the news of my enforced departure, and came to know at what time it would be convenient for me to pay my respects and say farewell to the Khan. Shortly afterwards I rode with him to the palace, when he first led the way to the treasury, and there presenting me with a dressing-gown, said that his Majesty had been pleased to beg my acceptance of this garment. It was a long robe, made of black cloth, reaching to the knees, and lined inside with silk and bright-coloured chintzes. Indeed, as I was afterwards informed, this is the highest honour that can be paid a stranger, and a halat or dressing-gown from the Khan is looked upon at Khiva much as the Order of the Garter would be in England.

The sovereign expressed his annoyance that I had to leave his capital so suddenly. He then remarked—

"You will come back again, I trust; and pray tell all Englishmen whom you may meet that I have heard from the envoy I sent to India of the greatness of their nation, and only hope that before long I shall see some of them in my capital."

He was very kind in his manner, and shook hands warmly when I took my leave; the impression being left on my mind that the Khan of Khiva is the least bigoted of all the Mohammedans whose acquaintance I have made in the course of my travels, and that the stories of his cruelties to Russian prisoners, previous to the capture of his city, are pure inventions which have been disseminated by the Russian press in order to try and justify the annexation of his territory.

Before leaving my quarters I endeavoured to persuade my host to accept a present in lieu of the handsome treatment my party and myself had received at his hands. However, this was a fruitless task; the Khivan at once declined, saying that I was the Khan's guest, and that his Majesty would be very angry if he were to learn that I had tried to requite his hospitality by giving a present to his servant. Indeed, when I made it a personal matter my attempt was equally fruitless, and I left the city slightly pained at not being able to leave behind some token or other to show how much I appreciated his kindness during my stay at Khiva.

CHAPTER XXXIV.

WE left the city by its eastern gate, and presently
passed by a building constructed with some regard to
taste, and surrounded by a number of large gardens,
all separated from each other by low walls. The house
belonged to the sovereign's brother, who, it was said,
had the intention of visiting St. Petersburg, so as personally to ask the Tzar to withdraw his troops from
the Khan's dominions.

It was a glorious bright morning, and one calculated to raise the spirits of myself and party, now very
much depressed at hearing that possibly we should
have to return to Fort Number One. Little Nazar in
particular lamented the idea of a return to the snow-
covered steppes, where there was nothing to eat, and

said that he had been obliged to take in his leather belt three holes, and that he was only just beginning to fill it out again.

The guide, too, dreaded the rod that might be in pickle for him at Petro-Alexandrovsk. I myself was suffering from a bilious attack, brought on either by eating melons, or by the letter of the Russian Commandant—bad news affecting one's digestive organs, in my opinion, quite as much as anything put into the stomach.

The road was now quite unenclosed, and a large tract of fertile country extended on all sides as far as the eye could reach. Presently we passed a small village about twelve versts from Khiva; and twenty-four versts further on, another village called Goryin, finally halting for the night at Anca. We had marched sixty versts, or forty miles, in six hours, our horses having gone all the time at a slow steady trot, the camels not reaching our halting-place till eight hours afterwards.

Anca is a large town, and has a bazaar and market, which are famous throughout the district. We had stopped at the house of the Governor, a Khivan, who had been sent by the Khan on a mission to Lord Northbrook, four years ago, just before the Russians invaded Khiva, and at the time when the Khan thought that an alliance with England would prove beneficial to his country.

The moment our host discovered that I was an Englishman, he squatted at my feet, and asked a hundred questions about India and the natives. He had heard of the Prince of Wales's visit to those regions, and in order to explain to me his own route, and what towns he had passed through on his road to Calcutta, he cut an apple in pieces. Taking one seed he placed it on the ground with the remark, "Khiva;" then for Herat he put down a second seed; whilst for Lahore and Lucknow he cut an apple into two pieces, and for Calcutta he put a large apple on the floor, endeavouring in this way to indicate to me his idea of the relative size and importance of the places which he had visited.

The soldiers in India, in his opinion, were magnificent men, with splendid uniforms. As to the Russian soldiers, they were nothing in comparison; and he spat on the ground by way of showing his contempt for the Cossacks.

"But they have a great many more soldiers than you," he remarked, "and could afford to lose as many men as you have in India, and begin again with double the original force."

"But the Russians like us," I said. "Their Emperor is a man of peace; and many people in my country say that it will be a good thing for India when she has a civilised neighbour on our frontier, instead of the Afghans."

The Khivan's face swelled with suppressed mirth, which he thought that it would be indecorous to give vent to, but checking his laughter as best he could, he merely said—

"If they like you so much, why do they prevent your goods coming here? Indian teas are either forbidden altogether, or have a prohibitory duty placed upon them; and I have often heard it said that if an Englishman were to go from India to Russia, he would be killed by the Russians, and that they would say we had done it, in order to stir up an ill feeling against us."

We started early the next morning, and rode across the Amou Darya at a spot about thirteen miles from Anca, and where the stream was nearly two versts wide; the ice being in some places more than a foot thick. Presently we passed by a Cossack cavalry station, called Lager. Here, in spite of the inclemency of the season, three squadrons were picketed out in the open, the horses having coats like bears, and looking exceedingly well, in spite of their exposure to the extreme cold.

We were now approaching Petro-Alexandrovsk, and a few dark spots on the distant horizon were pointed out to us as the recently erected fort. The emissary who had brought me the Commandant's letter spurred his horse forward, leaving his companion with my party and self. "He has only gone on to say that you are coming," was the reply to my inquiry, and a few minutes later we rode into Petro-Alexandrovsk. It has been built on the site of a house and garden, which formerly belonged to the uncle of the Khan of Khiva, the materials of his house having been used in constructing the wall which has been erected round the fort.

A clean-looking, well-built house stood in a small open space in the centre of the enclosure. A flagstaff at one end of the dwelling, and two sentries walking up and down in front of the doors, made me think that this was probably the house of the chief of the Amou Darya district. My guide, who was each moment more alarmed at the possible consequences to himself for his having taken us to Khiva, now informed us that here lived the celebrated Colonel Ivanoff.

The Commandant was out hunting, so a servant informed me. At that moment a young officer coming up accosted me by my name, and said, "We expected you before this. Come with me. There is a room prepared;" and he led the way to a small building inhabited by some of the officers in the garrison. Here I found several of them congregated in a small room, and was introduced in due form by my newly-made acquaintance. I then heard that the telegram which had arrived for me was from H.R.H. the Duke of Cambridge, the Field-Marshal Commanding in Chief, and that he required my immediate return to European Russia. The document had been waiting for me several days at the fort, and, in the event of my having gone first to Petro-Alexandrovsk, I should never have seen Khiva.

A little later an officer brought a message from Colonel Ivanoff, to say that he had returned from shooting and was waiting to see me. He is a tall man, considerably over six feet in height, but very thin, and of a German type, his whiskers having a decided Teutonic appearance. I was received by him at first a little stiffly, but his demeanour soon changed, and he began to laugh about my journey.

"Too bad," he said, "letting you get so far, and not allowing you to carry out your undertaking."

"It was lucky," I remarked, "that I did not come here first."

"Yes," said Ivanoff; "when I received the despatch, and found that you did not arrive, I sent back a special Tartar courier to Fort Number One, to say that you had probably gone on to Bokhara, and had thus given us the slip; but we should have caught you there," he continued.

"It is the fortune of war," I said. "Anyhow, I have seen Khiva."

The Colonel here winced a little.

"Khiva; that is nothing," he said. "Why, Major Wood, one of your compatriots, an officer in the Engineers, was here last summer; he could have gone to Khiva any day if he liked; indeed, I was a little surprised that he never asked me to let him go there."*

"Well," I remarked, "as I have to return to European Russia, there can be no objection to my going to St. Petersburg *viâ* Tashkent and Western Siberia, or by Krasnovodsk and the Caspian."

"My orders are very strict about this," said the Colonel. "You must go back the shortest way through Kasala. But you can write if you like to General Kolpakovsky, the officer commanding our troops in Turkistan: I will send on the letter with the same courier who leaves this afternoon to announce your capture; and then, if you return to Kasala in the course of three or four days' time, you will there receive the General's answer."

I dined at Ivanoff's that evening, and had the pleasure of making the acquaintance of the officers on his personal staff. They were all of them intelligent men, and, to my surprise, very abstemious, which is indeed a rare quality amidst the officers in European Russia.

---

* Apparently there was a slight misunderstanding between Major Wood and Colonel Ivanoff on this point, or possibly the atmosphere of Central Asia has somewhat affected the Colonel's memory. After my return to London from Khiva, I dined one evening with Major Wood, and asked him why he had not gone to Khiva. His reply was, "I wanted to go there very much; I frequently asked Ivanoff to let me, saying that it was a great nuisance to have come so far and not be allowed to enter the town. However, Ivanoff replied that he was very sorry, but he could not allow me to do so, as he had received a strict order from General Kauffmann on that subject."

We talked for a long time about England and Russia, the general tone of conversation being that England and Russia ought to be on the most friendly terms, but that our interests were so diametrically opposite that it would be impossible, sooner or later, to avoid a collision.

With reference to Merve, the Colonel remarked that he could take it at any time, provided his Government would allow him to do so, whilst he said that the fortress he would then build there would be a great deal stronger than the one at Petro-Alexandrovsk.

"In fact," he added, "here we hardly require a fort. You see it only consists of a low earthen parapet. The Khivans are quiet people, they do not give us any trouble, and they pay their tribute very regularly. The Turkomans, however, are quite another race; they were perpetually quarrelling with our Kirghiz. However, a few months since I caught an armed band, which had crossed the Oxus; I ordered two of my captives to be tried by court-martial, and afterwards had them hanged. Since then the Turkomans have been very quiet. However, they have got one of my soldiers a prisoner at Merve."

"Have they not tried him by court-martial and hanged him?" I inquired.

"No; but they want me to pay a ransom for him. The fellow has told them that he is an officer. In consequence of this they ask an exorbitant sum; any-how, I shall not grant it."

"We should have no difficulty whatever in taking Merve," observed another officer. "People talk of the difficulty of getting there; why, our Cossacks could be at Merve in a week if the Government would only allow us."

" It is too bad," continued a third; " our comrades at Tashkent and Kokan are getting all the rewards and decorations, and here we are doing nothing. When I came to Petro-Alexandrovsk I thought that it would lead to something."

The Colonel, it appeared, had risen very rapidly in the service; he was only thirty-two, and now commanded 3,000 men, whilst 1,000 of the Cossacks from Uralsk were shortly expected. They would make up the strength of the troops in the Amou Darya division of the Turkistan district to about 4,000 strong. The head-quarters were at Petro-Alexandrovsk, whilst detachments had been stationed at Lager and Nookoos, a small fort about eighty miles from Petro-Alexandrovsk, and on the right bank of the Oxus.

It was said that Ivanoff would shortly receive his promotion, and be made a general, which probably would take place when Kauffmann returned from St. Petersburg.

A newspaper was brought in later on in the evening. It was the *Russian World*, and it contained an article about the large number of German officers in high position in the Russian army, a number out of all proportion with the population of the Baltic Provinces, as compared with the rest of the empire.

It was easy to see, from the remarks which were freely passed, that not much love was lost between the officers in the garrison and the Germans, Ivanoff himself, in spite of his Teuton appearance, being very anti-Prussian, in which feeling he was joined by almost every officer in the garrison. Indeed, during my journey through Russia I was struck by the marked hostility shown by all classes to the Austrians and Germans, the conduct of the former Power during the Crimean war having left a very bitter feeling behind it, which is strengthened by the supposed antagonistic views of the two Governments with reference to Constantinople.

The Russian officers were unanimous in saying that the new military system in Russia was as yet in a state of transition, and that they were not prepared for war with so great a Power as Germany; the general remark being that if they could only have peace for five more years, that then Russia would be able to show her teeth.

As to Austria, she was spoken of in terms of great contempt, and alluded to as if she only held her place in Europe by reason of the sufferance of the Emperors Alexander and William; the Austrian army being looked down upon by the Russian officers.

However, I cannot help thinking that the latter will find out their mistake when the day arrives for them to attempt an invasion of Francis Joseph's dominions. Austria has profited by her defeat at Sadowa. Her officers and men are now as intelligent and capable as those of any army in Europe, whilst, though her exchequer is at a low ebb, it is really in not so bad a state as that of her neighbour, whose reckless borrowing to pay the interest of former loans is very likely to ultimately produce a national bankruptcy.

There were about thirty ladies in Petro-Alexandrovsk. These were the wives and daughters of the officers in the garrison; and once a week a dance was held at a club-house which had been recently built.

The ladies had reached the fort, having performed the journey in the summer months by the Syr Darya, the Sea of Aral, and Amou Darya (Oxus), in the steamers which ply between Tashkent and Petro-Alexandrovsk. The latter was a dull quarter, and the fair sex had done their best to enliven it by establishing this weekly dance. Colonel Ivanoff very kindly gave me an invitation for the one which was to be held the next evening, and I was told that the following day there would be some coursing with greyhounds and hawks, one of the chief diversions in Central Asia

CHAPTER XXXV.

THE following morning, after a hurried breakfast, an officer came and informed us that everything was ready for a start. I now mounted a little bay horse which, though hardly fourteen hands, danced about beneath me as if he had been carrying a feather-weight jockey for the Cambridgeshire.

There were horses and men of all kinds and shapes, long-legged men on short-legged horses, and short-legged men on giant Turkoman steeds. All the officers were in uniform, and some Bokharan and Kirghiz sportsmen, attired in crimson dressing-gowns, rode in the rear of our cavalcade.

Seven or eight greyhounds were led in couples behind the master of the hunt, a stout colonel, who was said to understand the ways and haunts of timid puss better than any other officer in the garrison ; and a stoutly-built Khivan, who rode a fine-looking chestnut, bore upon his elbow a graceful falcon, which, now hooded, was destined later on to play its part in the day's sport.

The Kirghiz made the welkin ring with their yells. Immense excitement prevailed. All the dogs in the

fort, attracted by the noise and commotion, were col-
lected round the *cortége*.

The hunting-ground was about eight miles distant,
and away we rode at a rattling pace ; the gallop to
cover being considered as part of the day's entertainment.

The country lay open and flat before. There was
not an obstacle to check our course, save now and
then a dyke, some eight feet wide, which the horses
took in fair style; the Kirghiz and Bokharans looking
back to see how the animal I bestrode would jump
with his heavy rider. Never a stumble, however, and
the hardy little beast could have carried Daniel Lam-
bert himself, if that worthy but obese gentleman had
been resuscitated for the occasion. Now a Bokharan
would race by me with a wild cry, and lash a flagging
mongrel, which, mingling with our pack, and soon outstripped by his fleeter brethren, had crossed the riders'
path.

All of a sudden the master pulled up his panting
steed, and, dismounting, told us that we had reached
the cover.

A narrow tract of bush and bramble-covered ground
was extended right and left of our party, whilst over
the low brushwood was seen a broad crystal streak,
like a Venetian mirror set in a frame of frosted silver.
The Oxus lay before us. The flakes of snow which
covered the banks and surrounding country marked
its breadth from shore to shore.

We now formed one long line, each horseman being
twenty yards apart from his fellow, and in this order
rode through the reeds and brambles.

Presently a wild shout from a red-gowned Kirghiz
announced that a hare had broken cover, and Russians,

Cossacks, Kirghiz, and self galloped in pursuit of the startled quarry. Straight at the river went the frightened animal, and after it, in hot pursuit, our heterogeneous pack. Down the bank our horses slid rather than scrambled, and across the river we raced, each man vieing with his neighbour. Half a mile from the farther shore lay another dense copse, and it seemed as if the greyhounds would be distanced in the chase.

But the rider who bore the falcon now launched his bird into the air. Another second and the hawk was perched on its victim's back, whilst the well-trained greyhounds, surrounding their prey, stood open-mouthed, with lolling tongues, not daring to approach the quarry.

The master now galloped up, and, dismounting, took possession of the hare, when, in a few minutes more, we were again in full cry. Five hares eventually rewarded our exertions, and then, after a headlong burst homewards, I found myself again within the precincts of the fort.

In the evening I went to the assembly-rooms. Here each week a dance is held, but on other days the building is used as a club by the officers of the garrison. A long but narrow room, the wooden floor of which had been brought from European Russia, was arranged for the ball ; an adjacent apartment was furnished with a well-spread supper-table, whilst a quantity of small tables, laden with bottles of the sweetest of champagne and bordeaux, were already occupied by some officers.

A brass band belonging to one of the regiments of the garrison was playing an inspiriting quadrille ; the Russians not dancing it as in England, but each man, first securing chairs for himself and partner, remains seated beside his lady until the moment arrives for them to take their turn in the figure. The last part of the dance, too, is different to anything ever seen in this country. London society would find itself singularly puzzled if invited to participate in a Russian quadrille.

Now the musicians struck up a valse, and round went the giddy couples; but the moments of bliss experienced by the cavalier are brief, for he is not allowed to dance the valse through with his partner; after taking one turn she leaves him, and in another instant is whirling round, encircled by the arms of a second cavalier, who in his turn gives way to a third.

Later on a mazurka was danced, not as we see it in this country, but with stately figures, accompanied by the jingling of spurs, each cavalier stamping lightly with his armed heel, and joining in the cadence of the music; the varied uniforms of the Cossacks and other officers lighting up the room, and making it difficult for me to realise that we were in Central Asia, and in the lately conquered Khivan territory.

I had despatched a letter to General Kolpakovsky, the Governor-General of Turkistan during Kauffmann's absence from his command. Colonel Ivanoff now informed me that two officers, with a Cossack escort, were about to march to Kasala. He also said that it would be as well if I were to accompany the party, and receive at Fort Number One the answer to my request to be permitted to return to St. Petersburg by Tashkent and Western Siberia, instead of by Orenburg.

Some theatricals had been arranged for that evening, with soldiers as actors. After dinner I went with Ivanoff and his staff to witness the performance. The majority of the spectators consisted of Cossacks and Kirghiz; the latter were not able to understand the language of the actors, but eagerly followed their gestures, and were highly delighted with the frequent pistol-shots and clashing of sabres which accompanied each act, the principal character in the piece being a robber chief. The performance ended by his capture and execution, the actor personifying the robber being brought on the stage. This man, who was an acrobat, inserted his feet into the noose of a rope, and was suspended by his heels, the executioner firing off a pistol in the air as a sign of the prisoner's dissolution. A plate was on a table by the door, and each officer on leaving put in a few roubles to reward the performers for their trouble.

I had a conversation with the colonel the next evening about the respective merits of the Kirghiz and English horses; and I left the good-natured officer in considerable doubt as to my veracity, neither his staff nor himself being able to believe that any English horse had ever jumped thirty-six feet in breadth; whilst Osbaldestone's feat of riding 200 miles in eight hours and a half was in their eyes nothing in comparison to the leap above mentioned.

People in Central Asia cannot be supposed to be so *au fait* with what goes on in the world as we denizens of the West, and I eventually succeeded in obtaining a certain amount of credence, by saying that no one in the room could tie me with a rope in such a manner that I could not free myself. An Artillery officer now stepped forward, and wished my assertion to be put to the proof. This was done, and the result disconcerted the audience, as the time I took in escaping from my bonds was not half so long as the officer had taken in tying me.

The following morning the Khan's treasurer arrived,

bringing with him several thousand roubles as an instalment of the war indemnity. He breakfasted with Ivanoff, and managed to eat his food with a knife and fork, though the management of the latter article appeared to give him a good deal of trouble.

In spite of his Mussulman creed the treasurer had a taste for champagne, which his sovereign also appreciates. A few dozens of this wine is frequently sent to Khiva from the fort; the scruples of the Khan having been allayed by the information that champagne was not known to the prophet, and that consequently he could not have laid down any law prohibiting its use.

Shortly before the arrival of the treasurer, an envoy from the Ameer of Bokhara had been at Petro-Alexandrovsk. There had been a misunderstanding about some nomad Kirghiz, who, it was said, used to cross the frontier and enter Bokharan territory when the Russian officials were about to collect the taxes. Some correspondence on this subject had ensued between the Ameer and General Kauffmann. The former, by all accounts, was not a very enlightened ruler, and it was said of him that on one occasion he sent to a Russian officer, who had been seen looking at the moon through a telescope, and inquired what it was he could see there. "Mountains and extinct volcanoes," was the answer. "Dear me!" said the Ameer, "how very curious. Pray, who is the Khan in the moon? I should like to make his acquaintance."

Whilst talking about Bokhara, an officer remarked that a Russian and German scientific expedition was about to visit that city, and subsequently survey the country between Samarcand and Peshawur; a railway to Central Asia being absolutely necessary for the purpose of quickly concentrating troops, should it be required. " To our next meeting !" suddenly observed a young officer, pledging me in a glass of champagne. "Where will it be ? " "Who knows ?" said another ; " I suppose sooner or later we shall meet on the battle-field." In fact, almost every officer I met in Central Asia was of opinion that ere long a collision would take place between themselves and our troops in India, the general remark being, " It is a great pity, but our interests clash, and though capital friends as individuals, the question as to who is to be master in the East must soon be decided by the sword."

In spite of General Kauffmann's dislike to foreigners travelling in Turkistan, a Prussian officer had been permitted to enter a Russian regiment, and was serving at Petro-Alexandrovsk. He had been all through the Franco-German War, where he had distinguished himself. Subsequently, however, to this, he persuaded one of the Tzar's German relatives to ask the Emperor to give him a commission in a regiment in Turkistan. In the course of conversation, I found that he had been educated at the same establishment as myself in Germany, and consequently knew several of my friends. The Russian officers spoke very highly of his military capacity, though many of them remarked that it was a great mistake, allowing him to serve with them, as he would know too much, should war break out between Germany and themselves, when of course he would return to the Fatherland. It must at first have been somewhat disagreeable for this young German officer, being thus thrown in constant contact with a body of officers who, to a man, detested his nationality.

I was now busy with Nazar making preparations for our return march to Orenburg, and laying in a supply of provisions for the journey. I had purchased two dozen pheasants, these birds being found in great profusion in Khiva, where they can be bought for five-pence each.

My little Tartar had a doleful expression on his countenance, and on inquiry I found that he was living with Ivanoff's soldier servants, and that they sold their own rations and lived principally upon fish, which could be purchased for a mere song at Petro. Nazar had found that this diet did not agree with him. He was too stingy to spend some extra money I had allowed him as board wages, and preferred to mess at the expense of the servants. The latter protected themselves by not letting him know the dinner-hour, and only calling him when nothing was left of their repast save bones.

" Look here ! " said my servant, " I'm a skeleton."

"Why do you not buy something with your board wages ? " I inquired.

" Buy ! " he replied, much surprised at my question, " I'm not such a fool as to buy so long as I can get anything to eat without paying for it ; but they are greedy, those dogs of servants, sons of animals that they are;" and the little man walked away not at all pleased with the hospitality of his *confrères* in the kitchen.

I was now introduced to the two officers who were to accompany me to Fort Number One. One of them, Captain Yanusheff, was an Artillery officer, who had distinguished himself in the Khivan expedition, and he now commanded the entire Artillery force in the Amou Darya district. He was going to Kasala to buy some remount horses from the Kirghiz. His companion was a Cossack *Saül* or Captain ; he was returning to

Tashkent to join his squadron. These two officers would take with them an escort of ten Cossacks, and the start was arranged for the following morning. The weather had become much warmer; indeed, when that afternoon we rode over to Shurahan, a Khivan town which has been annexed to Russia, our road lay no longer over snow, but over sand. According to all accounts the ice on the Oxus would soon begin to melt. My companions, who did not fancy a ride to Kasala, determined to take advantage of this change in the weather, and travel in a tarantass drawn by horses, until they should arrive at a place where snow had fallen; the horses could then be sent back, and camels be harnessed in their stead.

CHAPTER XXXVI.

OUR start the following morning was a curious sight to witness. First came the tarantass, an extraordinary vehicle peculiar to Russia. It resembled a hansom cab without the wheels, and the carriage then fastened in a brewer's dray.

There were no springs of any kind to prevent jolt-ing, whilst some small but very solid wooden wheels supported the body of the cart. Harness made of cables was attached to six Kirghiz horses, whose united efforts could barely move the vehicle more than five miles an hour. Several officers of the garrison accompanied their comrades for a mile or so, and then wished them "God speed" on their journey, which, in spite of the change in the weather, was looked upon as anything but a light undertaking. Soon after leaving the fort we came to a large village. Here we found several ladies ; amongst others, the wife of the Artillery officer, who had come to say farewell to her husband. Champagne and bottles of vodki were lying on the ground, and a bonfire had been lit, by which the ladies sat warming their feet.

The last adieux had been said. Yanusheff had torn

himself away from his fond surroundings, and we were once more *en route*. In a few hours or so we came again upon the snow. It covered the ground so thickly that the horses in the tarantass had to be taken out, and a couple of camels harnessed in their place.

In the meantime I had ridden on with my guide and Nazar. Presently we halted by the ruins of an old castle, which had been built by one of the Khan's ancestors to defend his country against a Russian invasion.

After waiting some time for the tarantass, which did not arrive, we continued the journey, hoping to encounter our baggage camels, which had been sent forward the previous day with the Cossacks. After marching for another hour we stopped at a well, about forty miles from Petro-Alexandrovsk. It was bitterly cold, there was a great deal of wind, nothing to eat, and what was worse, the brambles and brushwood were too damp to make a fire. "What had become of our baggage camels?" was the question each man put to his neighbour; "had we passed them in the dark, or were they still in front of us?"

It was useless going on or going back, and the only thing to do was to sit it out and persuade ourselves that we were neither cold nor hungry. Imagination is a wonderful thing, but it has its limits, and the more I tried to persuade myself that I had just dined, the more I thought of the fleshpots of Egypt and all their accompaniments, while visions of turtle soup and champagne came floating up before me, and sharpened afresh the keen edge of a ravenous appetite. The guide cursed his fate, and to cheer up his spirits commenced singing a ditty about the beauties of a sheep and the delights of roast mutton. However, the night sped by, and lying down on the snow we got what sleep we could, till at daybreak we were joined by the officers in the tarantass.

My fellow-travellers, who had slept in the carriage, and were provided with thick furs, had passed the night a little less uncomfortably than ourselves, although they too cursed the cold in no very measured terms.

Soon afterwards we came up with the Cossacks and baggage camels, the escort having bivouacked a few versts beyond the well.

The Artillery captain ordered his driver to stop, and getting out of the vehicle, proposed that we should have breakfast.

Presently he produced from the boot in the tarantass a square tin box, with a large cork inserted in one of its sides. The vessel contained about four gallons of the strongest vodki. He then took a beaker, which held about half a pint, and called out, "Children, come here!"

The Cossacks, who were looking on at the operation with great interest, ran up; my companion, filling the measure, gave each man in turn a dram. This the soldiers tossed off at one gulp, and then returned to their horses. I tasted some of the vodki, which was more like liquid fire than anything else to which it can be likened, and spirits of wine or naphtha would have been a cooling draught in comparison. However, the Artillery captain had no intention of testing the strength of the Cossacks' fire-water. His servant, bringing up some bottles of madeira, and vodki of another quality, poured us out a less potent stimulant, which, in the keen air we were then breathing, was not unpalatable, though in England two or three glasses of the mixture would have put most men under the table.

The Cossacks were fine well-built fellows, averaging about eleven stone in weight. Their marching weight was over eighteen stone, this including twenty pounds of barley for their horses (barley being preferred to oats in those parts), and six pounds of biscuits, a sufficient ration for a man for four days. For arms they carried short breechloading rifles and swords, and they were shortly to be supplied with the Berdan carbine, which is spoken of very highly by the Russian officers.

The Cossacks do not receive much pay—about four shillings every third of a year, or a shilling a month, being all a man has for pocket-money. However, they are well fed and clothed. The daily ration is two and a half pounds of flour and one pound of meat; one hundred soldiers receiving one pound of tea and three pounds of sugar per diem, whilst each man is credited with half a kopeck a day for vegetables. His horse, uniform, arms, &c., are his own property, or the property of the district which has equipped him, and sent him forth to fight for the White Tzar. He receives about two pounds fifteen shillings a year from the State, and is obliged to keep his kit in repair with this sum, which the military authorities say is sufficient for the purpose, although the soldiers are of a different opinion.

These data were given me by the Artillery captain, who, leaving his companion asleep in the tarantass, occasionally stretched his legs by walking a few versts over the snow. He had seen a good deal of service in

Turkistan, and expected very shortly to obtain his promotion. Amongst other things, he told me that when Russia was at war with Bokhara, a Cossack officer was taken prisoner. The Ameer sent for him, and asked if he could make powder. He said, " Yes, but not for them." On their asking why, he declared that it was manufactured with brandy and pigs' fat, and that this made the powder so strong. " The Ameer," continued my companion, " regards the Sultan with feelings of the greatest veneration, and has the honorary title of Grand Officer to the Porte. He used to look upon England as the first nation in the world, but he is beginning to fear us now, and he believes more in our troops, who are close at hand, than in those of the Sultan at Stamboul."

It was getting late, and Yanusheff gave strict orders to the sentry who was posted over the horses to awake him an hour after midnight. The man, however, neglected his duty, and was punished by having to walk the whole of the next day and lead his horse, the culprit being much laughed at by the other Cossacks, who look down upon all foot-soldiers with supreme contempt.

It was a picturesque sight, the march from this encampment. First, the Cossacks, the barrels of their carbines gleaming in the moonlight, the vashlik of a conical shape surmounting each man's low cap, and giving a ghastly appearance to the riders. Their distorted shadows were reflected on the snow beneath, and appeared like a detachment of gigantic phantoms pursuing our little force. Then the tarantass, drawn by two huge camels, which slowly ploughed their way through the heavy track, the driver nodding on his box but half awake, the two officers in the arms of Morpheus inside, and the heavy woodwork creaking at each stride of the enormous quadrupeds. In the wake of this vehicle strode the baggage camels. The officers' servants were fast asleep on the backs of their animals, one man lying with his face to the tail, and snoring hard in spite of the continued movement; another fellow lay stretched across his saddle, apparently a good deal the worse for drink. He shouted out at intervals the strains of a Bacchanalian ditty. Nazar, who was always hungry, could be seen walking in the rear. He had kept back a bone from the evening meal, and was gnawing it like a dog, his strong jaws snapping as they closed on the fibrous mutton.

I generally remained by our bivouac fire an hour or so after the rest of the party had marched, and seated by the side of the glowing embers, watched the caravan as it vanished slowly in the distance.

My guide was utterly crestfallen; he had been severely reprimanded at the fort for taking me to Khiva, and was now kept in such order by the Cossacks, that his usual air of importance had entirely disappeared.

Yanusheff had already given his camel-driver an idea of discipline. The man had been very dilatory in saddling the camels. My companion, observing this, called a Cossack, and ordered him to beat the refractory individual. Seeing, however, that the whipping was not sufficiently severe, the captain took the knout from him, and with his own hand administered the chastisement, at the same time telling the soldier that if this occurred again, he should order him to be beaten by his own comrades for not carrying out orders properly.

We now arrived at a spot on the road where the snow was so deep that the camels were unable to draw the vehicle. In this dilemma the Cossacks proved useful; for attaching some lassoes to the tarantass, and spurring their horses, they succeeded in dragging it slowly forwards. At this place we met a Kirghiz who was taking the post to Petro-Alexandrovsk. He rode one horse and led another, carrying his letters, food, and forage on the spare animal. The man, however, would change his horses every two or three hours, and expected to arrive at Petro-Alexandrovsk in about ten days from the time he had left Perovsky, the next fort the Russians hold on the Orenburg and Tashkent line, after passing Kasala.

On the following day we rode by an old Kirghiz chapel, built in memory of some celebrated warrior. It was used in summer time for praying, and in winter as a sheep-pen, the Kirghiz being indifferent about such matters. Finally we arrived at a landmark known as being seventeen miles from Kasala.

Yanusheff and I determined to let the camels follow us, and to gallop on ourselves ahead of the caravan. The Cossack officer resolved to do the same. My companions selected the best horses they could find from amidst the escort, at the same time ordering the dismounted Cossacks to ride the camels. The snow still slightly covered the ground, but not enough to stop our animals, which, probably knowing that they were close to home, raced against each other the whole way. We galloped across the frozen surface of the Syr Darya, and pulled up at Morozoff's hostelry at twelve o'clock mid-day, February 12th.

We had ridden 371 miles in exactly nine days and two hours, thus averaging more than 40 miles a day! At the same time it must be remembered, that with an interval of in all not more than nine days' rest, my horse had previously carried me 500 miles. In London, judging by his size, he would have been put down as a polo pony. In spite of the twenty stone he carried he had never been either sick or lame during the journey, and had galloped the last seventeen miles through the snow to Kasala in one hour and twenty-five minutes.

A room was unoccupied at the inn. It was not a very luxurious apartment, the furniture consisting of a rickety table, a few chairs, and a wooden sofa or divan; however, it was like Mohammed's seventh heaven after the steppes.

A young officer who was residing at the inn now entered the room, and told me all that occurred since my departure. There had been a duel, in which several officers had participated, and he had been under arrest in consequence.

An *emeute* had taken place amongst the Uralsk Cossacks. It appeared that the 2,000 exiles had become very discontented at the way in which they had been treated, and from grumbling had proceeded to threats; some of them had been overheard, and it was said that a few of the malcontents had expressed a wish to cut the throats of all the officers in the fort. As the Uralsk Cossacks outnumbered the garrison, and the officers slept in private lodgings and not in barracks, it was perfectly possible that the exiles might be able to carry their threat into execution. For several nights each officer had a guard stationed round his quarters. The District Governor had reported the affair to the Governor-General at Tashkent. The latter officer had despatched one of his subordinate generals, with full powers of life and death, to investigate the matter, and report said that several of the malcontents were to be shot.

Amongst the many rumours which were rife at Kasala, was one to the effect that the Tzarevitch would probably visit Tashkent in the course of the summer, when he would perhaps join in an expedition to be despatched against Kashgar. It was remarked that a campaign against Yakoob Bek would afford the Prince a capital opportunity for winning his Cross of St. George, a military order which must be won on the field of battle, and which the Tzar wears.

In confirmation of the rumours of a summer campaign, it was stated that a division of 10,000 men from the Orenburg district was now on the march to Tashkent. This was a source of annoyance to some of the officers in Turkistan, who did not like the idea of the field for gaining crosses and promotion being too much enlarged. In their opinion the forces in Central Asia were ample for any expedition that might be despatched against Yakoob Bek.

CHAPTER XXXVII.

I now called upon the District Governor, and found him at home, surrounded by a bevy of officers in full uniform. He told me that a Cossack colonel had recently died of consumption, and that the funeral ceremony was then going on inside the church. The men of the regiment were all mounted, and drawn up facing the holy edifice. The cold was very great, and the troops had every facility afforded them for sowing the seeds of their colonel's malady. Indeed, the frost was so severe that the District Governor and his friends had found it inconvenient to remain inside the church, and had returned to drink tea at home, until such time as the service was concluded.

Amongst the guests was a naval officer who had frequently cruised in the Sea of Aral; he said that there was an island in it which was forty miles round, and that no fresh water could be discovered, although antelopes and foxes abounded. Some sheep had been turned out on the island a year previous, but since that time no one had seen them. According to my informant, there were hardly any rocks in the Sea of Aral, and navigation was not at all dangerous.

The possibility of gaining the Amou Darya and Syr Darya, by means of the Jana Darya, was next discussed ; but most of the officers seemed to think that in this case there would be too little water left in the Syr Darya for the steamers to pass from Orenburg to Tashkent.

When I had the opportunity of speaking privately to the Governor, I inquired if he had received any communication with reference to the letter which I had despatched from Petro-Alexandrovsk to the Commander-in-Chief at Tashkent, in which letter I had asked to be allowed to return to European Russia *via* Western Siberia. However, the Fates were unpropitious; no reply had been sent, and I had to return to the inn without any knowledge as to what would be my next movements.

My quarters at Morozoff's were not quite what a Sybarite would have selected, unless like myself he had been confined to Hobson's choice. The pipes of the stove were out of order, and if it were heated, there was an escape of charcoal-gas into the room I inhabited, a frightful headache being the consequence.

If, on the contrary, I desired the servant not to light the stove, furs had to be worn day and night to keep out the cold.

The waiter was the most phlegmatic of his species.

When I complained of the gas he never moved a muscle of his countenance, but simply observed—

"One of noble birth, at Morozoff's it is always so." If I upbraided him on account of the cold he returned a similar answer.

Yanusheff now came to say good-bye ; he had not

been able to find any good artillery horses at Kasala. He intended to start the following morning for a large village in the neighbourhood of Perovsky, and visit the Sultan of the district, a Kirghiz chief, who owned 1,500 horses.

Yanusheff was going to dine out on that evening, and as he had a large sum of money which he had brought to purchase the necessary animals, and did not care to carry it about with him, he asked me to take care of his roubles until he returned from dinner. I could not help remarking that he was placing a singular amount of confidence in a stranger, particularly as there were several Russian officers at the inn; but I agreed to take charge of the money, as he said he preferred leaving it in my care.

The following morning I saw my fellow traveller for a moment, and returned him the packet. He was in his sleigh, *en route* for Perovsky, and we cordially shook hands. I parted from him with regret; he was an agreeable companion, besides being a well-read and highly intelligent man.

A little later in the day I received a letter from General Kolpakovsky. It was to this effect: that as I had received orders to return immediately to European Russia, he could not sanction my proposed journey *viâ* Tashkent and Western Siberia, for this would not be the shortest route; and that the permission which I had received from General Milutin to travel in Russian Asia had been cancelled. Presuming that the reasons given would convince me of the necessity of my immediate return to European Russia by the postal road to Orenburg, he asked me to believe in his complete respect, and had the honour of being, &c. &c.

The letter was very conclusive, and there was

nothing to be done save to pack up my traps, order horses, and start for Orenburg.

The District Governor now called. He had also received a letter, insisting on my immediate departure from Kasala. Although it was a holiday, and all the official departments were closed, he said that he would at once send to get me a podorojnaya (a road pass).

I wanted to change some gold before I started on my journey. A Bokharan offered to take a few of the Russian half-imperial pieces, but on looking at them he refused to give the same value for all the coins, as some of them were three and four years old, and this, in his opinion, deteriorated their value. I eventually disposed of my half-imperials, and also of a few English sovereigns, to the District Governor. These were looked upon as a curiosity by the Russian officers in Central Asia, and whenever it became known that I possessed some, everybody was eager to change them for me.

The sleigh was packed; the horses were prancing at the door; I had paid my bill and sold my horses, &c. My little black had not been a dear purchase. I bought him for forty roubles (about five pounds), and had sold him for three pounds ten shillings. He had carried me nearly 900 miles, and I had no reason to complain of my bargain.

Getting into the coffin-like sleigh, I said farewell to my friends. A wild huzzah from the Tartar driver to stimulate his horses, accompanied by a stinging reminder from his whip, and we were off.

Later on I met a Jew and a Greek, who were going to Tashkent. The latter, when I inquired how he had obtained permission to travel in Central Asia, told me that on arriving in Russia he had a Greek passport, but after a little while he managed to procure a Russian one, and was then permitted to cross the Ural. The Jew was a Russian subject, so of course no difficulties had been thrown in his way.

There is a great deal of sympathy between the Russians and Greeks, probably owing to the hatred these Powers bear the Porte, and to their similarity in religion. The character of the inhabitants of both these countries is also strongly marked with Oriental peculiarities; the Russian being of a highly suspicious nature. The Greek is equally suspicious, but he has more brains, and is sure to get the best of the Muscovite in a bargain.

On arriving at another station the inspector informed me that a rich young Kirghiz widow was in the waiting-room. He wished to know whether I had any objection to her presence, as some Russian travellers disliked the natives sharing the same apartment with them. To this I replied by sending the lady a formal invitation through Nazar, who was desired to say that an English traveller had heard of her presence in the station, and hoped that she would drink tea with him.

Nazar departed with a broad grin on his countenance, this attention on my part to the young widow of the steppes striking him as rather remarkable. "One of noble blood," he remarked, as he quitted the room, "you cannot marry her; she is of a different religion." Presently he returned, leading in a decidedly good-looking and prepossessing girl, apparently about eighteen years of age. She was clad in a long grey dressing-gown, her tiny feet being encased in Chinese slippers; and her head covered with many yards of white silk, worn in the form of a turban.

On my offering her a chair, she sat down, and by the means of Nazar we speedily commenced a conversation.

There are a good many ways of telling a woman she is pretty, but it is always difficult to do so through a third party; and the compliments which I paid her in Russian I have no doubt lost considerably in being translated into Tartar, though Nazar assured me that the expressions he selected were the most poetical with which he was acquainted.

As, however, his ideas of poetry were like my late guide's, limited to songs about the beauty of a sheep, and the delights of roast mutton, I fear that when he was desired to tell her that she was the most beautiful of her sex, Nazar translated it as follows :—

He says " that thou art lovelier than a sheep with a fat tail "—this appendage being a great delicacy amongst the Tartars—" that thy face is the roundest in the flock, and that thy breath is sweeter to him than many pieces of mutton roasted over bright embers."

On Nazar informing her that I was not married she was a little astonished, and then observed that she was not married, but would be so in two years' time.

It appeared that, according to the laws of her tribe, she must become the wife of her late husband's brother. The latter was only twelve years of age, and she would have to wait till the boy was fourteen before the marriage could take place. The lady did not much like the idea of so young a husband, and was curious to know how widows managed in my country, being very much surprised when I told her that they chose for themselves.

A few hours sped away very agreeably as I was chatting with the fair widow, when her future husband, a chubby-faced lad, entered the room, and announced that the camels were ready, and that it was time for them to start for their *aúl*.

On receiving this information she gave the boy a sharp stroke across the shoulder, but left the room; and the future husband will doubtless get many a whipping from her previous to their marriage, which he will probably pay back with interest at some later period.

On nearing Orsk I learnt from an inspector that 800 Cossacks had already left Orenburg, and were on their way to Tashkent. He added that he had received orders to have some kibitkas pitched for them close to the station-house. Many more battalions would shortly follow, and they would have been at Orsk before if it had not been for the weather, which this winter had been more severe than he ever remembered to have experienced, several Tartar drivers having been frozen to death.

Nazar now informed me that his wife lived at a small village a few miles from Orenburg, with her father; and, as my little Tartar was very eager to see his lady, I promised to halt there for the night. We drove up to his house about 12 P.M. The inmates, who were not aware of Nazar's return, had all gone to sleep. My follower tried the door; it was bolted; then he hammered against the portals.

After about five minutes thus spent waiting in the cold, his father-in-law came out, and, hearing that I had arrived, asked me to sleep there for the night. In the meantime, Nazar's wife, who was a good deal taller than himself, had got up, and was welcoming her husband. On looking around me, I found that only one room was well warmed, and that the others had no stoves. The bedroom was occupied by Nazar's father-

in-law, his wife, their daughter, and two other children.
Nazar would sleep with them. I felt that my presence
might be slightly *de trop*, although Nazar himself was
not at all particular about privacy. The apartment was
in a filthy state; and thousands of cockroaches were
crawling about on some wooden platforms, which
served as beds for the family.

The room did not offer any attractions, so I
determined to leave my servant and drive on to the
next station. This was filled with travellers; the
commander of a battery, and a surgeon of artillery,
with their families, occupied all the available space,
so the inspector took me to his own quarters where
his wife was sleeping. The woman looked up with a
smile as I entered, not being at all disconcerted by the
presence of a stranger.

In the morning I made the acquaintance of the
commander of the battery and his wife. They were
travelling in a large sleigh, and were many versts in
front of the troops. The commander had occasionally
carried despatches from Tashkent to St. Petersburg,
and on one occasion he had performed the journey in
twelve days. He remarked that he could post from
Tashkent to Samarcand in one day and a quarter,
and could be in Bokhara in five days after leaving
Tashkent.

Nazar now arrived with his father-in-law, the latter
bringing a fat goose, which he laid down at my feet.
Nazar informed me that this was his way of showing
respect, remarking that it was a fat bird, and that he
would eat it if I did not. The father-in-law could
speak a little Russian, and inquired about Nazar's moral
behaviour during his journey, patting the little Tartar
on the back when I said that his conduct had been

most exemplary, and that to the best of my belief he had not brought back a Khivan lady.

Not far from this station we met two companies of infantry on the march to Tashkent. They were all in sleighs, some drawn by camels, others by horses, five and six men being in each vehicle. The troops were being hurried on as rapidly as possible. The men seemed to be young and healthy, and were singing in chorus to pass away the tedious hours. Later on, when passing through a village, we encountered more soldiers, several of them much the worse for drink.

The officers with the troops had brought all sorts of reports from Orenburg, the last rumour being that Kryjinovsky was to be the Governor-General at Tashkent, Kauffmann to be Minister of War, and Milutin to be Commander-in-Chief in the Caucasus.

CHAPTER XXXVIII.

I HAD made up my mind not to stop at Orenburg, but continue my journey straight to Uralsk, a large town on the Ural river, the capital of the district from which the Cossacks in Kasala had been so recently banished. Uralsk was off the main road to Sizeran, but by taking this route I should have the opportunity of seeing a new line of country.

The following day I encountered an inspector who was more suspicious than any I had previously met with.

He looked at my pass—"So you have come from Khiva?"

"Yes."

"You are English?"

"Yes."

Here the man looked at me very fixedly, and continued, "Will England cede (*oostoopit*) us Kashgar?"

This question rather amused me, and I replied, pointing to a horse that was being led by the station, "Will you cede that horse to me?"

"He is not my property," said the man, looking a little astonished at the question.

"Well, Kashgar is not an English possession, and

how can we cede to Russia what does not belong to ourselves ? "

" Then England will not fight with us about Kashgar ? " inquired the inspector.

" I really don't know, but I wish she would," I replied, becoming a little annoyed by this evident attempt at cross-examination. " Anyhow," I continued, " if you put your noses into Afghanistan you will very likely get them pulled for you."

" Afghan ! " said the man ; " oh, very good ! " and taking a piece of paper he wrote down—" If Russia should take the Fortress Afghan (*Krapost Afghan*) there will then be war between England and Russia." " I have noted your words down," he said.

" So I see," was my remark ; " but Afghan is not a fortress."

" That does not signify," said the inspector ; " it is something, and you have said that if we take it there will very likely be war."

A friend of his now entered the room, and asked a great many questions about England.

"Are the English Christians ? " he inquired.

" Yes."

" Have you images (obrazye) like those ? " pointing to some tawdry pictures of saints which hung on the wall.

" No ; we do not believe in images."

" And yet you call yourselves Christians!" said the man, the Protestant religion instantly falling one hundred per cent. in his estimation.

" Do you believe in Christ ? "

" Yes."

" And in the saints ? "

" No ; not as being able to perform miracles in

our own days, whatever they might have done before."

"Horrible!" said the man; "you are as bad as the Mohammedans."

The distance from Orenburg to Uralsk is about 280 versts. On arriving at the last-mentioned town I drove to the inn. It was tolerably clean, although bed-linen was a luxury unknown to the proprietor.

My first inquiry was for a bath; and not being able to obtain this article on the premises, I drove off to the bathing establishment. Here I was told that no washing could be done on that day, for it was a Friday, and not a washing day. No one in Uralsk ever washed on a Friday, and if I wanted a bath I must come there the next afternoon. The offer of four times the usual price had no effect on the proprietor, and in return to my entreaties the man merely exclaimed, "Little father, go away; to-morrow the bath will be beautiful and hot. Go away, for the sake of God, and do not be angry."

On returning to the hotel I found that the Chief of the Police in the town had already been to see me, and had left word that he would call again. Shortly afterwards he was announced, when in the course of conversation he told me that he had heard of my being likely to visit Uralsk, having received the information from Orenburg.

The next morning Nazar came into my room with a beaming countenance. "We shall have such a spectacle to-day, and all for nothing," he said; "a man is to be beaten to death. Let us go to the market-place; a scaffold has been erected there." On inquiry I learned that a Kirghiz had murdered a Cossack officer about twelve months previous, and that the assassin had been found guilty, and was to be punished. On arriving in the square we found the ground partly occupied by a scaffold, on which stood a large solid black cross. A few ropes and cords were lying on the platform; the scaffold was surrounded by lines of infantry, who kept the people off, and from time to time dropped the butt end of their rifles on the toes of the bystanders, if they attempted to approach too closely.

Presently a low hum, which gradually swelled to a deep bass roar, announced that the *cortége* with the prisoner was in sight. The culprit could be plainly seen mounted on a block of wood, placed in a dirty old cart, which was drawn by a mule; a guard of soldiers followed the criminal, whilst an escort went in front and opened out a road through the crowd of bystanders. On arriving at the platform, the prisoner was made to ascend it. He turned deadly pale when he saw the cross, but quickly recovering himself, his countenance resumed its original expression, and carelessly looking at the people, he nodded to some of his acquaintances.

The officer in command of the soldiers now gave an order, and two of the men, seizing the prisoner, tied him up to the cross. A magistrate, who was standing on the scaffold, took a document from his pocket and commenced reading the proceedings of the trial and the sentence, which was to the effect that the culprit would be sent to Siberia.

The man did not move a muscle of his face as the sentence was read out, but Nazar was considerably disappointed. "And so we are to have no performance," said the bloodthirsty little Tartar; "it is too bad of the authorities cheating us in this way."

Capital punishment has been abolished throughout

European Russia, save for treason ; however, it must not be thought that on this account the culprits are more leniently dealt with. Forced labour in the mines of Siberia rapidly puts an end to the criminal's existence, and it is said that the strongest man will succumb after two or three years' confinement.

The inhabitants of Uralsk, who had most of them some near relation or dear friend in exile in Central Asia, were so depressed that they hardly ventured to look us in the face as we met them in the streets. Some of the Ural Cossacks were said to be still in hiding, and waiting for an opportunity to escape from the country ; but their fate could not be doubtful for a moment. When the cold season was over they would be caught, and despatched in gangs to their relations in Kasala.

Such are the delights of living in a country where a despotic form of government prevails. Such is the civilisation which certain people in England are eager to see forced upon the inhabitants of Central Asia.

There was nothing of note to be seen at Uralsk, so I left for Sizeran. This was reached after a thirty-six hours' continuous journey. It was the middle of March ; my sleigh journey was now over. Shaking hands with the faithful little Tartar, who had accompanied me to the last, I said good-bye to him, and, as far as my travels are concerned, must say farewell to the reader.

APPENDIX A.

THE RUSSIAN ADVANCE EASTWARD.

THE same rule which applies to natural phenomena is equally applicable to nations; the smaller body is attracted towards the greater, and the tribe, khanate, or kingdom, to the more powerful empire which they adjoin.

Russia in the days of her weakness was overrun and dominated to a great extent by her warlike neighbours, the Tartars. She is repaying them in their own coin.

Forty years ago she had taken from Persia 70,000, and from Tartary 270,000 square miles of territory. Since that time she has conquered the Bokharans—Khiva and Kokan; whilst her frontier is rapidly striding forward towards the Hindoo Koosh.

During the early part of this century she had stretched out a long line of outposts, let us call it her left arm, in the direction of Western Siberia, and had gradually penetrated farther and farther, until she spread herself nearly over its entire extent. Military settlements, forts, and chains of detached posts extended from the rivers Ural and Irtish to the valley of the river Ili, whilst her right arm, but half extended, reached from Orenburg to Orsk, and then by the north of the Sea of Aral to Fort Perovsky, which is about 200 miles from the mouth of the Syr Darya, the Jaxartes of ancient history.

This extension of the right arm had been attended with numerous difficulties. The line of strongholds stretching from Fort Orsk to Zvarinogolovsk had cut off from the Kirghiz of the Little Horde their best grazing ground. It had been given to some Cossacks. An endless feud ensued between the new and the old occupants. It is impossible, if you are bent upon conquest and despoliation, to prevent those nations which feel themselves aggrieved from resorting to hostilities.

As Russia stretched her right arm past the north of the Sea of Aral, the Kokandians and Khivans became alarmed. Would they not too some day have to succumb?

The Bokharans, Khivans, and Kokandians felt, thirty years ago, as Russophobists in India feel in the present day. Which was the best course for the Kokandians and Bokharans to pursue—to check the invader's progress at the outset, or allow him to establish his depôts and push forward to their frontier?

They elected the former. Constant raids were made on the Kirghiz—now Russian subjects—and the Russians captured the enemy's stronghold, Ak Mechet. The name of the victorious general was given to this fort henceforward known as Perovsky. Forts Numbers One, Two and Three were then built at Kasala and on the sites of two Kokand forts. Thus was founded the Syr Darya line, the extremity of the half-bent right arm which Russia was gradually extending towards Tashkent.

In spite of the chain of forts which stretched along the Western Siberian and the Syr Darya lines, the country between them was only half subdued. It was felt that the newly-acquired territory could not be deemed thoroughly secure until the two lines joined. The right hand must grasp its fellow of the left ere the wished-for result could be obtained.

In 1854 a committee of officers was ordered to assemble and deliberate on this proposed step. It was then stated that the junction could not be effected without having a collision with Kokan and Bokhara, which would eventually lead to the subjection of these khanates. This idea was not displeasing to the authorities at St. Petersburg, and it was determined to join the Syr Darya and Western Siberian lines.

The Crimean War now came on, and occupied all Russia's attention. But as soon as peace was proclaimed preparations were at once commenced for carrying the original proposal into execution.

The Ili was crossed, the Kokan forts Pishpek and Tokmak were destroyed by General Zimmermann, and Forts Vernoe and Kastek constructed on the northern slopes of the Ala Tau mountains. This was between 1854 and 1860. Armed reconnaisances were next made of the district lying between the Chú river and the Aulieta fort. The fingers of the left hand had not been idle. They were gradually circling round in the direction of the Syr Darya. The right arm, which in 1859 had reached forward to Djulek, where a fort had been constructed, was pushed onwards to Yany-Kurgan. The Syr Darya valley and Karataù mountains had been carefully surveyed.

Everything was prepared for uniting the two lines. It was determined that simultaneous movements should be made by Major-General Tchernayeff with the Siberian army, and by Verëvkin with the

Orenburg troops. The former was to occupy Aulieta, the latter to march from Djulek along the Karataù ridge, and to take possession of Suzak and Chulak Kurgan.

General Verëvkin thought that it would be more satisfactory if the frontier line embraced the town of Turkistan, thus pushing forward the boundary 130 miles beyond Djulek ; but General Tchernayeff—thinking that as it was a mere question of advancing the frontier eastwards, the more territory secured for Russia the better—suggested that the line should include Chemkent, a Kokan fort 100 miles beyond Turkistan, or 230 from Djulek. This proposal was duly carried into execution.

There had been but little bloodshed on the Russian side. The large towns of Turkistan and Chemkent had been taken at the expense of about fifty killed and wounded. The loss experienced by the Kokandians, according to the official accounts, was immense.

This was satisfactory to the Russian military authorities, but indecision still reigned at St. Petersburg as to how far the limits of the empire should be extended. On the 30th of July the following general order was published :—

"His Imperial Majesty has been pleased to command that all the forts erected on the newly occupied extent of country from the river Chú to the Syr Darya as far as the Kokand fort, * Yany Kurgan inclusive, be considered as temporarily forming a new Kokand line of frontier, to the command of which his Majesty has been pleased to appoint Major-General Tchernayeff, who is to have chief command of all the troops along it; those of Western Siberia as well as those of the Orenburg region."

General Tchernayeff took possession of Chemkent

* Between Djulek and Turkistan.

on the 22nd of September; the news of his success soon reached St. Petersburg, and on the 21st of November the same year (1864) the world was favoured with Prince Gortschakoff's despatch. The Chancellor states in the First Article of this celebrated document :—

"It has been judged indispensable that our two lines of frontier, one reaching from China to Lake Issyk Kul, the other from the Sea of Aral along the Syr Darya, should be united by fortified points, so that all our posts may be in a position to mutually support each other."

The Chancellor continues in the Third Article :—

"We have adopted the line between Lake Issyk Kul and the Syr Darya, besides fortifying Chemkent, which has been recently taken by us. We find ourselves in the presence of a more solid, compact, less unsettled, and better organised social state, fixing for us with geographical precision the limit up to which we are bound to advance, and at which we must halt, because, on the one hand, any further extension of our rule, meeting as it would no longer with unstable communities such as the nomad tribes, but with more regularly constituted states, would entail considerable exertions, and would draw us on from annexation to annexation with complications which cannot be foreseen. It is unnecessary for me to call attention to the evident interest that Russia has in not extending her territory. Of late years people have been pleased to assign to Russia the mission of civilising the countries which are her neighbours in the Continent of Asia. The advancement of civilisation has no agent more efficient than commercial relations. These last, to become developed, require order and stability, but in Asia this necessitates a complete change of customs. Asiatics must be made to understand that it is more to their interest to favour and insure the trade of caravans, than to pillage them. These elementary notions can only penetrate the public conscience, when there is an organised society and a government to direct and represent it. We accomplish the first part of this task in advancing our frontier to the limit where these indispensable conditions are to be found. We accomplish the second by endeavouring henceforward to prove to the neighbouring states by a firm system, so far as the suppression of their ill-dealings is concerned, but at the same time by moderation and justice in the employment of force, and by respecting their independence, that Russia is not their enemy, that she entertains towards them no ideas of conquest, and that peaceful and commercial relations will be more profitable than disorder, pillage, reprisals, and permanent warfare. In consecrating itself to this task, the Imperial Cabinet is inspired by Russian interests. It believes that at the same time it serves the interests of civilisation and humanity. It has the right to count on an equitable and loyal appreciation of the steps which it pursues, and of the principles by which it is guided."

After the promulgation of this despatch, it seemed clear that the Imperial Government at St. Petersburg had set its face against any further annexation in the East; that Chemkent was the limit of its boundary line, and that the authorities at St. Petersburg were really desirous to live at peace with the inhabitants of Central Asia; that the Cossack swords were to be turned into reaping-hooks, and that everything was to be done to promote commerce and the interests of civilization. The millennium had apparently commenced in Russia. The Cossacks and Kokandians were to stroke beards and lie down peacefully side by side. This would have been a most refreshing spectacle, and the peace at any price party in England went into raptures at the idea. However, it was not so pleasing to the Governor-Generals who represented the Emperor in the Orenburg and Western Siberian districts. The despatch was diametrically opposite to the system which, according to Colonel Venukoff, has always been adopted by Russia in her dealings with Eastern nations; for this gentleman, in his military review, observes, " In Central Asia, that is to say, there where it is easy to apply the principle *divide et impera*, by making use of the rival antagonisms of the Bashkirs, Kirghiz, and Calmucks, the Orenburg and Siberian Governors have taken for their guidance the rule to weaken each one of these troublesome nations by the means of the others." We cannot be surprised, then, that the Generals looked upon Prince Gortschakoff's literary composition as so much waste paper, in so far as they were concerned, and intended merely to blind the eyes of Europe to the ulterior intentions of their Government. The promotion of discord amidst their neighbours was much more likely to be the policy pursued by the conquerors of Turkistan than the promotion of peace, commerce, and civilization.

At all events, General Tchernayeff, who directed the military operations in Turkistan, did not think that he was bound to maintain peaceful relations with the inhabitants of Tashkent, a large town containing 78,165 inhabitants, and seventy miles from Chemkent; for, considering it necessary to obtain a more intimate* knowledge of the state of affairs in Tashkent before the winter set in, the General advanced upon that city. In this reconnaissance, on the assumption that the numerous but unwarlike population would not be able, suddenly attacked, to defend the entire length of their walls (about sixteen miles), Tchernayeff stormed the most accessible part of the town. Contrary, however, to expectation, the attempt failed.

It is a strange way of living at peace with your neighbour—first making a military reconnaissance of the city, then playfully throwing a few shells within his walls, and finally storming the most accessible part of the town. Indeed, if we take General Tchernayeff's own report, we find that the reason assigned by him for his attack upon Tashkent is

---

* See General Romanovsky's "Notes on Central Asia." This work has been translated into English.

singularly vague. He writes, in a despatch to the Minister of War, which is dated the 19th of October, 1864, "At last, as I have already had the honour of acquainting your Excellency, information was received which has subsequently been confirmed, that Tashkent had entered into relations with the Ameer of Bokhara."

Now, Bokhara was at peace with Russia, and the authorities at St. Petersburg wished to live at peace with their neighbours ; so the reason which is given by General Tchernayeff for his attack upon Tashkent is not very satisfactory. Some European statesmen thought that this little ebullition of feeling on the part of General Tchernayeff would have been followed by the authorities at St. Petersburg gently remonstrating with the energetic warrior. However, the Russian Minister of War was at that time so soothed by the peaceful notes in Prince Gortschakoff's declaration, that he could not find it in his heart even to forward a reprimand. The Government contented itself by refusing to give its sanction to the General's project of conquering Tashkent, but took care to furnish him without loss of time with strong reinforcements, on the plea that it would then be easier to defend the district already occupied.

In an order of the day from the Minister of War, dated 12th of February, 1865, we read—" The advanced line established last year in the Trans Chú region is to be connected with the line of the Syr Darya, and one province to be formed, under the title of the Province of Turkistan, of the whole of the territory bordering the Central Asiatic possessions from the Sea of Aral to Lake Issyk Kul. The administration of the new province is to be entrusted to a special military governor, who shall at the same time command the forces stationed within the province."

General Tchernayeff was punished for his attack upon Tashkent, made only five months previously, by being appointed Governor of the region, and Commander of the Forces. Fresh troops were sent to him from Orenburg and Western Siberia.

Tchernayeff, three months after he had been appointed Governor of Turkistan, reported to the Minister of War at St. Petersburg that the Ameer of Bokhara was marching his troops in the direction of Ura Tube, a town about sixty miles south of Tashkent. The General concluded his despatch by saying that this movement could only be interpreted as a desire on the part of the Ameer of Bokhara to take advantage of the difficulties of the khanate, and mix himself up in its affairs.

The magnanimous Tchernayeff was alarmed lest another might take possession of some territory which did not belong to Russia. There was no direct evidence as to this intention on the part of the Ameer. The General, however, thought—in spite of the disapproval expressed by the Imperial Government about his attempt to annex Tashkent—that the authorities would be glad if this were an accomplished fact. He advanced with his troops to Fort Niazbek, which commands the water supply of the city, and summoned the Governor to surrender. This fortress is situated sixteen miles north-east of Tashkent, and is on the left bank of the river Chirchik. It was one of the most formidable strongholds in the khanate, and yet it capitulated after a few hours' fire from the Russian batteries. The Tzar's troops suffered no loss in killed, and only seven Russians were slightly wounded. From this we can see that no great difficulties in the shape of opposition from the Kokandians could be anticipated. Prince Gortschakoff's despatch and the Kokan forces were equally impotent to restrain the invader.

Russia had indeed advanced her right arm during that last twelve months. From Djulek, where it had been intended to draw the boundary line, to Niazbek, is more than three hundred miles. Fort Vernoe was more to the east than even Niazbek. The right arm must again reach forward.

After taking Niazbek Tchernayeff determined to take possession of Tashkent. This town was stormed on the 14th of July, 1865. The Russians had 1,951 men and twelve guns exposed to a force of 30,000 defenders. In spite of this discrepancy in numbers, there were only twenty-eight Russian soldiers killed and eighty wounded. No officer was amongst the slain. Thus one of the most populous and important cities in Central Asia was added to the dominions of the White Tzar.

The Ameer of Bokhara was extremely well disposed towards Russia. The Bokharan merchants in days gone by had received special privileges and an exemption from custom duties in their tradings with the Emperor's subjects; but shortly after the capture of Tashkent, Tchernayeff found that he had serious cause to complain of the Ameer's conduct. This sovereign, simultaneously with the seizure of Tashkent by the Russians, had actually dared to enter Hodjent, a town about six days' march from the city.

Hodjent is a most important military post. It is situated on the Syr Darya at a point where the stream turns sharply to the south. Here the roads to Kokan, Tashkent, Bokhara, and last, but not by any means least, Balkh, cross each other. The possession of Hodjent by the Russians would enable them to sever Kokan from Bokhara, and afford a most advantageous position for an attack upon either of these countries.

If Tchernayeff had intended to respect the despatch which the Russian Chancellor had sent to the different Courts in Europe, the General would not have troubled himself about Hodjent; but the temptation was too great, and Tchernayeff fell. Hodjent did not belong to Russia; but this was no reason why it should belong to Bokhara. Thus the General argued to himself; any little scruples he might have had as to whether the conscientious Chancellor at St. Petersburg would be grieved at his proceedings were speedily quelled, and he issued an order to arrest all the Bokharans who could be found within his province, and to seize their property. The order was extended to Orenburg. General Kryjinovsky was requested to co-operate in carrying Tchernayeff's edict into effect. The merchandise of every Bokharan found in that town was also sequestrated.

This was in July, 1865, only six months after the promulgation of Prince Gortschakoff's famous despatch, in which he said that Russia wished to live at peace with her neighbours, and promote commerce and civilization in Central Asia.

In my account of the way a rupture was first brought about between Russia and Bokhara I adhere strictly to General Romanovsky's statements in his " Notes on the Central Asiatic Question."* As this officer accompanied General Kryjinovsky in a journey which the

* See page 13 Romanovsky's " Notes on the Central Asiatic Question."

latter made at this time to Turkistan, in order to study the position of affairs in that province, he ought to be well acquainted with the facts of the case. Terentyeff, in his work on " England and Russia in Central Asia," says that Tchernayeff arrested the Bokharan merchants because the Bokharans had demanded the evacuation of Tashkent and Chemkent pending the receipt of the final decision of the White Tzar, and that in the event of a refusal they had threatened a holy war, or, in other words, a general rising of all Mohammedans.

It is very possible that some report as to the contents of the celebrated Gortschakoff document had reached Bokhara. The Ameer might have learned that the Russian General had exceeded his instructions. But even if the demand were made as Terentyeff states, it was a strong measure for Tchernayeff to adopt, and one more characteristic of Eastern than of Western civilization. Perhaps, indeed, I am wrong in using the term Eastern, as the laws of hospitality are rigidly observed by Mohammedans in Asia, and the Russian in this respect is sometimes behind his first-cousin, the Tartar. It does not, however, signify whose version of the circumstances is correct. The Bokharans were arrested ; General Tchernayeff's main object was attained; he had wished to have a *casus belli* against Bokhara. His wish was realised, for the Ameer at once retaliated by arresting all the Russian merchants who happened to be within his city.

In spite of the aggressive measures commenced by the Russians against Bokhara, the Ameer did not attempt any hostilities. Tchernayeff, too, had not many troops at his disposal, so he satisfied himself for the moment by occupying the Trans-Chirchik region, a fertile district close to Tashkent.

In the meantime the Bokharan sovereign despatched a mission to the Emperor at St. Petersburg, in order to remonstrate about the imprisonment of the Bokharan merchants and the seizure of their goods. The Ameer could not understand this system of promoting the interests of commerce and civilization. However, he would not long remain in ignorance. He was about to undergo a course of education in the doctrines of civilization as understood in Russia.

Kryjinovsky met the mission at Fort Number One. He would not allow the Bokharan envoys to go to the capital, the reason assigned being that he was himself empowered to negotiate with them. We need not be astonished at General Kryjinovsky's refusing to allow the Bokharan envoys to go to St. Petersburg. Their mission was to complain of his conduct, and if their story had reached the Tzar's ears the Governor of Orenburg might have lost his appointment. Shortly afterwards the two Generals, Kryjinovsky and Tchernayeff, met. They were not in accord about what was to be done with Tashkent. Tchernayeff wished to annex that city to the empire, whilst Kryjinovsky was for reducing it to a state of vassaldom, and not for occupying the newly-conquered district with Russian troops.

It is interesting to mark this difference of opinion between the two Generals, as towards the end of the year 1865 Kryjinovsky was recalled for a time to St. Petersburg. It will be curious to note how this visit to the capital subsequently influenced him in his treatment of the question. The Bokharan envoys were still detained by the Russian authorities, and at the end of October, 1865, General Tchernayeff sent a Russian mission to Bokhara. This he did ostensibly with the object of establishing friendly relations, and of re-opening that trade which had been brought to so abrupt a conclusion by his own act of arresting the Bokharan merchants.

There were several military as well as civil officers attached to this mission. It bore such a military as well as political aspect that the Ameer, who was highly dissatisfied that his own envoys to the Tzar had been arrested, actually had the audacity to detain the Russian gentlemen. He was undoubtedly wrong in committing so illegal an act, and one so contrary to the law of nations. The Ameer was not wise in his generation. He did not discern that the old saying, "What is sauce for the goose is sauce for the gander," did not apply in his case. The Russians had detained his mission, it is true, but then the Tzar was more powerful than the Ameer, although the latter potentate had this still to learn. Might gives right in the treatment of one country by another. The Ameer was rash in applying the Mosaic law, "An eye for an eye, a tooth for a tooth," to the Christianizing and civilizing power on his frontier.

Tchernayeff now crossed the Syr Darya, at Chinaz, with fourteen companies of infantry, nine hundred Cossacks, sixteen guns, and twelve hundred camels. His object was to march across the hungry steppe to Djizzak, so as to force the Ameer to release the envoys. However, the latter sovereign declined to do so unless his Bokharan subjects were permitted to return. A battle was the consequence, and the Russians had so much the worst of the encounter that their expedition had to retreat to the Syr Darya.

That Tchernayeff had the worst of this encounter is clear, from his report to the Commander-in-Chief, at Orenburg, dated March 19th, 1866, in which he urgently asked for reinforcements. However, the authorities at St. Petersburg were not pleased at the check their arms had received. An order was issued to recall the beaten General, and General Romanovsky was appointed to replace him in the command.

Soon afterwards the Russians had a force of three thousand fighting men in Tashkent. In an engagement that took place at Irdja the Bokharans were utterly routed. General Romanovsky followed up the advantages he had gained by a fresh victory in the same neighbourhood. The Ameer's army was annihilated, and the sovereign had to take refuge in Samarcand.

The Russian General did not think that he had sufficient forces to capture the city of Samarcand, so he determined to take possession of Hodjent. This town was stormed after a siege which lasted eight days. The Commander-in-Chief then resolved to retain all the territory he had occupied on the left bank of the Syr Darya, and on the Kokan side he expressed his wish to take possession of the large town of Namangan. This, in Romanovsky's opinion, would have been most convenient, as the boundary line could then have been drawn along the river Naryn, which lies south of Lake Issyk Kul.

General Romanovsky was not permitted to carry out his project of occupying Namangan, and of pushing the frontier to the south of Lake Issyk Kul. It was felt at St. Petersburg that this step would have been premature, and that the English nation might have been aroused from its state of lethargy, the object of the Russian Government being always rather to take advantage of events than to force them.

The General was on the best of terms with Hudoyar Khan, the Prince of Kokan, who had promised to faithfully obey the commands of the Russian authorities. In Romanovsky's own words the Khan had most conscientiously fulfilled his promises. However, General Kryjinovsky, after his arrival at St. Petersburg, sent a despatch to Tashkent, in which he stated that he considered it necessary to occupy the entire khanate of Kokan, and extend the Imperial dominions to the Celestial mountains and the Bolors. He recommended General Romanovsky to assume a high tone towards Kokan, and to treat Hudoyar Khan as a man who by his position should be a vassal of Russia. Should he take umbrage and operate against us, wrote the Governor-General of Orenburg, so much the better; it will give us a pretext to close with him. With reference to the Ameer of Bokhara, everything must be demanded of, nothing conceded to, him; and Kyrjinovsky still refused to allow the release of the Bokharan merchants, who were detained at Orenburg. Doubtless he did this in their own interests, and in order to accustom them to the new order of things, as stated in Prince Gortschakoff's declaration of 1864. The Russian merchants had long since been sent back from Bokhara. This did not affect Kryjinovsky's treatment of his prisoners. They required civilizing *à la Russe*. He determined to civilize them.

It was well known that this Governor-General had been honoured a short time previous by being admitted to an audience with some high authorities in the capital. A few people in London expressed their belief that the celebrated despatch was all humbug, and said that the Chancellor wished to annex more territory. These men, however, were contradicted by the wiseacres of the English community, who contented themselves by pointing out the distinctness of the Chancellor's statements, which, they said, ought not to be impugned by even the shadow of a suspicion.

Kryjinovsky returned to Tashkent. It was stated that he was desirous to bring matters to a head. He shortly afterwards manifested his ideas on this subject by forwarding an official report to St. Petersburg recommending the immediate commencement of hostilities against the inhabitants of Kokan. The Governor-General of Orenburg grounded his report on an attack which had been made on the Russians by a party of robbers, and on the Khan having concentrated his forces in his own territories.

In Romanovsky's opinion the Khan had not the means to stop the inroads of predatory parties. The General thought that the concentration of native troops was merely the very natural consequence of the concentration of the Russian troops in Hodjent. This had commenced immediately after the arrival of the Governor-General of Orenburg in the province of Turkistan.

It was deemed politic to throw a colour of justice over the acts of violence which had been perpetrated. Some of the inhabitants of the conquered districts were induced to ask for permission to become vassals of Russia. Sixty-two natives of Tashkent signed a document asking for their town to be annexed to the Tzar's dominions. A few inhabitants of the Trans-Chirchik District and of Hodjent did the same. All the country occupied up to May, 1866, became incorporated with the Russian Empire.

Shortly after this event the Ameer of Bokhara sent an emissary to Kryjinovsky to conclude a treaty of peace. However, the Governor-General of Orenburg demanded 100,000 tillas as a war indemnity. The emissary would not accede to these terms. His Mohammedan mind was too obtuse to see the justice of the demand. The case was a clear one. The Governors of Orenburg and Tashkent had first of all arrested some Bokharan merchants, and sequestrated their goods. The Ameer of Bokhara had been so wicked as to resent this proceeding. It was as if a strong savage had set fire to a weak savage's wigwam, and the strong man had afterwards asked for an indemnity because he had slightly burnt his fingers whilst creating the conflagration. The facts had been made out, the weak savage could pay, but would not pay, so he must be made to pay ; and Kryjinovsky determined to attack Bokhara.

His subordinate, Romanovsky, was ordered to prepare for an immediate campaign in the Ameer's territory. The frontier was crossed, and the forts of Ura Tube and Djizzak were taken by storm. Singularly enough the day after the capture of Djizzak, Kryjinovsky received a telegram from St. Petersburg, in which the Government stated its disinclination to extend the limits of the Empire, and at the same time called his attention to the order of 1866, which was to the effect that should the inhabitants of Tashkent and of the other conquered districts renew their request to become Russian subjects, so as to obtain protection against the Ameer of Bokhara, it was to be granted them. But this had already been done. Sixty-two out of the 78,165 inhabitants of Tashkent had expressed a desire to belong to Russia ; the remaining 78,103 individuals were, *nolens volens*, subjects of the Tzar.

Kryjinovsky started for Orenburg on the 10th of November, 1866. The troops were put into winter quarters, and a strong garrison was left in Djizzak, the recently-conquered town, which was some distance from the left bank of the Syr Darya, and on the high road to Samarcand. In the spring of the following year (1867), a Bokharan fort, called Jani Kurgan, not far from Djizzak, was taken by the Russians. Shortly afterwards an Imperial decree was issued, separating the Turkistan province from the Orenburg Government, the residence appointed for the Governor-General being in Tashkent. The newly-formed province was in its turn divided into the Syr Darya and Semirechensky districts; the two together containing a population of about 1,500,000 inhabitants.

A fresh Governor (General Kauffmann) replaced Romanovsky on the 17th of November, 1867. The new officer commenced his reign by destroying the Bokharan town of Ukhum, and in April, 1868, he marched through the valley of the Zerafshan to Samarcand. This far-famed town at once surrendered to the Russian arms. Katye Kurgan, forty miles from Samarcand, and on the high road to Bokhara, was next taken, and on the 2nd of July, the Ameer, with all his army, was utterly defeated on the Zerabulak heights. The Bokharan sovereign now felt that he was impotent to resist the invader's progress. Muscovite civilization was too much for him, and the defeated monarch was obliged to sign a treaty of peace. By this he bound himself to pay an indemnity, and to acknowledge the right of Russia to all the territory won by her since 1865.

Territorial aggrandisement had always been contrary to the expressed wish of the authorities at St. Petersburg. They must have been deeply grieved to find themselves compelled to annex so much Bokharan territory. However, Kauffmann was not recalled, like his predecessors Tchernayeff and Romanovsky had been; a scapegoat was not required this time. England was too much occupied in money-making to cast a thought upon the affairs of Central Asia; and although a few members in the House of Commons and the *Morning Post* might grumble a little, the British Government did not trouble itself much about the matter.

By the possession of Samarcand, the Russians held Bokhara completely at their disposition; they had full control over the waters of the Zerafshan, and, in consequence, over the crops of Bokhara. The knowledge of this fact now stirred up a little the British Cabinet, but the Russian Chancellor, eager to throw oil on the troubled waters, promised to restore Samarcand to the Ameer. Our Ministers placed credence in the statement. Their minds were tranquillised about the matter. They once more lay down to slumber. The Cabinet had excited itself a little more than was its wont, for some Afghans—that warlike race, which were looked upon as our surest safeguard in the event of a quarrel with Russia—had actually fought under the Tzar's standard, and with the Christians, against the Bokharans.

The facts were as follows :—The ruler at Balkh had sent 286 Afghan soldiers under Sekunder Khan, the grandson of Mohammed Khan, to aid the Ameer of Bokhara. The Ameer had not been able to pay these auxiliaries with regularity, and Sekunder Khan quietly left his ally and attached himself to the forces under Kauffmann. Afghans, combined with Russians, were in arms against the followers of the prophet. Soldiers of fortune have not many religious scruples. They will fight for the power which pays best or is able to offer the greatest bribe. It had just dawned upon the few people in Great Britain who take an interest in the affairs of Central Asia, that the chance of looting the rich cities of the plains in India might prove an irresistible attraction to the inhabitants of Afghanistan if it were proposed to them, of course in the interests of civilization, by any Russian agents. Sekunder Khan, who is the nephew of Shere Ali, became a lieutenant-colonel in the Tzar's army. He soon mastered Russian and French; however, he found that there was no chance of his rising higher in the Russian service, his nationality told against him; and being furthermore aggrieved at the treatment received by one of his followers, Rahmed Khan, an ensign in the Russian army, from the adjutant of his regiment, Sekunder called out the last-mentioned officer. The challenge was not accepted. The infuriated Afghan, who announced his determination to horsewhip his adversary on the first opportunity, was put under arrest. He resigned his commission and came to England, where, according to Mr. Terentyeff, he has been well received, and assigned a liberal pension.

The Ameer of Bokhara was under the impression that Samarcand would be restored to him. It is said that he signed a treaty granting special privileges to Russian traders, and pledged himself to pay a war indemnity of £75,000, on the understanding that Samarcand would be evacuated. This the Russians did not do; however, they restored the Ameer's authority, which had been shaken by an insurrection headed by one of his sons, for, marching upon Karshi, they drove from it the rebel and his supporters. They then advanced against two chiefs in Shahr i Subz, and, conquering them, restored the district to the Ameer.

The last expedition the Russians have made in that part of the world was to the sources of the Zerafshan to the mountainous country to the south-east of Bokhara. There they reduced to their own rule the Bekships of Urgut, Faraf, Macha, Kshtut, and Maghian. What was of no use to Kauffmann he gave back to the original owners; what was worth retaining the General kept for Russia.

In the north-eastern division of Turkistan the Tzar's officers had not been idle. Some troops had been despatched from Vernoe to the Naryn, the main branch of the Syr Darya. Here they constructed a bridge, erected a fort, and made a road, thus opening a carriage-way in the direction of Kashgar.

Kokan was now entirely cut off from the adjacent khanates, and lay at the mercy of the invader.

Shortly before this the Russian relations with China had become complicated; a revolution had occurred in that empire, and all Eastern Turkistan emancipated itself from the Chinese yoke. Bands of Russian Kirghiz marched into Chinese territory, and freely pillaged the inhabitants. This led to the destruction of the Russian consulates and factories in Kulja and Chuguchak. Yakoob Bek, the ruler in Kashgar, formed of Kashgaria an independent state, and as he found that the Taranchees and Dungans were not at all submissive, he occupied some of the Dungan towns, amongst others Karashar and Turfan.

In order to defend the Russian Kirghiz from the Taranchees, which was a capital excuse for an advance, the Governor-General of Turkistan, at the end of August, 1870, ordered the slope from the Muzart Pass to be occupied. This is a pass in the Tian Shan range which unites the province of Ili with Altishahr.

The Russians having possession of the Muzart Pass, were enabled to prevent Yakoob Bek from annexing Kulja. They did this in the most effective manner by taking possession of it themselves.

The St. Petersburg official journals declared that Kulja was only to be temporarily occupied, and that it would be given up as soon as the Chinese authority could be re-established by reinforcements of troops from China. Negotiations about the restoration of the province of Ili (Kulja) were said to have been carried on between Jung, a Chinese commissioner, and a Russian general. However, all was to no purpose; there was no intention to give anything back, and in spite of the statements issuing from official sources, Kulja, like Samarcand, became permanently annexed to the Tzar's dominions.

A little later a revolution in Kokan, brought about by Russian agents, afforded the long-wished-for opportunity. Some of the inhabitants expressed a desire to become subjects of the Emperor, and General Kauffmann was so kind as to accede to their wishes. By the entire possession of this khanate the Russian right arm had reached far eastward, but Kulja, the extremity of her left arm, was still a long way in advance.

In Lieut.-Colonel Lusilin's map of Turkistan, 1875, the boundary line between Kokan and Kashgar is not dotted in. Does this mean that a fresh movement forward with the right arm is imminent? It will have to reach well out to shake hands with its fellow at Kulja.

A natural boundary of mountains separates Kokan from Kashgar, but General Kauffmann is not likely to be deterred in his advance. Eastward, south-eastward! is the cry, and Kashgar will inevitably succumb unless England intervenes in her behalf.